THE WAY OF
THE PIRATE

THE WAY OF
THE PIRATE

Who's Who in Davy Jones' Locker

ROBERT DOWNIE

ibooks
new york

DISTRIBUTED BY SIMON & SCHUSTER

THE WAY OF THE PIRATE

Acknowledgements

I am indebted to all of the following people. Without their care, friendship, love, encouragement, approval and support I would not have survived the bad times. Bless you all.

Dr Stephen Adams
Jenny Beadle
Nana Breum
Mark Brewer
Joyce and Geoff Brookes
Frazer and Hayden Pearce
Maurice Milne-Redhead
Menai Roberts
Jenny and Martin Ruddle
Ann Tame
Caroline Therrien
Pam and Alvin Tull

But most of all my wife and children, Ann, Helen and Lance.

A Foreword

To produce what one intends to be an authoritative reference book from sources as dubious as those I have used is perhaps foolhardy. And perhaps that's why more scholarly researchers have avoided the attempt. My only excuse can be that I offer this volume as the opening statement of a conversation. I hope that it will stimulate readers to make their own researches, search their own libraries or track down local legend and folklore. I honestly look forward to being corrected by anyone who feels inspired to do that. You will find a blank letter-form at the end of the book.

My biggest quandary was just who to include and who to exclude from this directory. Many men were hanged for piracy who were clearly innocent. Conversely, several men were acquitted at trial, while obviously as guilty as sin. In the end I decided that all these tales added to the sum of knowledge about pirates, so I put 'em all in. One of your responsibilities as a reader is to decide what you want to believe.

If I offend any of the descendants of these characters then I am a bit surprised, I would happily accept any of them as an ancestor of mine. After a couple of centuries the buccaneer genes you have inherited will probably only surface when you are given a parking ticket or correspond with the Inland Revenue.

The seventeenth century was not an era noted for its political correctness. If I offend persons of any particular race, religion, nationality or gender, then I can only swear that it was not my intention to do so.

A Brief History of Piracy

Piracy did not end when Blackbeard's head was severed at Ocracoke Inlet in 1717. Year by year the number of reported pirate attacks on shipping increases.

Lloyd's insurance underwriters repeatedly warn the captains of great container ships to be alert for small, swift pirate boats in the Malacca Straits and much of the South China Sea. Owners of luxury pleasure craft in the Caribbean are aware of the danger of their vessels being taken by drug-runners. Once the owners and crew are disposed of, the innocent-looking vessels are ideal for the smuggling of narcotics. Currently Albanian brigands are cutting-out useful vessels from marinas and harbours on the Greek Isle of Corfu and along the mainland coast. These instances fall well within my own definition of the word 'piracy'.

Neither did piracy begin on the eastern United States seaboard nor the Caribbean. The Greek and Roman empires, spreading from the Mediterranean shores, were bothered by these sea-borne thieves. Julius Caesar himself wrote unkind words about them.

The maritime kingdoms of northern Europe were harried and tormented by Viking pirates. Eventually many of countries were ruled by the descendants of these nautical vagabonds. William the Norman, conqueror of much of northern France and Britain, was the son of a Viking raider.

Royal navies from the times of Alfred the Great onwards made attempts to reduce piracy around the wealthy and fertile fringes of Europe's countries. These attempts were always single-nation defences. The pirates' answer was to base themselves in another country, whose ruler was not unhappy to see his neighbours' shipping decimated. In effect these pirate visitors were adding to the strength, defence and economy of his own realm. These unofficial forces were the first privateers.

PRIVATEERS

Monarchs are traditionally not keen on the idea of paying out of their own pockets to defend their monarchy. Over the years they encouraged the idea that their subjects should pay for the defence of that country against invasion and rule by another monarch. This has always been a bone of contention between ruler and ruled. Citizens, very sensibly, are normally more interested in the price of a loaf of bread than the colour of their ruler's flag, or his/her religion.

The idea that a private ship could be used as a man-of-war and licensed by a monarch to sink or capture his enemies must have been a dream come true for many of Europe's rulers, and a great relief to their taxpayers. Privateers sailed without any expense being incurred by the crown. The Captain or financier of the vessel was responsible for providing the ship, arms, victuals and crew. If the vessel was captured or sunk the King lost nothing. If the vessel broke international law or treaty the King denied knowledge of it. If it were successful the King claimed a percentage of the prizes. If the Captain became a national hero the King would give him a title, which cost the King nothing.

Privateering in Britain reached a magnificent peak in the reign of Queen Elizabeth I. She so skillfully managed her privateer captains that their names are writ large in world history still. Exploration and conquest, as well as predation of enemy fleets, were the glorious deeds of these Elizabethan heroes. Drake and Hawkins, their kinsmen, officers and crews performed incredible tasks for Elizabeth at minimal expense.

In the age of expansion into the Americas, when Spain first, then the other European powers, began to colonise the new continent, privateers carried their country's flag. Islands, rainforests, savannahs, rich seams of gold and silver were gathered into embryonic empires; all at almost no expense to Europe's rulers. Africa, Asia and the Far East were carved into colonies and client-states, but the richest prize by far was the Caribbean and its surrounding lands.

Privateers still flourished in later years and you will read that respectable citizens like Samuel Pepys and Sir William Penn (father of the Penn of Pennsylvania) were commonly investors in privateering ventures. More adventurous souls like Tom Paine (perhaps writer of the US constitution and certainly writer of the French constitution) and Lancelot Blackburne (made Archbishop of York in 1724) sailed as privateers in their formative years.

EUROPEAN PIRACY

The earliest well-documented period of European piracy was in the early 17th century. King James I's accession to the English throne coincided with a brief period of general peace throughout Europe. The naval and land forces of most European countries was drastically reduced. England alone dismissed over 50,000 sea-going officers and men.

Though some would have been pleased to return to homes and families, there was often no work in town or countryside for them to do. The country's economy had been geared to equipping and provisioning a huge army and navy. Now it was contracting to a peacetime economy. A host of unemployed officers and sailors were available in every seaport, eager to turn a hand to whatever adventure came their way.

This general reduction in European navies meant that commercial shipping was largely unprotected and that pirates stood little chance of capture. De-commissioned vessels were plentiful, could be 'bought for a song' or cut loose on a dark night.

Fleets of pirate ships began to capture trading vessels. The two areas that had dense concentrations of shipping were the Straits of Gibraltar and the Western Approaches to the English Channel.

Those pirates who worked the Straits based themselves in the harbours of Morocco's Atlantic coast. There the local rulers allowed them shore facilities and a market for their plunder in exchange for a percentage of their profits. This arrangement spread to the Mediterranean ports of Algiers and Tunis.

The pirate fleets that preyed on the commercial traffic in the Western Approaches were generally based in the Southwest of Ireland, in Bantry Bay. There the large anchorage and many islands made a safe refuge for them. Wines, spirits, chandlery and female company were shipped from England to provide for their needs. The water there was the sweetest in Europe and the beef was excellent.

By 1614/15, the Dutch especially had lost patience with the pirates. They concentrated their own naval forces and encouraged England (as the other great sea-going nation) to join them in driving out the pirates. No doubt many of the pirates, who had been sailors in the previous century, felt it time to retire. Those who opted to remain in the trade took service with the Barbary Corsairs for a time.

Within a year or two, piracy in European waters was a rare occurrence once more. This period of robbery and murder on the high seas was over.

THE CARIBBEAN

When Columbus returned to Europe with his news of the discovery of the New World, it was vital to Spain that these new lands, and the treasures they held, should belong to Spain alone. As the greatest and most-favoured Catholic power at that time, Spain insisted that Pope Alexander IV decree that all the lands across the Atlantic were to belong to Spain.

This edict dismayed Portugal, the other great Catholic nation of explorers and navigators. The Azores were across the Atlantic, and the Azores were already Portugese. Pope Alexander amended his edict to say that a line must be drawn, to run north and south, three hundred leagues beyond the Azores. All lands 'beyond the line' were to be

Spanish. The 'line' kept the peace between Spain and Portugal for many years.

Spain proceeded to settle the New World. They began with the nearest islands, those on the eastern side of the Caribbean, to 'windward'. The Spanish took sheep to the islands, and they died. They took cattle that thrived, but the land was mostly forest and unsuitable for ranching. They took seeds of all the grains that grew well in Spain, but the seed rotted in the hot, moist, tropic earth. More importantly, the islands bore little or no gold or silver.

As the mainland of South and Central America was explored and subdued, it became obvious that there was where treasure and fortune were to be found. The outer islands were slowly abandoned in favour of the mainland. The abandoned cattle and hogs flourished in the wild. Those Spanish farmers determined enough to carve a ranch from the forests moved to the larger islands of Cuba and Hispaniola. Spains' need for the gold, silver and emeralds that the mainland produced moved most of the colonists there.

Local Spanish Governors of colonies had very little autonomy, they were in place to carry out the instructions of the Spanish Government. Spain's colonial ambition was to fill a treasure fleet once or twice a year with enough bullion to prop up an ailing economy. The occupation of useless outer islands was considered a waste of manpower.

At this point, let me remind you, if I may, of the weather in the Caribbean and the nature of old sailing ships.

The easterly tradewinds blow steadily and fairly reliably into the Caribbean from the Atlantic. The Windward Islands are almost always just as their name implies, to windward. Those who sail will know that to be to windward of one's objective is ideal, to be to leeward of it is always inconvenient, sometimes disastrous. A sailing ship of the 16th century might take weeks to work its way against the wind from Mexico to Jamaica. A Jamaican vessel sailing the other way might strike anywhere along the Mexican coast with hours.

The Governors of the Spanish colonies knew this. They were able sailors and sound tacticians. The ministers in Spain, however, refused to see the problem and ignored it. The Pope had drawn the 'line' which excluded all other nations. What was there to fear? Who would defy the Pope?

The Protestants of Holland, Britain and those of France as well. They would happily defy the Pope's ruling on anything. Far more vehemently anti-Catholic than we can now understand, these Protestants regarded defiance of the Pope's ruling as a religious duty.

By the time of Queen Elizabeth I's reign in England, Spain was reaping the rich rewards of her colonisation of the Americas. Great fleets left Spain for the growing and exclusive markets of the Spanish Main. On

4

their return, these ships brought back treasure. They brought gold and silver, in ingot, artifact and coin. They brought emeralds and pearls.

The Protestant countries of Northern Europe, better manufacturers of most goods than Spain was, wanted at the very least a chance to sell their products to the new colonies. As things stood, they were obliged to sell them to Spanish traders who were allowed to export them to the Americas, but charge ten times what the products cost in Delft, Bristol, Bruges or Rouen. Spain steadfastly refused to allow any trading by foreigners 'beyond the line'.

Drake and Hawkins from England, with the blessings of their Queen, other adventurers from France and the Netherlands, all went to plunder their share of the fabulous treasures. The Queen got her share of treasure too. These were the first privateers. They were technically not pirates because they had the permission of, and a commission from, their monarch or government. They had permission to rob and capture Spanish Catholic vessels and they did it with great vigour and relish.

The coronation of James I brought little change until he decided that his son should marry the Spanish Infanta and a peace was made with Spain that lasted for nine years. (The marriage never happened and the son became Charles I. A district of London, across the river from Execution Dock, is called Elephant and Castle, this was the Cockney interpretation of La Infanta de Castille.)

This outbreak of peace caused the withdrawal of privateer commissions which was not accepted by the sea-rovers or the men who financed them. Many Englishmen obtained a French or Dutch commission and continued their profitable plundering. The only loser, apart from Spain, was King James. The Spanish forces in the Caribbean executed all privateers that they caught, whether commissioned or not. Some privateers operated without a commission from anybody, and technically were pirates.

The Northern Europeans began to make settlements on the neglected, outer islands of the Antilles. Thomas Warner made a settlement on St Christopher (now St Kitts) in 1623. This was the first non-Spanish community in the Caribbean. The Dutch and French soon followed. Barbados was settled in 1624, Nevis in 1628, Antigua and Montserrat in 1632. The French settled Guadeloupe and Martinique in 1635 and the Dutch settled St Eustatia, Tobago and Curacao in 1632/34. Jamaica was settled by the British in 1635.

Note: A cautionary note: I have to keep reminding myself that in writing about privateers, buccaneers and pirates it becomes automatic to regard the Spanish as 'the enemy'. The facts don't bear this out. Go ashore in any of the former Spanish colonies, Honduras perhaps, or Nicaragua. See how far you have to walk to find a person of Native American origin, speaking a semblance of their native tongue or playing an American musical instrument. Not far? Try the same exercise in one of the former English colonies, Boston or Jamaica. Then ask yourself whom you have preferred to colonise your country? Sorry, back to the plot.

Cromwell's Commonwealth took advantage of the new colonies to rid themselves of many prisoners of the civil war. Later, magistrates' courts provided shiploads of people who were deemed criminal, vagrant, unemployed, orphaned, or just down on their luck. Planters in the growing colonies needed labour to clear forest and to plant sugar and tobacco crops. Anyone drawing any sort of welfare payment was likely to be shipped as an indentured servant. Many people volunteered for this period of slavery in exchange for a passage to the colonies.

Another note: It is interesting that Scottish and Welsh surnames predominate in the West Indies. Perhaps this just reflects the poverty and hardship in those countries in the 17th century.

The new, mostly Protestant, colonies flourished, but not without much hardship. Diseases, unknown in Europe, ravaged whole communities. Hurricanes could destroy years of planting and building.

The only naval power in the Caribbean was Spanish. The northern European monarchs would not finance fleets so far from home-waters. The settlers were left to defend themselves as best they could from the threat of Spanish retaliation. What the settlers needed was a large volunteer army of tough, self-reliant men who could live off the land when required, and work for no pay other than what they could seize for themselves. As luck would have it, just such a force existed.

THE BUCCANEERS

Most of the people who went, or were sent, to the new colonies were totally unsuited to pioneer agricultural life. Most were sold into bondage to a planter or a trader in the colony. As soon as their term of bondage was over, or much sooner in many cases, they left their masters. Black slaves began to arrive from Africa to replace these white slaves and it soon became obvious that they were far fitter and stronger, far better workers, and far better suited to the tropics than the undernourished poor of Europe's large cities.

The 'no longer required' Europeans soon found places and a lifestyle to suit them better. They drifted to the smaller islands and the uninhabited shores of Hispaniola, to places that were less suitable for large plantations. Many of these places had become the habitat of the Spanish cattle and hogs, which now roamed wild.

By hunting these animals, shooting them, skinning them, preserving the meat and curing the hides, they could make a living of sorts. The beef and pork was cut into strips and dried over a fire of the fat and bones of the animals. It acquired a distinctive, savoury taste and was called Boucan. Thus these people became known as Buccaneers. They made temporary camps for the slow grilling of the meat. The camps were called after the native Carib name of 'barbacoas'; thus the 'buccaneers' 'barbequed' their meat. The preserved meat and hides were traded with the colonists for the buccaneers few necessities of life; muskets, powder and lead for shot being the most important.

Jamaica had become the major trading and wealth producing colony in the Caribbean. When the island was threatened by rumour of an approaching Spanish fleet, privateer commissions were offered to the buccaneers and ships were provided for them. They came flooding in from the smaller islands that are

now well-known holiday resorts. They banded together, regardless of nationality or religion, to fight the Spanish.

The buccaneers were not seamen, though many would have had experience in small boats. Their strength was that most of them were marksmen with a musket and they could all fillet a beast in quick time with their ever-handy cutlass. They weren't sailors though, nor fighting seamen. To make best use of them they had to be employed as a land force.

France too had a large number of dispossessed and displaced men in the Caribbean who had taken up the buccaneer way of life. They didn't call themselves by the French-derived word 'buccaneer', that would have been too easy. Instead they took the Dutch term 'frij-booter', which the English changed to 'freebooter'. The French pronounced themselves 'filibusters'. Dutchmen came to the Caribbean in almost as large numbers as the French and English. They had suffered Spanish rule in their homeland and felt even more strongly about Spain than the English or French Caribbeans did.

This multi-national, polyglot community, known as 'The Brethren of the Coasts', worked in crews or gangs that were seldom divided by nationality, language or class. Black men from Africa joined them, a few at first, but more as freed or escaped slaves learned the European languages. The English buccaneers, most of whom had been slaves themselves, would certainly not have returned slaves to their owners. Well, not unless the price was right.

7

Who's Who in Davy Jones' Locker?

In the 1660's the buccaneers found exactly the right man to lead them. Henry Morgan was a seasoned soldier of Welsh descent who had settled on the island of Jamaica and already owned more than one plantation. A disastrously bad sailor, Morgan rarely set sail without losing his ship. On one occasion the Governor of Jamaica gave him a navy frigate as a flagship for his fleet. Morgan had a party aboard to celebrate the gift. The frigate's magazine blew up, killing most of those at the party. That was typical of Morgan's luck with ships. He must be chuckling now to hear himself referred to as 'Captain' Morgan.

A charismatic character, silver-tongued and an entertaining drinking companion, Morgan drew adventurous men to him like a magnet. He raised buccaneer armies over a thousand strong for raids on towns and cities along the coasts of the Spanish Main, including Maracaibo, Portobello and Cartagena.

Under the leadership of Morgan, and others before and later, the buccaneers became seamen as well as land-soldiers. The musket was never discarded, but they found that a pistol was a better weapon on the crowded deck of a ship, until an enemy came within cutlass reach. They avoided the standard naval battle-tactic of exchanging broadsides until better gunnery and discipline won the day. The buccaneer tactic was to swoop from windward, grapple alongside and board, relying on fearsome countenance, ferocious fighting and daring deeds to overpower the victim vessel.

For the next quarter-century these irregular forces dominated war and politics in the Caribbean. They were a force that could be quickly summoned in great numbers and dismissed at no expense. They were enormously useful in defending the precarious colonies of England, France and Holland in the Spanish-dominated Caribbean.

At first the buccaneers would return to their occupation as killers of wild cattle in times of peace. Inevitably this way of life came to an end as the wild beasts grew fewer and the woodland was turned into plantation. The men grew accustomed to an exciting life at sea, large rewards for their efforts and a riotous time ashore between voyages.

When the organised raids along the Spanish Main became no longer necessary or acceptable, the seas of the West Indies were still under the sway of these seaborne soldiers who had grown to fill a need that their countries no longer had. It was obvious that many of them were going to continue a way of life that was so rewarding to them. It was not surprising that some were going to become pirates.

They had been trained and organised to take foreign shipping. They had been rewarded with much treasure and made heroes in the communities that they had defended. Little surprise then, that they continued to use their skills to their own account.

Naval forces were still very thin on the ground and the chance of being caught were slim at first. Only when naval power increased did the risk become greater, until the game finally became 'not worth the candle' and piracy dwindled to almost nothing.

For a brief generation though, pirates ruled the seas of the Caribbean and the eastern seaboard of North America. For a time they really lived the lives that Victorian novelists and Hollywood film-makers have portrayed for us. They were colourful, larger-than-life characters. They were cruel and bloodthirsty, vain and posturing, humorous and quixotic, gentlemanly and savage. They were also our ancestors.

THE PIRATE WAY OF LIFE

Most men came to piracy by being captured by a pirate vessel. A common seaman or a deep-sea fisherman was the ideal recruit to a pirate crew. For most seamen, capture by the pirates was a blessed relief from a life of grinding hardship and brutality.

A few senior officers in naval or merchant services seem to have decided that they no longer wished to operate with normal maritime law. In some cases wealthy landsmen, like Stede Bonnet, having dreamed of being a pirate for years, bought a ship and a black flag and sailed 'on the account'.

Often reluctant crewmen on a pirate ship would gradually become integrated. The freedom of the life, the lack of discipline and the chance of great wealth that it offered must have been near irresistible.

The early Caribbean pirates had been privateers or buccaneers originally. They were used to capturing ships and towns of enemy nations for their own gain. To take property of friendly nations or their own country is only a small step from privateering. No great change in philosophy was needed.

Once a man was absorbed into a pirate crew there were some immediate lessons to be learned. The first of these was that, as a crewmember, he owned a share of the ship and any prizes that it captured. The new pirate was suddenly living in a sort of democracy, an unknown experience for common people in the early 18th century. He must also learn quickly that his vote and his share brought responsibility, towards his ship and his ship-mates.

Our new pirate would have been required to sign the Articles of Agreement that had been written by, and for, that particular ship. The Articles didn't vary much from ship to ship. Here is a good example:

ARTICLES FOR CAPTAIN BARTHOLOMEW ROBERTS'
"ROYAL FORTUNE"

1. Every man has a vote in the affairs of moment; has equal title to the fresh provisions, or strong liquors, at any time seized, and may use them

at pleasure, unless a scarcity make it necessary, for the good of all, to vote a retrenchment.

2. Every man to be called fairly in turn, on board of prizes, because (over and above their proper share) they were on these occasions allowed a shift of cloaths; but if they defraud the company to the value of one dollar, in plate, jewels, or money, marooning was the punishment. If the robbery was only betwix one another, they content themselves with slitting the ears and nose of him that was guilty, and set him on shore, not in an uninhabited place, but somewhere, where he was sure to encounter hardships.

3. No person to game at cards or dice for money.

4. The lights and candles to be put out at eight o-clock at night; if any of the crew, after that hour, remain inclined to drinking, they were to do it on open deck.

5. To keep their pieces, pistols, and cutlasses clean, and fit for service.

6. No boy or woman to be allowed amongst them. If any man were found seducing any of the latter sex, and carry'd her to sea, disguised, he was to suffer death.

7. To desert their ship, or quarters in battle, was punishable with death or marooning.

8. No striking one another on board, but every man's quarrel to be ended on shore, at sword and pistol.

9. No man to talk of breaking up their way of living, till each had shared £1000. If in order to his, any man should lose a limb, or become a cripple in their service, he was to have 800 dollars, out of the public stock, and for lesser hurts, proportionably.

10. The Captain and Quartermaster to receive two shares of a prize; the Master, Boatswain and Gunner, one and a half, and other officers one and a quarter.

11. The Musicians to have rest on the Sabbath Day, but the other six days and nights, none without special favour.

You will see from Article 1, that every crewman may vote on each important issue. This did not apply when the ship was engaged in battle or running away. Article 1 also shows that limiting fresh food or strong drink was only done when absolutely necessary. This alone would have been a great inducement for men to join the pirates. On their last vessel, edible food and alcohol of any kind would have been reserved for the officers, or rigidly rationed.

Article 2 tells us of the fondness that pirates had for fine and colourful clothing. In an age when the poor dressed in rags, they loved silks and velvets, preferably in bright red, but any gaudy colour would do. John Rackham was an exception because he always wore cotton, a sensible thing in the tropics, but it earned him the nickname 'Calico Jack'. One can well understand this love of finery when one considers that their youth was probably spent inadequately clad, through freezing northern winters.

The second part of Article 2 tells us how scrupulously the shares of any plunder must have been divided. Nothing would turn a crew rebellious quicker than a suspicion that they had been cheated. When Basil Ringrose wrote of Captain Bartholomew Sharpe's return from the Pacific, he said that the division of the spoils took several days. One pirate in the Indian Ocean complained that although his one diamond weighed just the same as other crewmen's handfulls of diamonds, he felt cheated. They broke his diamond into smaller pieces to please him.

I suspect that Article 3's ban on gambling may have been peculiar to Bartholomew Roberts' ship. He was a sober, Godfearing man.

Lights and candles, mentioned in Article 4, must have been a constant worry, especially when handled by crewmen who were not very sober. Fire was ever a terror to seamen. In wooden ships, loaded with all the gunpowder they could obtain, the potential for disaster was enormous. If a man chose to drink on into the night, then it was just as well that the man at the wheel or the look-outs could keep a brotherly eye on him.

It is unlikely that any of the old hands needed reminding to keep their firearms and cutlass clean and in good working order. They would have known well enough that their weapons must fire when the trigger was pulled. Pistols were treasured by pirates and the reward for sighting a good prize was the best pair of pistols on that vessel. Newcomers to a pirate crew would not have been the excellent marksmen that the ex-buccaneers were. No doubt they practiced for many hours in the cleaning, loading and firing of their weapons before they began to compare with their older brethren.

Article 6 speaks for itself. Most Captains would not take women captives. If they did they were guarded very carefully, because nothing would ruin discipline quicker than the fight for female captives. It seems most unlikely that a woman could live aboard a pirate ship disguised as a man, until we consider Mary Read.

Article 7 is the same for pirates as for an other body of fighting men, desertion or cowardice cannot be allowed.

Article 8 is good common-sense. Disputes between crewmen were put aside until there was opportunity for them all to go ashore. That might have been months in the future, the dispute may have been long forgotten. If they determined to settle a dispute by arms, then it was arranged as a spectator sport, providing justice and entertainment at the same time. The Quartermaster was in charge of the event. He would set the duellers back-to-back on the seashore, then count the designated number of paces. Both men turned and fired on the Quartermaster's word. If they hesitated, the weapon was struck from their hand. Should they both remain unmarked, they would draw their cutlasses and fight until the first blood was drawn. The Quartermaster then declared the winner and the dispute was over.

A Captain's fear, with an ill-disciplined crew, was that they would collect a little plunder and then want to go away and spend it. Article 9 holds the crew together long enough for those who wish to save to start a respectable business ashore to do so. It also provided a large pension for those injured during their service. Sadly, most pirates could spend a thousand pounds quicker, and in more imaginative ways, than any landsman could understand or believe.

Article 10 is self-explanatory. I imagine that many reluctant crewmen decided to sign the Articles the first time they saw a crew weighing buckets full of gold coins, or measuring emeralds or pearls in handfuls. The larger shares for the more senior officers gave incentive for promotion. I have read of only one pirate captain, Charles Vane, who is said to have cheated his crew on the share-out of plunder. He was a repugnant man in every other way also.

Article 11's ban on music on Sundays may either have been a reflection of Bartholomew Roberts' religious leanings, or on the quality of his players. If they weren't good then possible the crew needed a rest from them on Sundays. Music was valued on any ship, pirate or not, and several pirates were noted as good singers.

THE CAPTAIN

The Captain of a pirate vessel was appointed by a vote amongst the crew. At any time, except when in pursuit of a prize, in the heat of battle, or when running away, a vote could be called and he could be replaced by another. This wasn't a very common occurrence, but it did sometimes happen.

To hold onto his captaincy, a man needed to be a popular and successful leader. More captains seem to have been dismissed for timidity than for foolhardiness. Most pirate crews did not appreciate great cruelty and more than one captain lost his command for being too hard with captives, Perhaps pirates had suffered more than enough cruelty themselves before they took to the profession.

The Captain had to dispense justice that was obvious to his crew. One pirate said that "less law made for more justice", and he was probably right. Crew members had to apply to the Captain for permission to fight each other. A common punishment for a minor offence against the ship was that the offender got one stroke of the lash from each crewman.

The Captain allotted shares of the booty, and that would not have been an easy task. Goods seized could be in any form, currency or coinage. They could be in bullion, the value of which had to be guessed, or in baled goods or barrels of supplies, sometimes even slaves were taken as booty. Tact and diplomacy of a high standard were required to satisfy each man that he had received an equal share. A Captain could not afford to alienate more than one or two of his crew, otherwise he might lose the next election for leadership.

Some detailed knowledge of the world's trade routes was necessary for the Captain. He had to keep abreast of events in the new-forming colonies, new wars and alliances and general trends of freight movement. He got news of the world from prize vessels that he took and used that information for his ship's survival and profit.

The best of the pirate captains were great natural leaders. Often illiterate, but always articulate, they inspired great loyalty. The best of them, that is. Some were mere brutes who ruled other brutes through violence, fear and threat.

A pirate Captain received two shares of all the plunder that his ship captured.

THE QUARTERMASTER

On a man-of-war, the Quartermaster and his team steered the vessel. A pirate Quartermaster had very different responsibilities, though steering the ship was part of them.

A pirate Quartermaster was always the Captain's right-hand man. He took the role of the Chief Mate on a merchantman, or the First Lieutenant on a man-of-war. It was the Quartermaster who saw that the Captain's orders were carried out, by promise of rewards where possible, by threat if necessary.

The Quartermaster maintained discipline among the pirate crew, as much as was necessary. He also kept control of the prisoners that pirate ships frequently carried. The Quartermaster normally conducted business for the Captain, ashore or on another vessel, a pirate Captain being too important to be summoned from his ship.

Another of the Quartermaster's responsibilities was to conduct duels between crewmen who violently disagreed. Fights were not allowed aboard, so duels had to wait until the crew could get ashore.

A pirate ship's Quartermaster received two shares of the ship's plunder, just as the Captain did.

SAILING MASTER, OR MASTER

The Sailing Master on a pirate ship was the officer who was most expert at setting the sails and deciding the course for the ship to sail where the Captain ordered.

Pirates, the Captains included, did not necessarily have any great nautical skills. Some, like Major Stede Bonnet, had no sea-going experience at all. These Captains relied on their Master, who told them not only what a ship could do, but how to arrange the rigging and canvas to make that possible. Each vessel had different characteristics, and if a Master could be captured with a new vessel, or persuaded to join their crew, then the new vessel would be easier to manage.

An 18th century sailing ship under wind-power could, with an able Master and a weed-free bottom, sail just a few degrees into the wind on either tack. To sail nearer to the direction that the wind came from was impossible. Thus, to sail to windward, a vessel had to sail for a measured time on its closest tack, then change its direction and sail close-hauled on the other tack for a corresponding period. The alternative, often possible on a pirate ship because of the huge crew that they carried, was to launch a couple of boats and tow the ship into the wind, with seamen rowing.

Pirate Captains preferred to capture the Master of a prize ship with it. His intimate knowledge of the ship's ability was valuable information. The captured man would be well looked after by the pirates and many of them eventually joined the pirate crew and took their share of the plunder. If the Master joined them, he received a share and three-quarters of the ship's prizes.

NAVIGATOR, OR ARTIST

A Navigator was usually known on board ship as the Artist. This was because the science of navigation, not very accurate in those days, was regarded by most of the men on board as a complete mystery, or a natural gift.

Often pirate ships would sail in a fleet because they only had one navigator between many vessels. If a good navigator was captured with a prize ship he would rarely be released, even if the vessel was. Many navigators were held by the pirates for years and some inevitably became crew members, attracted by the great rewards of pirate life.

18th century navigation was certainly a 'hit or miss' affair and the principles of it were not understood by many. At best, a reasonable Navigator of that period could calculate on what latitude his vessel sailed. That is, how far above or below the Equator they were. Navigation to a desired port required the ship to sail to the right latitude and then go East or West until they reached their destination, or somewhere near. The circulating ocean currents had not been charted then, though the tradewinds were common knowledge.

A successful Navigator could bring his vessel a few miles upwind of where the Captain wished to be, allowing the vessel to drift down to its destination. To arrive downwind of the ship's destination could be a total failure. One pirate vessel crossed the Atlantic from the West Indies to the Cape Verde Islands, came within sight of their destination but could not make headway against the tradewind. Their only option was to run back with the wind to South America. They had been out of water for two days, and were on the point of death from thirst when they sighted Surinam after their double Atlantic crossing.

BOATSWAIN OR BOSUN

The bosun of a pirate ship was one of the key men in the crew. He was responsible for the maintenance and repair of all the ship's standing and running rigging. The bosun was also responsible for the repair and the working of the simple machinery that the ship possessed. He must have a knowledge of setting up blocks and tackles to lift and move heavy weights, not simple in an age when all weights had to be guessed and men's lives depended on his guesswork.

The Bosun was also responsible for making working parties for any task assigned by the ship's officers. Forays ashore for water, firewood or fresh food would be led by the Bosun. He would be well to the fore-front of the action when the crew boarded another vessel.

His additional duties were the storage and maintenance of the cordage and canvas that the ship must carry; the maintenance and manning of the ship's boats, and the direction and manning of all work on the sails, spars and rigging of the ship.

Normally the Bosun would have been the most senior, experienced, genuine sailor on the ship. An inexperienced Captain could manage if he had a good Master and Navigator, a landlubber could get by as a Quartermaster if he had an experienced Bosun. The Bosun's appointment was different. A ship without a truly experienced Bosun could not be viable or successful, it would not even be safe.

CARPENTER

A pirate ship's Carpenter was nothing at all like a carpenter ashore. He was neither a house-builder nor a maker of fine furniture.

A pirate ship's carpenter was responsible to the Captain for the water-tight integrity of the ship's hull and the soundness of its masts. That was his prime function. He had to know in detail how the ship was con-structed, and how to repair it in the heat of battle.

In action, the carpenter would be ready with his damage-control team, to rush to any part of the ship to repair a leak. Ship's pumps were simple hand-pumps, and to get rid of a large amount of water could take days. A leak had to be stopped quickly or the vessel would lose way and sink.

Old spars, baulks of timber and spare canvas were all used by the carpenter to stop leaks. They would be propped against any strong part of the ship and driven tight with wedges. The carpenter's need for spare timber would often put him at odds with the Sailing-Master and the Bosun. In battle, the Master would order the Bosun to cut free any fallen mast, spar or rigging that would impair the sailing ability of the vessel. There must have been some instances when the Bosun was trying to jettison what he considered rubbish, while the Carpenter tried to save valuable materials.

Unlike a normal ship's carpenter, the pirate carpenter could not put off the more difficult tasks until the ship was dry-docked. Pirate ships rarely went into port and never had access to dockyard facilities. All repairs had to be carried out while the ship was afloat, or beached, and so they were, until the vessel became in such a bad state of repair that it had to be replaced.

When a new vessel was captured, the Carpenter would do an instant survey for the Captain to determine whether it would be better for them to keep the new vessel as their own and give their captives the old vessel to sail away with. This happened quite often.

All of this meant that the ideal pirate Carpenter had to be very much better than a shore-based colleague or a normal ship's Carpenter. He was the man who had to determine that their vessel was no longer seaworthy, and that they must seek a replacement.

Almost as a sideline, on most ships, the Carpenter would perform amputations of arms or legs, though the safety of the ship always came first. For this reason, I don't suppose anyone begrudged him the time that he spent sharpening or setting his saws.

GUNNER

My guess is that the pirate Gunner was almost always a deserter from a man-of-war. Few merchant ships would carry a gunner who compared in training and experience with a man whose trade it had been on a fighting ship.

Naval Gunners would quite likely have started as a Powder-Monkey at the age of 10 or 11, straight from the Poorhouse or Foundlings' Home. He would have worked through each position in a gun-crew until he became a gun-captain. By this time he would have been profoundly deaf and badly scarred by powder-burns.

On his pirate ship he would be expected to oversee all aspects of gunnery, from the safe stowage and handling of powder and shot, to the safe and efficient working of all the guns that the vessel carried.

Long-range battles, using ships' great guns, were not the pirate Captain's favoured method of fighting. Neither was it what they were best at. Musketry and nose-to-nose combat with cutlasses were the pirates strongest tactic. Pirates always ran away from a gunnery contest with any man-of-war, unless the odds were vastly in their favour. They did use their great guns to bring many a merchantman to a standstill, either with a warning shot across their bows, or with chain-shot to bring down some canvas and rigging.

The Gunner had to be able to train and practice his gun-crews in the loading, laying and firing of all the ship's heavy weapons. He needed the skills to keep the guns maintained and the leadership qualities to keep his gun-crews firing, in the heat of battle, without the threat of punishment that always prevailed on a man-of-war.

A good pirate Gunner well deserved his share and a half of the ship's plunder.

SURGEON

In the 17th and early 18th centuries, few ships would have carried anyone with any formal medical knowledge at all. In some cases, notably on men-of-war or troopships, a person with some knowledge of stitching, splinting or sawing of bones would have the title of Surgeon. Such a man was highly prized and would certainly have been held by a pirate ship if they happened to capture one. Often any person of education and common-sense was kept as a surgeon, and they probably did no more harm than a trained doctor of those times.

If no surgeon was aboard a ship, then the Carpenter did any job that required sawing (and many of them did). The Sailmaker was the obvious man to do the sewing, and it was the Bosun's largest axe that was heated red-hot to cauterise wounds and stumps.

Death from disease was very common, Captain Bartholomew Roberts once lost over one hundred men while careening his vessel on a swampy African river-bank. That was not considered unusual. Venereal diseases also ravaged pirate crews and the accepted treatment was with mercury, highly prized for its magical powers.

COOPER

In these days of cheap, watertight containers, it's easy to forget the importance of a ship's cooper. On early sailing ships the only container that could hold more than a bottle was a barrel.

The making and repairing of barrels was always a specialized task and coopers served a long apprenticeship to learn the skill from a master-craftsman. Barrels were not only used to carry liquids, they were the only way of keeping stores dry. Most foodstuffs were kept in barrels to keep them free of damp and ruin. Many meats and fish were preserved in salt to last for a long time; some were pickled in brine, so had to be kept wet.

The most valuable commodity of all, water, needed to be stored in as large quantities as possible. The loss of other stores was an inconvenience that had to be lived with, but the loss of water was a catastrophe.

The ship's cooper regularly inspected the barrels to discover any that leaked. These, he would empty into a sound barrel while he repaired the leaker. If a ship was fully laden, then space for more storage could be made by knocking apart barrels as they became empty. The bottom, wooded staves, lid and iron hoops could be stored, taking far less space than complete barrels.

When a pirate ship approached a watering place (somewhere that had fresh water running down to a deserted beach), the cooper would have a very busy time re-assembling barrels. Perhaps plunder would have to be buried there to make room for newly-made, newly filled, water barrels.

MUSICIAN

Music has always played a great part in the life of sailors throughout the ages. Manual work at sea also benefitted from a song or a tune. A slow, heaving rhythm helped hauling work on halliards and sheets, and a tramping beat aided capstan-turning.

Pirate crewmen tended to have more spare time than other seamen, for several reasons. They sailed mostly in the tropics where the steady trade-winds blew almost constantly from the same direction; thus the task of constantly altering sails as winds backed and veered was unnecessary. Much of the mundane, routine work on the ship would have been done by captives. Also, the lack of stern discipline meant that work was done as necessary, not as a punishment.

This increased leisure time was all the better enjoyed with a jug of rum and a skilled musician or two. The idle hours would pass more easily with good music. Dreams of home and family, or dockside doxies could be conjured more easily to a tuneful ballad. A few pirates were 'more celebrated as ballad-singers than as fighters.

Good musicians were highly valued and awarded a share-and-a-quarter of the plunder on most ships. If they were captives, they were rarely released until a better musician was found.

Captain John Smith's crew, pillaging in the Orkneys, refused two daughters of one house but took away the bagpiper. With no descriptions of the characters concerned, I can only guess that the local whisky and the piper's kilt confused them. Maybe all three had ginger beards, I can't say. What is certain, though, is that good musicians made for a happier ship.

THE PIRATE SEAMAN

The common seaman on a pirate vessel was normally a man recently released from the hardship and degradation of life under a tyrannical regime aboard a merchant ship or a man-of-war. He had become a member of a free society, where his skills and bravery were rewarded with an equal share of the profits made. He was released from much of the drudgery of day-to-day shipworking because a pirate ship probably carried captives who did not wish to turn pirate. These prisoners would do the boring, heavy work, leaving the pirate crewmen to supervise and guard them.

Strong drink was limited only by its availability and was not restricted to the ship's officers, as it had been on the seaman's last vessel. Many crewmen thought it best to go into action roaring drunk because if an injury resulted in an amputation, then it was better not to know too much about it. In spite of that, most prizes were taken with only a warning shot fired. Pirate vessels had such large crews that the sight of a hundred drunks, waiting to board a merchantman whose crew were a handful of reluctant men, most of whom wanted to join the pirates, probably drove all thought of resistance from the merchant skipper's mind.

One of the incentives for a seaman to turn pirate was the opportunity for revenge on his former captain and officers. The pirate quartermaster would organise a mock trial for these officers, and pirate crewmen would become the prosecution and defense lawyers. The punishment was normally a flogging by their ex-crewmen. I suspect that this might have been the first time that those officers realised how hated they were.

Pirate ships had to have a clean bottom to outsail the merchant ships that were their prey. Much time was spent in quiet bays and creeks, with guns ashore to protect them, scraping the ship's bottom. If there were local native people, they usually preferred pirates to the European settlers, who wished to enslave them. They probably also liked the pirates rum and riotous living. Some of the loveliest resorts in the Caribbean are those places where pirates careened and caroused ashore.

The pirate crewman had to be ready to change from one vessel to another quite quickly. All his possessions were contained in one container, his sea-chest. So sacred was another man's property, that stealing from someone's sea-chest was punishable by death. In more than one instance, a man's chest was lost on a sinking ship because others would not touch his property, so rigid was the rule.

When a pirate seaman wished to retire ashore he would be 'given a ticket' by his Captain. This meant that he was given a document which stated that he was not a willing member of the pirate crew and had received no share of plunder. A 'ticket' rarely saved a pirate from the gallows if he was caught.

TAKING A PRIZE

Pirate Captains always wished to have the element of surprise in their favour when confronting another vessel at sea. If the vessel was a man-of-war they would run, if it was a merchantman they would swoop quickly onto it. For this reason, a pirate ship kept a very vigilant lookout. The man who first espied a prize was awarded the best pair of pistols that the prize vessel carried.

Pirates had no wish to exchange broadsides of cannon-shot with any vessel they were capturing. They wished for both vessels to have as little damage as possible. Their advantage lay in generating terror in their victims, simply by firing a warning shot and showing an oversized black flag.

In the majority of cases the merchant ship would heave-to at the sight of the pirate ship's colours (sometimes a scull-and-crossbones, sometimes a complete skeleton, often a plain, black flag). The merchant Captain would hope to escape with the loss of a few crewmen, some of his cargo, and little else. In many cases it worked that way, if the pirates did not decide to take the vessel, and the Captain to act as a navigator for them.

The pirates tried, when it was possible, to come under the stern of a vessel they were taking. No great guns could bear on them that way. If the vessel tried to run away the pirates could shoot away the rudder, leaving the ship with no steering.

Merchant ships who offered resistance to the pirates were normally in for an unpleasant experience. Many of the pirates were ex-buccaneers and marksmen with a musket. The merchant ship would be raked with accurate musket-fire as they neared, then with pistol shots as the pirates boarded. The final stage, cutlasses at close-quarters, was rarely won by anyone but the pirates.

The approach of a pirate vessel whose bulwarks and ratlines were crowded with gaudily-clad, cutlass-waving, drunken vagabonds must have been a heart-chilling sight. Most merchantmen would have realised that resistance was futile.

Another favoured tactic of the pirates was to capture ships while they lay at anchor in harbour. Many tales of trickery, cunning and audacity are quite true. Most of these adventures involved muffled oars, the silent overpowering of sentries, and climbing up anchor cables. All of these things really happened. None of the adventure tales that you have read, or seen in movies, is any more exciting than the real lives of the real pirates.

PIRATE SHIPS

Pirates never built ships, and I know of only two that ever bought them, so it's speculation to say which type they preferred. Some pirate Captains seem to have preferred to exchange their vessels constantly for bigger ones as they progressed; others preferred to acquire more vessels, divide their crewmen among them and create a pirate fleet. I believe it depended upon whether a Captain felt he had the authority and charisma to hold a fleet under his command, or whether he preferred to keep all his men under his personal attention.

A pirate's choice of vessel depended on what appeared over the horizon and fell into his clutches. Here are some of vessels that pirates most commonly used:

Canoe or Pirogue or Peroagoa

These were copies of the native Carib canoe, made from a hollow tree-trunk. They were not the tiny canoe that we see in National Geographic with two Amazonian Indians in it. These vessels could be a hundred feet long with six feet of beam. They were finely hewn. They had a dagger-board or some other arrangement of keel and would sail in a clumsy sort of way. Normally they were paddled. These primitive vessels were quite sensible for shore-based pirates among the shoals and reefs. Being paddled, and with tiny draught, they could go well to windward and escape a pursuing man-of-war through shallows of coral or mangrove. Many pirates began with a canoe and graduated to full-rigged ships.

Barque or Barquantine

The Barque was a small trading vessel, used in Europe for coastal or cross-channel work. They were never as popular in the Caribbean as they were in Europe. Single-masted, they carried a square fore-sail and a large gaff-rigged main. They were considered too much of a blunt-nosed workhorse to appeal to pirates and their slow speed would have brought few prizes. They were the nautical delivery trucks of the 17th and 18th centuries.

Brig or Brigantine

Larger than a barque, two masted, a brig normally carried square-rigged sails on the foremast with one large, gaff-rigged sail on the mizzen, trisails and flying stay-sails filled-in between the masts. Some pirates used brigs as 'make-do' vessels in their progress towards their ideal ship. Like the barque, the brig was a bit too pedestrian to make a very successful pirate ship.

Galley

Not to be confused with the Spanish Galleon, the galley was a square-rigged sailing ship that could be assisted with the use of long oars or sweeps. Each oar could be pulled by two or three men, but they were rarely the main means of propulsion. Their real use was to enable the vessel to make way to windward for a short time. This enabled the pirates to come alongside, or run away from, a vessel that relied on wind-power alone. When being rowed, the sails would be furled. If the galley was sailing close-hauled, the sweeps could be manned on the leeward side to point the ship's head closer to the wind, giving the galley an advantage over her rivals. Many pirates found the galley ideal for their purposes. The large crews that most pirates carried meant that the manning of the sweeps was seldom a problem.

Sloop

The sloop was the ancestor of the modern sailing yacht. It was developed in the Caribbean into the ideal vessel for pirates. Sloops were built in all sizes; from two-man fishing and turtling boats, right up to Royal Navy ships which carried a dozen great guns. The attraction of the sloop was its simple rig, with one mast and most of the running rigging leading down to the foot of the mast. Sail handling was done from the deck and the only man needed aloft was the lookout. Sloops could stay at sea and make way when bigger, square-rigged ships had to stay in harbour or lie-to because of the weather. The sails of the sloop were 'fore-and-aft' rigged. The effect of this was that the winds action, over the curved surfaces of the sails, drew the bows closer to the direction of the wind. Simply put, the sloop sailed better against the wind than any square-rigged ship and this gave it an advantage in either capturing another ship, or running away. It is noticeable that the Royal Navy's greatest successes in taking pirates were performed in sloops.

Spanish Galleon

At first glance, with its high castles of accommodation at forepeak and stern, the galleon looks a most unwieldy, unweatherly vessel. And so they were. They were built to cross the Atlantic in a large fleet, with the tradewind pushing them. Their return journey was with the reciprocal winds on the northerly route. They could, however, present an enormous array of cannon to an enemy, and carry a huge payload. Several pirates, notably those who crossed to the Pacific on foot, captured these vessels. Their carpenters were given free-rein, a large crew and several days to do their work. The upper storeys were cut away and discarded. The galleons were then useful, seaworthy, weatherly craft. Several Spanish prisoners, having watched tons of beautiful carving and sumptuous accommodation vanish overboard, agreed that the vessels were hugely improved. There is no evidence of the Spanish authorities learning from these conversions, but the pirates who 'customised' galleons were well satisfied.

WEAPONS

Cutlass

The pirate's main weapon was his cutlass. It was a rough, broad-bladed, single-edged, slashing or hacking weapon. It relied on its weight and the strength of its owner's arm, and would snap a naval officer's fancy sword at a blow. Its chief advantage lay in the fact that it was strong. It was nothing at all like the elegantly curved, silver-basketted, sharkskin-gripped, dress sword so beloved of His Majesty's Navy. Though the cutlass was based on the naval issue weapon for seamen, in buccaneer and pirate hands it was a tool as well.

A man could fell a large tree with a cutlass. He could, and did, open coconuts, skin cattle, strike a spark for a fire, hack through an anchor cable or split an opponent down to his wishbone. Whatever firearms a pirate favoured, he would always have his cutlass hanging about his person somewhere.

Cutlasses have not disappeared, nor have they changed. Visit anywhere in Central America. Everyone employed in the forests or in agriculture still carries a cutlass, though each country has a different name for it.

Pike

The hand-pike or halberd was still used by the Spanish long after the conquest of the New World. In order to fight a man with a pike, another pike is needed. The early buccaneers would carry racks of pikes along the bulwarks of their ships. Only gradually did their Captains appreciate the skill-at-arms of their buccaneers. The ex-cattle-hunters proved that not only could they shoot far straighter than reluctant garrison soldiers, but they could re-load quicker too. The pike was eventually left at home, making the deck of a ship a far safer place for a man to get roaring, rolling drunk.

Pistols

Pistols were highly prized. Not just for their usefulness at close quarters, but for their balance, accuracy and ornamentation. The pride in ownership of such a fine object, perhaps with silver lock-plate and fittings, was enormous.

A pirate could not have too many pistols. Remember that they were muzzle-loaded and quite slow to re-load. In effect they were a 'one-shot' weapon. In action a man would carry all the pistols he owned, loaded and primed, hanging about him. They would be tied at the end of sashes or scarves of coloured silks.

Muskets

Muskets were usually made in huge quantities for the national armies of Europe. These would have been brought to the emerging colonies and bought or stolen by pirates. It was desirable that the muskets on a ship were from the same source, because then they were likely to be of the same calibre. With each prize taken, a ship would hope to standardise, or at least rationalise, its armoury. The complications of making, storing and issuing different sizes of ball for many different weapons would have been an unnecessary complication.

The buccaneer and pirate era was an 'overlap' time for firearms. Among the European armies, the wheel-lock mechanism was giving way to flintlock. The newer firing mechanism improved the chance of a weapon firing when the trigger was pulled, but only when everything was right.

Muskets were still muzzle-loaded. The men who lived (and often died) by firearms each had their own idea of how much powder was right for them, and how tight the wad should be tamped. The more fussy marksmen, or the most perfectionist, would make up a dozen prepared charges consisting of powder, wad and shot. Each charge would be held in a small leather or wooden purse and hung on a leather cross-belt which went from shoulder to hip. These dozen charges, in their pouches, were called 'apostles', whether for their number, or a prayer that they would fire, is anyone's guess.

The Great Guns

The main armament of a fighting ship in the 17th and 18th centuries was its muzzle-loading cannon. In principle, they were little different from the ordnance pieces that land armies trundled with them from one battle to the next. The real difference lay in their handling and limitations. A land artillery piece was dug into an emplacement of earth which enclosed it, or had its long drawbar spiked into the earth, so that the energy of its recoil could dissipate harmlessly. Some field pieces simply ran backwards until the soft earth stopped them. That was easy, provided you had room enough.

On the crowded gun-deck of a ship the energy of a gun's recoil becomes a major problem. Tiny wheels and a heavy wooden 'truck' discouraged the gun's backward run, but a smooth, scrubbed oak deck could not dissipate its force as soft earth did. To restrain the guns and absorb the energy, a system was made of ropes and blocks which attached the gun to the ship's side with some elasticity.

We can start to see already the factors which limited the size, and therefore the range and effectiveness, of a ship's guns. First was the strength of the deck and its ability to carry the number and size of cannon required. Next the ability of the 'walls' of the ship to stand the simultaneous and repeated recoil of several guns. Finally there was the ability of the ship to carry so much weight, so high above its keel, without turning over. (King Henry VIII's vessel Mary Rose was an example of a new, over-gunned ship which turned-turtle soon after her launching.)

Consequently, a pirate sloop (and sloops became favourite because of their handling and speed) would normally carry just one pair of great guns on either side of her maindeck. Neither buccaneers nor pirates were keen on an artillery duel. The more disciplined naval vessels were just so much better adapted to gunnery fights. Speed and precision at gunnery were the result of unthinking discipline and the unlimited use of the cat-of-nine-tails, neither of which appealed to the 'brethren of the coasts'.

A warning shot across the bows of a merchantman was the most effective use that pirates had for their great guns. If that failed to stop a prize vessel, then chain-shot through the rigging would dislodge a spar or two and slow them down. Pirates had no wish to damage any vessel that they were capturing, it might become their next home.

So the size of the great guns was limited by what a pirate ship could safely carry and fire. The guns were rated according to the weight of a roundshot that fitted its barrel. The largest were 32-pounders, huge pieces for the very lowest gun-decks of mighty men-of-war, not pirate ships. More probable on a pirate ship would have been 8 or 12-pounders, far more sensible for an ill-disciplined gang to work.

The Swivel-Gun

The pirate's most-favoured piece of ordnance was the swivel-gun. It was nicknamed 'the murderer', with good reason. Made of brass or bronze, with two handles on its barrel, the swivel-gun could be carried by two strong men and fitted at any point along the ship's sides. They could also be mounted in any of the ship's boats. This made them very versatile and dangerous. Loaded with many pistol-balls or scrap metal, the 'murderer' could sweep clear the deck of a prize vessel as the pirates came alongside. Quick to load, easy to aim and fire, the swivel-gun was a deadly weapon in pirate hands.

An Armed Pirate

We can start to get some idea of what a pirate would look like when he was prepared for action.

His cutlass always hung at his side. He called it his 'hanger'. He probably also wore a broad leather cross-belt, hung with his 'apostles'. Swinging about him would have been his pistols, several, each hanging on a coloured silken sash. His musket would have been cast aside by the time he was ready to board a prize vessel.

Under all his weaponry he wore a dirty velvet coat. A sweatband or kerchief would be wound round his brow to keep the sweat from his eyes and on top of that would be his wide, black, tri-corn hat, if he possessed one.

Our pirates face would blackened from the powder of his musket or the ship's great guns. If he had made several ocean voyages it is likely that he would have lost all his teeth to scurvy. It's likely too that he would no longer have all the eyes, ears, hands and feet that he was born with.

All in all, he was not the sort of person you would wish to encounter if you were the Captain of a Spanish treasure ship, or an honest merchant carrying your goods to the colonies to sell.

The average pirate's resemblance to Douglas Fairbanks Jnr, Errol Flynn or Mel Gibson was, I'm afraid, very slight.

THE GALLOWS

The end for many pirates was a trial and the gallows. Most of the pirates named here ended their lives that way, and that's why a record can still be found of their existence. Very many more pirates died of disease than were ever caught. Many more retired to become squires, traders, publicans or beggars.

It seems brutal to us, that so many seafarers were publicly hanged without very much of a trial. More especially when we realise how little choice most of them had.

I think the pirates' view of hanging was best given by the woman-pirate Mary Read, "that if it was put to the pyrates, they would not have any punishment less than death, the fear of which kept some dastardly rogues honest; that many of those who now cheated the widows and orphans, and oppressing their poor neighbours, who have no money to obtain justice, would rob them at sea, and the ocean would be crowded with rogues, like the land."

The place of execution was always visible from the sea-approach to a harbour, where the hanged bodies would swing in the wind as a warning to the crews of all passing ships. Trials for piracy were conducted on behalf of Their Lordships the Admiralty, often by the Governors of colonies. The land below the high watermark along the shores was the jurisdiction of Their Lordships, so it was appropriate that the gallows were erected there.

Custom varies on the disposal of the pirate corpses. At Execution Dock in London, three tides had to wash over the bodies before they were removed. In Boston they were hanged on the foreshore, then the bodies removed to be displayed at Nix Mate, an island in the harbour. Famous pirates were often coated in tar to preserved the bodies, then displayed for many years as a gruesome reminder to all passing seamen.

I recently made a winter pilgrimage to the site of Execution Dock. It was just before dusk on a biting-cold, dark afternoon. The open square is now neat gardens, but it needed no great leap of the imagination to picture pirate corpses turning in the icy wind blowing off the River Thames.

The colonies of Britain followed the motherland in their manner of execution, probably because the rule of the Admiralty extended to those new shores. The Spanish favoured garrotting as a method of executing pirates, but that was, until recent years, their national method of execution ashore too.

The way that pirates faced their deaths is characteristic. Brave men died bravely, while some who had dealt out death to many others had to be dragged, struggling and crying, to the gallows. Many met their death with resigned humour. One of my favourites is Captain Richard

Thomas, who, asked if he was sorry and repented, said, "Yes. I repent that I had not done more mischief, and that we did not cut the throats of them that took us, and I'm extremely sorry that you ain't hanged as well."

Dennis Macarty was another gallows humorist. He said, "Some of my friends said I should die in my shoes. To make 'em liars, I kicks them off."

There was huge public interest and attendance at the hanging of more famous pirates. I guess that people of property watched with some relief that their ships and trade were a bit safer; while the poor chuckled silently that some of their own had managed to buck the system.

Bartholomew Roberts, probably the most successful pirate, used to say, "In an honest service, there are commonly low wages and hard labour; in this – plenty, satiety, pleasure and ease, liberty and power; who would not balance creditor on this side, when all the hazard that is run for it at worst, is only a sour look or two on choking? No – a merry life and a short one, shall be my motto!"

For those who don't wish to think about such a morbid subject, I recommend that you think of the successful pirates who retired with great wealth. Many titled and landed families, many multi-national companies and great trading empires were originally funded by a sea-chest or two of buccaneer or pirate gold, silver, emeralds or pearls.

BEFORE PIRACY – AN ORDINARY SEAMAN'S LIFESTYLE

The daily life of a common seaman in the 17th and 18th centuries was far harder than we can easily understand. Even by the harsh standards of his country cousin, his life was grindingly hard, ill-paid and very dangerous. Serious injury was commonplace and diseases caused by malnutrition, privation and tropical infections were rife.

A merchant ship was usually under-crewed, to keep down the costs. The only machinery used on a vessel were blocks and tackles, windlasses or capstans; all man-powered. Where horses, mules, oxen, elephants or llamas might be used ashore for heavy work, on board a ship it was all done by men's muscles alone.

The cordage used for lifting and hauling was all of natural fibres, handmade and untested. It rotted quickly in the marine atmosphere. When it broke, something heavy fell from aloft, or flew free, or ran loose across a pitching deck, often causing horrific injury.

A merchant vessel carried no doctor or surgeon. On some vessels the Captain or one of the Mates would have experience in dealing with injuries, but no formal training. Often quite minor injuries would lead to infections and many times a small cut on hand or foot led to a painful death some days later.

The seaman on a man-of-war lived with all these same hazards, but with the added dangers of a fighting ship. Naval gunnery was almost as dangerous for those behind the guns as it was for the enemy. Gunners waved lighted fuses around lads scampering with buckets or bags of gunpowder. The tackles which restrained the great guns often parted, or the eye-bolts pulled out of the ship's side, allowing 'a loose cannon' to crush anyone in its path.

Men-of-war sometimes spent months on station, blockading a port or stretch of coastline; while a merchantman would aim for a safe and swift passage. Discipline was even harsher in the naval service than it was in the merchant marine. It had to be so because many, if not most, of the common seamen had not wished to go to sea. They would have been impressed (press-ganged) into the service at some port along the way.

Impressed men could never be allowed ashore, except in places so inhospitable that no-one would contemplate desertion. When a vessel or a fleet returned to the Solent or the Medway, outbound ships would take off their impressed men at Spithead or the Nore. Thus life was one continuous voyage for the pressed men.

Seamen in the 18th century used to say, with good cause, that they would have been far better off in prison, where the food was better, the quarters were better, the life was easier and there was no chance of drowning.

A brutal regime of cruel punishment was the prospect of every seaman who didn't 'look lively' at all times. Flogging was routine and encouraged as a spectator sport by the ship's officers. Flogging and pickling (if the galley could spare the vinegar) wasn't uncommon. A naval Captain could hang a man from a yard-arm after the briefest of trials and the corpse be left for the seabirds as an example to the rest of the crew.

There were two ways that a seaman could escape his miserable life at sea before he was too old or ill to be any more use. The first was to be injured seriously enough; when he would be put ashore at the next convenient place. Convenient to the ship, that is, not the seaman.

The seaman's other hope of rescue from misery was that by capture or desertion from the ship, he might join a pirate crew.

In spite of the pirate's chance of being hanged, the pirate seaman had a good chance of living well for two or three years. That was as good a life expectancy as he could hope for if he stayed in the Navy.

ADAIR

James ADAIR. b. Scotland. A retired Indian Ocean pirate, who, with John PLANTAIN and Hans BURGEN established a stockaded fortress at Ranter Bay, Madagascar. It became a famous stopping place for pirates and trading vessels. They lived in great style, each with an exotic harem. Eventually their establishment was dispersed by growing naval strength in the area, probably in 1720.

AISA

AISA. A famous Mediterranean Corsair in the 16th century.

An admiral in the fleet of the Turkish pirate DRAGUT. AISA was probably involved in the Siege of Malta.

ALCANTRA

Captain Mansel ALCANTRA. A Spaniard. He commanded the brig *Macrinarian*. ALCANTRA took the Liverpool packet *Topaz* near St Helena, en route for Boston in 1829. The same year he took *Candace* from Marblehead. A passenger on *Candace* was an actor who happened to have a priest's costume in his baggage, he donned it and sat telling his beads as the pirates boarded. The pirates crossed themselves and left him in peace while they robbed everyone else on board. No further knowledge of ALCANTRA.

ALEXANDER

John ALEXANDER. A Scot. A buccaneer with Captain Bartholomew SHARP's expedition to plunder the Pacific. He drowned on 9 May 1681 while ferrying tools from shore to ship at the island of Chira. His body was found three days later and buried at sea.

ALI BASHA

ALI BASHA, of Algiers. He conquered Tunis in the 16th century, capturing many Maltese galleys. He organised and developed piracy in the Mediterranean. At the Battle of Lepanto in 1571, ALI BASHA commanded a fleet of 250 galleys. He was defeated, but escaped alive.

ALLESTON

Captain ? ALLESTON. A buccaneer captain in the Caribbean. He took his ship of 20 tons and 24 men to join Captain Bartholomew SHARP's expedition to plunder the Pacific coasts in 1680/81.

ALWILDA

A Scandinavian royal woman pirate in the 5th Century. To avoid an arranged marriage to Prince ALF of Denmark, ALWILDA and some of her companions dressed as men, stole a boat and sailed off. They encountered a pirate crew who were leaderless and ALWILDA's natural leadership qualities soon won her command of the whole force. Her band of pirates made such a reputation for themselves in the Baltic that Prince ALF was despatched to destroy them. After a pitched battle ALWILDA was captured by the Prince, but was so impressed with his gallantry that she agreed to marry him. ALWILDA eventually became the Queen of Denmark. A romantic legend? What if it is?

AMEER

Ibrahim AMEER. Commanded an Arabian pirate fleet in the Red Sea. In 1816 he captured four British merchant ships en route for Surat.

ANDRESSON

Captain Cornelius ANDRESSON. A Dutchman. He left Boston in 1674 in *Penobscot Shallop* with Captain ROGELIO, to take English ships on the coast of Maine. Caught and tried at Cambridge, Mass. and sentenced to death, but later pardoned. He fought for the English colonists against the Indians.

ANDRIESZOON

Captain Michael ANDRIESZOON. A Dutch freebooter and a subordinate to De GRAAF. In 1683 he joined De GRAAF's huge fleet to sail against Veracruz. As part of his reward

ANDRIESZOON received a Spanish prize vessel which he named *Mutine*. The next year ANDRIESZOON and WILLEMS blockaded Cuba on De GRAAF's orders. In 1685 he sailed again with De GRAAF, by this time he commanded his own fleet of 5 vessels.

ANGORA

The Sultan of Timor. He refused to let the East India Company garrison his island, and was driven out of all but his chief town, which was also called Angora. He turned pirate and captured the vessel carrying orders to the garrison on his island. Captain HASTINGS, commanding the vessel (a relative of Warren HASTINGS) had already dropped the despatches overboard and was hanged by ANGORA. The remainder of the crew were imprisoned on the island and poisoned. The same fate awaited the crew of the next captured vessel, the East Indiaman *Edward*. ANGORA took several more English vessels, then a Burmese ship with a rich cargo. He drowned all on board except one beautiful woman whom he kept for himself. He took a Malay vessel, drowning the crew, then blew up the fortress at Bombay. After taking the English packet *St George* he returned home to find *HMS Victorious* waiting for him. He managed to slip away to Ceylon, where the East India Company left him to settle in peace.

ANGRIA

The brother of ANGORA, Sultan of Timor. When ANGORA retired to Ceylon, ANGRIA took over his vessel of 38 tons and wrought vengeance upon the English. He took *Elphinston* with a crew of 47, some 80 miles off Bombay. The crew were put in an open boat without water and only 28 were still alive when they reached Bombay. He continued to take vessels of all nations and claimed to have murdered over 500 Englishmen. He was eventually chased to Timor by *HMS Asia* and besieged there for a year. ANGRIA was shot by one of his own men in the end.

ANNAND

Alexander ANNAND, of Jamaica. A crewman to Major Stede BONNET. Captured with BONNET on the Cape Fear River on 27 Sep 1718. Tried at Charleston. Found guilty of piracy and hanged on 8 Nov 1718.

ANSTIS

Captain Thomas ANSTIS. Sailed from Providence in the sloop *Buck* with Dennis TOPPING, Walter KENNEDY and Howel DAVIS. This was the beginning of the great pirate company that Captain Bartholomew ROBERTS eventually commanded. They took the vessel *Morning Star* near Bermuda. With ROBERTS they lay at an uninhabited island '20 leagues to windward of Jamaica' to await

their joint petition for a pardon from the King. It never arrived. They ran from the man-of-war 'Hector' in the Cayman Islands and sailed to a small island off the Honduras coast, where they careened and refitted in Dec 1722. Their next careening was ashore in Tobago, where *HMS Winchelsea* surprised them. ANSTIS in *Good Fortune* fled, leaving the other two vessels on the beach. The majority of the crew were angry at ANSTIS' mismanagement and he and other leaders were shot. The crew sailed the vessel to Curacao. Those who had rebelled against ANSTIS were acquitted, the rest were hanged as pirates.

APTHORP

Edward APTHORP. A reluctant crewman to Captain William FLY. APTHORP was taken from the prize vessel *John and Hannah*. After the capture of FLY's vessel, APTHORP was tried at Boston on 4 Jul 1726, but was quickly acquitted.

ARCHAIMBAUD

Captain ? ARCHAIMBAUD. A French filibuster in the Caribbean. In 1681/2 he sailed in a fleet of buccaneers which included COXON, SHARP and Le SAGE. They took 14 Spanish merchantmen off Riohacha. William DAMPIER called him Monsieur ARCHEMBO and joined his crew for an attack on the town of Coretaga (Costa Rica). DAMPIER says of his crew, "the saddest creatures that ever I was among; for though we had bad weather that required many hands aloft, yet the biggest part of them never stirred out of their hammocks, but to eat or ease themselves." DAMPIER and the other Englishmen soon left ARCHAIMBAUD.

ARCHER

John Rose ARCHER. A crewman to BLACKBEARD. He later joined Captain William PHILLIPS as Sailing Master. PHILLIPS and his crew were overpowered by captives and reluctant crewmen on 14 Apr 1724. The vessel was sailed to Boston by the reluctant crewmen and the pirates were tried. Archer was found guilty and hanged on 2 Jun 1724. It is revealing that before his execution, ARCHER spoke to those who had come to see him die. He said, "I could wish that Masters of vessels would not use their men with such severity, as many of them do, which exposes us to great temptations." An indictment against the cruelties of merchant ships Captains towards the common seaman.

ARGALL

? ARGALL. A buccaneer who operated with a privateer's licence from one of the Governors of the colonies. He is believed to have buried a vast treasure in the Isles of Shoals, New Hampshire, in the 17th century.

ARMSTRONG

Robert ARMSTRONG. A deserter from *HMS Swallow*, he joined Captain Bartholomew ROBERTS' *Royal Fortune*. He had the astounding ill luck to be captured by *HMS Swallow* off the West African coast on 10 Feb 1722. He was shipped back to London and hanged as a deserter from the yardarm of HMS Weymouth.

ARNAUGHT

John ARNAUGHT. A captive (he said) on Captain James SKYRM's vessel *Ranger*. Captured by *HMS Swallow* off the West African coast on 1 Feb 1722. He was tried at Cape Corso Castle on 28 Mar 1722. ARNAUGHT's defence was that he had been taken from the prize vessel *Tarlton* less than a month before his capture and was not a volunteer. He was acquitted.

ARNEWOOD

? ARNEWOOD. A Dorset-based pirate in the reign of Queen Elizabeth I.

ARNOLD

Sion ARNOLD. One of the pirates who settled, or was marooned, on the island of Madagascar. He was picked up by a Captain SHELLEY in 1699 and brought back to New England.

ARTHUR

Captain ? ARTHUR. An English pirate captain in the early 17th century. In 1611 he was sailing the North Atlantic and New-foundland Banks with a large fleet of pirates which included Captains FRANCKE, STE-PHENSON and SMITH.

ASHPLANT

Valentine ASHPLANT. b. Min-ories, London, 1690. Sailed as crew-man to Captain Howard DAVIS. Later a crewman on Captain James SKYRM's *Ranger*. Cap-tured by *HMS Swallow* off the West African coast on 1 Feb 1722. He was tried at Cape Corso Castle on 28 Mar 1722. ASHPLANT was found guilty and hanged.

ASHTON

Phillip ASHTON. Of Marble-head, Mass. A reluctant crewman to Captain Edward LOW. He was taken from a fishing shallop on 15 Jun 1722. ASHTON escaped from LOW's vessel to a desert island in the Caribbean where he spent several months. He was eventually rescued by a man-of-war and returned to Salem. ASHTON gives an excit-ing current account of the pirates lifestyle in that period.

ATKINSON

Captain Clinton ATKINSON. b. London. A Dorset-based pirate captain in the late 16th cen-tury. ATKINSON was the son of a Puritan clergyman who fled from England to escape the Catholic purges of Queen Mary. Clinton's godfather was the Earl of Lincoln. ATKINSON first sailed as a privateer for the King of Portugal, but after his commis-sion expired he continued to take French and Dutch vessels. His local protection was insured by favourable dealings with the Dorset authorities. In 1582 ATKINSON rowed ashore with his pirate colleagues to cut down the body of their fellow-pirate Captain John PIERS, who had been hanged on the shoreline at Studland Bay as a warning to others. ATKINSON was cap-tured in 1583 at Sandwich Bay and held for trial. He paid bribes to the Dorset authorities to ensure a trial within the county (which would have meant an acquittal) but the Admiralty tried him in London. Despite the efforts of his godfather, (by then the Lord Admiral) ATKINSON was condemned. He was hanged at Execution Dock in 1583.

ATWELL

? ATWELL (or ATWILL). Stew-ard of *Vineyard*. Plotted with another crewman, Charles GIBBS to overpower the officers and take over the ship. Drowned off Rhode Island in 1831.

AUGER

Captain John AUGER. Surrendered in exchange for a pardon to Woodes ROGERS on Providence Island, Bahamas, in 1718. Given command of a sloop by ROGERS to go for supplies, he immediately took the sloop to continue his piracy, taking 2 other sloops as prizes. Driven by a storm onto Long Island, Bahamas, he was captured by ROGERS men. AUGER was tried and hanged at Providence.

AURY

Luis AURY. Real name Louis-Michel AVERY, b. Paris, France. 1788? AURY joined the French Navy as a boy and later served on privateers. In his early 20's he was a Lieutenant with substantial prize-money. In 1810 he bought a schooner in New Orleans. The US authorities seized the vessel as a privateer. AURY then became part-owner of a Swedish schooner which he named *Vengeance* for obvious reasons. In 1811, in Savannah, locals set fire to *Vengeance*, thus reinforcing AURY's dislike of the US. AURY next based himself in Colombia and raised a fleet against the Spanish. After very limited success and much ill-luck, AURY decided that Mexico next needed his help. He took Spanish ships in the Gulf of Mexico. In Galveston, AURY's crew rebelled, stabbed him in the chest and sailed off

with his fleet. AURY reappeared at Amelia Island, Florida, where his men took the town of Ferdinandina from the Spanish, and from 21 Sep to 23 Dec 1817, he ruled the Island under the title of the 'Republic of the Floridas'. US President MONROE sent troops to Amelia Island. They raised the US flag over Ferdinandina and detained AURY for a couple of months before releasing him. AURY returned to his task of ridding South and Central America of the Spanish. A strange and complex man, AURY died in 1821 as a result of having been thrown from a horse, and that was typical of his luck.

AUSTIN

James AUSTIN. A crewman to Captain John QUELCH on the brig *Charles*. Arrested in Portsmouth, Mass. He escaped for a while but was caught again and imprisoned at Piscatagua. AUSTIN was tried in the Star Tavern in Boston in Jun 1704. AUSTIN was one of the 15 crewmen who pleaded guilty in exchange for 'the mercy of the court and being allowed to join the Queen's service'.

AVERY (or EVERY)

Captain Henry AVERY. (Known as Long Ben AVERY, because he was over two yards tall). b. Nr Plymouth, Devon. One of a seafaring family. AVERY served as a mate on a merchantman. He joined the vessel **Duke**, part of a small squadron fitted out at Bristol on Spanish orders to stop French smugglers between Martinique and the South American mainland. While the vessel lay at Coruna, AVERY organised a mutiny. About half of the crew, including the captain, GIBSON, didn't want to join AVERY. They were sent ashore in a boat. AVERY sailed for Madagascar and fell in with two other pirate sloops who were en route from the West Indies. They formed a pirate squadron. In the Indian Ocean they took a vessel belonging to the Grand Mogul. It was loaded with rich pilgrims bound for Mecca and the Grand Mogul's daughter was one of the passengers. As a result of this piracy, the Grand Mogul threatened war on the English settlements in India. Avery persuaded the vessels accompanying his own that his was the safest vessel to transport their huge treasure. Naturally, AVERY lost the other two vessels in the night. He headed for the Bahamas, where he sold the sloop and bought another vessel. AVERY sailed first to

Boston, then to Northern Ireland. He made his way to Bideford, Devon, where he decided to settle. He had a great wealth in diamonds and contacted someone who offered to sell them for him. Foolishly, he parted with the diamonds against a token payment, never receiving the rest of the cash. For a while he lived on the verge of starvation, but soon sickened and died.

Note: A play was written about AVERY, called The Successful Pirate, telling how he had married the Grand Mogul's daughter and lived in splendour like a prince. While the play ran, AVERY was starving under an assumed name in Devon.

AYLETT

Captain ? AYLETT. A buccaneer captain in the Caribbean. He attended Henry MORGAN's great feast on the frigate **Oxford**, to celebrate the buccaneer fleet having been given a naval vessel. During the feast, the **Oxford's** powder magazine blew up. The vessel was wrecked and AYLETT was amongst those who were killed. MORGAN survived.

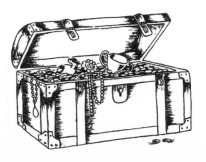

BAKER

Captain ? BAKER. A captain in the fleet of the pirate chief GASPARILLA. They cruised and plundered the Gulf of Mexico until they were dispersed by the US Navy in 1822.

BAKER

Thomas BAKER. Crewman to Captain John (Calico Jack) RACKHAM. He joined RACKHAM's vessel at Negril Point, Jamaica, on the day of its capture. Tried at St Jago de la Vega on 16 Nov 1720. His trial was adjourned until 24 Jan 1721 for want of evidence. No further evidence was found but they found him guilty anyway. Hanged at Gallows Point, Port Royal, on 17 Feb 1721.

BAKER

Thomas BAKER. b. Flushing, Holland. A crewman to Captain Samuel BELLAMY. BAKER was given command of a prize pink by BELLAMY. The pink went aground on Cape Cod on the night that BELLAMY's *Whydah* was wrecked close by. BAKER was taken prisoner and brought to trial at Boston. He was hanged there on 15 Nov 1717.

BALDRIDGE

Adam BALDRIDGE. A Jamaican buccaneer who fled to the islet of St Mary's, Madagascar, with a party of other buccaneers.

BALDRIDGE was wanted for murder in Jamaica and was running from justice. He established himself in this defensible harbour and a trading community grew up there. Being the first and best established pirate in the area, he became known as "The King of Pirates". St Mary's became a stopping place for pirates and trading ships bound into and out of the Indian Ocean. A popular ditty of those days asks:

"Where is the trader of London Town?
His gold's on the capstan
His blood's on his gown,
And it's up and away for St Mary's Bay,
Where the liquor is good, and the lasses are gay."

In 1697 the native inhabitants of Madagascar rose against the pirate community at St Mary's and drove them out. BALDRIDGE took his wealth to New York where he settled and lived to a ripe old age.

BALL

Roger BALL. Crewman to Captain James SKYRM on *Ranger*. Blown up in a powder explosion when *Ranger* was captured by *HMS Swallow*. He died of his wounds the next day, 2 Feb 1722.

BALLENTYNE

? BALLENTYNE. Crewman to Captain Thomas GREEN on *Worcester*. Falsely imprisoned, tried, sentenced and hanged at Leith, Scotland, in Apr 1705.

BALLET

John BALLET. A Caribbean buccaneer. He had been a ship's surgeon on one of DAMPIER's voyages. Later he was third mate on Woodes ROGERS ship, the *Duke*.

BALTIZAR

Captain ? BALTIZAR. A notorious pirate in the Gulf of Mexico in the early 19th century. He was captured and brought to Boston in 1823. At that time, US juries were a lot more squeamish about imposing a death sentence against pirates. Some were shipped to Jamaica, where the colonial government was keener to set a good example to its citizens. BALTIZAR was one of those who were tried at Kingston, found guilty and hanged.

BANISTER

Captain ? BANISTER. Sailing Master to Captain William LEWIS and Darby McCAFFREY. Hanged in Jamaica.

BAPTIS

John BAPTIS. One of the three Frenchmen who were reluctant crewmen on Captain William PHILLIPS' vessel. PHILLIPS eventually took more captives than he could control and they took over the vessel and sailed it to Boston. BAPTIS was tried in Boston on 12 Apr 1724 and acquitted.

BARBAROSSA

Kheir-ed-Din BARBAROSSA. d.1546. A famous Barbary Coast corsair. He established his headquarters in Tunis in 1504. He paid the Sultan of Tunis one fifth of all his prizes for the right to stay there. He preyed on shipping of all nations in the Mediterranean. In 1512 he assisted in the attempt to retake the town of Bujeya from the Spanish. After losing an arm BARBARROSSA gave up the siege. In 1516 he moved his base to Jijil, took command of an army of 6000 men with 16 vessels and captured the Spanish fortress of Algiers, of which town he became Sultan. Eventually Charles V of Spain sent an army of 10, 000 men against him and he was slain in battle.

BARBAROSSA

Aruj BARBAROSSA. d. 1518. A Barbary Coast corsair. Brother of Kheir-ed-Din. Active from early 1500s to his death.

BARLICORN

Richard BARLICORN. Crewman to Captain William KIDD on the galley *Adventure*. He surrendered with KIDD for pardon in New York. Was shipped with KIDD to England and tried at the Old Bailey in May 1701. BARLICORN was found not guilty of piracy because he was an indentured apprentice to the vessel.

BARLOW

Jonathan BARLOW. A crewman to Captain Edward LOW aboard *Merry Christmas*. The Massachusetts State House holds a statement from crewman BARLOW that LOW was cast adrift by his crew. This seems to nullify the rumour that LOW survived to enjoy his fortune.

BARNARD

Captain ? BARNARD. A Caribbean buccaneer. In June 1663 BARNARD sailed from Port Royal, Jamaica, to the Orinoco River. He plundered the town of Santo Tomas, returning to Jamaica in May 1664.

BARNES

Captain ? BARNES. A Caribbean buccaneer. Sailed with Captain John COXON to sack the town of Santa Marta, on the Spanish Main, in 1677. They kidnapped the Bishop and took him to Jamaica as a hostage. Lord VAUGHAN, Governor of Jamaica, hired a vessel to take him back home. The Bishop was "exceedingly pleased".

BARNES

Henry BARNES. b. Barbados, 1701/2. Crewman on Captain

Charles HARRIS' *Ranger*. Captured by *HMS Greyhound*. Tried at Newport R.I. in Jul 1723. BARNES was found not guilty and acquitted.

BARROW

James BARROW. Barrow kept chickens aboard the snow *Martha*, and the murder of his chickens by the pirates seems to have convinced him to join Captain James SKRYM's *Ranger* and sign the Pirate Articles. Captured off the West African coast by *HMS Swallow* on 1 Feb 1722. Referred to the Marshalsea for trial, he was probably suspected of being a Navy deserter.

BARROW

Captain Thomas BARROW. A New Providence based pirate captain in the year 1715.

BARRY

Captain Lording BARRY. An English pirate captain in the early 17th century. Notable, because when he anchored at Berehaven, Bantry Bay, one of his crew was a young black girl. He returned to England in 1615 to seek a pardon.

BART

Captain Jean BART. A French privateer and pirate in the Caribbean who achieved fame during the Nine Years War (1690s).

BARTOLOMEO

BARTOLOMEO el PORTU-GUES. (Bartolomew the Portugese) A buccaneer in the Caribbean in the 1660s. BARTOLOMEO worked out of Jamaica in a time when few non-English did so. He was not very successful and Esquemelling "saw him dying in the great wickedness of the world", whatever that meant.

BASTFIELD

Captain Lambert BASTFIELD. b. Liverpool. An English pirate captain in the 1600s. He was surprised and taken by a Dutch naval squadron while careening in a remote Irish Bay.

BAUGHE

Captain William BAUGHE. Another English pirate captain in the early 17th century. He cruised in company with Captains WALKER and MILLINGTON. They took vessels off the Atlantic coast of France. In 1610 BAUGHE's ship and its cargo were taken by Dutch pirates. He was soon back at sea and took a Flemish ship that he suspected of having money aboard. He took hold of a prisoner and 'sawed his throte with a dagger untill the blood ran downe'. He finally surrendered to the authorities at Kinsale, Ireland in Jun 1612. Most of his men were back at sea very soon.

Note: This man might just be the VAUGHN who was a Dorset-based pirate in the 1580's, BAUGHE was an alternative spelling of VAUGHN in Elizabethan times.

BAYLY

Job BAYLY. b. London. A crewman to Maj Stede BONNET. Captured with BONNET on 27 Sep 1718 at Cape Fear River. Tried at Charleston and found guilty. BAYLY was hanged on 8 Nov 1718.

BEAUREGARD

Captain Charles-Francois Le Vaseur BEAUREGARD. A leader of French filibusters in the Caribbean. He was the subordinate of De GRAAF, the great filibuster, but by 1694 BEAUREGARD commanded his own force of 6 ships. In April that year he was chased from the Jamaican coast by HMS Falcon. When he reached Petit Goave a few days later he found DUCASSE amassing a naval and filibuster force to invade Jamaica. BEAUREGARD joined them, as did De GRAAF. The pirate ELLIOTT's warning forearmed the Jamaican defences and the invasion had only limited success. On 28 July 1694 the filibusters landed at Cow Bay, Jamaica. BEAUREGARD led the successful assault on the small garrison there. For a few days they foraged ashore, taking 1600 slaves and some plunder. They returned to Petit Goave. On 11 Oct 1694 BEAUREGARD helped to repel the English force from Jamaica that had sailed to Petit Goave looking for vengeance.

BELLAMY

Captain Samuel BELLAMY. b. Devonshire, England. Began his piracy in Nassau under the command of Captain Benjamin HORNIGOLD, the old pirate Captain who also trained BLACKBEARD. HORNIGOLD refused to take British as prizes and no other vessels appeared. By this stage in HORNIGOLD's career he was considering a pardon and retirement. BELLAMY, however, wanted action and treasure. He got the crew to vote for him as Captain to replace HORNIGOLD and gave the first vessel that they took to HORNIGOLD as compensation. BELLAMY changed vessels twice and settled with *Whydah*, a ship-rigged galley, an ideal pirate ship. BELLAMY's plan was always to return to his sweetheart, Maria Hallet, who lived in New England. He captured over 40 vessels during his piracy. Taking the prize vessel *Mary Anne* at Nantucket on 26 Apr 1717, he ordered the Master of the prize to lead him between the shoals, showing a stern-light to guide him. Instead, the Master led him aground. In his rage,

BELLAMY killed all the prize's crew, but they may have died in the wreck along with BELLAMY. The survivors of *Whydah's* crew were captured ashore, tried at Boston and hanged on 15 Nov 1717. Maria Hallet gave birth to BELLAMY's child after his death and was cast out of her village to live in the dunes. That was not unusual in those times.

Note: BELLAMY's vessel is reported at different times as *Whidah*, *Whidaw*, *Whido*, *Whydaw* and *Quedah*. From this distance in time, no-one is going to come up with an authoritative spelling. My guess would be that the vessel was named after the African slaving port of Whydah. You choose.

BELVIN

James BELVIN. A crewman on the galley *George* out of Rotterdam. The vessel was taken over by the Mate, John SMITH, and the crew on 3 Nov 1724. BELVIN sailed with the vessel until it ran aground in the Orkneys in Feb 1725. He was taken to the Marshalsea. Tried in London and found guilty, BELVIN was hanged at Execution Dock, Wapping, on 11 Jun 1725.

BEME

Francis BEME. A Baltic pirate who cruised off the mouth of the River Scheldt, Holland, in 1539, waiting to take English merchant ships.

BENAVIDES

Vincent BENAVIDES. b. Chile. d. 1822. An irregular soldier with the Spanish forces during Chile's struggle for independence. BENAVIDES was in a group who were executed in Santiago, by firing-squad in 1818. Wounded, he pretended to be dead and was dumped with the corpses for the vultures to devour. He later allied himself with the Araukan Indians and went to Santa Maria, an island where shipping that had rounded Cape Horn would put in for fresh water and to catch seals. There BENAVIDES took two American ships, *Hero* and *Herculia* (Boston whalers, I think). He used the sails to make uniforms for his rag-tag army and the copper sheets from the ships' bottoms was beaten into trumpets. He manned the *Herculia* and took an English whaler *Perseverence* and the American brig *Ocean*. BENAVIDES was eventually captured in the harbour of Topocalma and hanged in the town-square. His hands were removed from his corpse and displayed, pointing towards the scenes of his most notorious crimes.

BENBROOK

James BENBROOK. A reluctant crewman to Captain William FLY. BENBROOK was tried at Boston on 4 Jul 1726 and was acquitted.

BENDALL

George BENDALL. Crewman to Captain John AUGER. He had probably already surrendered to Woodes ROGERS on Providence Island in 1718. He was taken prisoner with AUGER's crew when their sloop ran aground on Long Island, Bahamas. Tried and hanged at Providence Island.

BENNETT

Captain Edward BENNET. (alias Benito of the Bloody Sword, alias Don Pedro, alias Benito Bonito.) BENNETT was formerly a Royal Navy officer. As the Mate of a Portugese trader off the West African coast, he led the crew to mutiny. They took the slaver *Lightening*, moved aboard her and renamed her *Relampagos*. They killed all the crew of the slaver except the crewmen THOMPSON and CHAPELLE, then sailed for the Americas. BENNETT and his crew captured a fortune in silver coin ashore in Mexico and reportedly buried it ashore on the Cocos Islands. His vessel was captured by the corvette *Espiegle* near Buena Ventura, Mexico. BENNETT shot himself through the head rather than be taken.

BENNET

Captain John BENNET. A Jamaican buccaneer who commanded a brig and 20 men, BENNET took the Spanish ship *Buen Jesus de las Almas* in April 1675. The ship carried 46,471 pieces-of-eight, the wages for the garrison of Santo Domingo. The Spanish complained to England at ambassadorial level, but it fell on deaf ears.

BENNET

William BENNET. A British soldier who deserted from Fort Loyal, Falmouth, Maine, in 1689. He joined the pirate Captain Thomas POUND. BENNET was captured and imprisoned in Boston. He died in prison.

BERNARD

Thomas BERNARD. b. Bermuda. BERNARD was a crewman to Captain Samuel BELLAMY on *Whydah*. BERNARD is believed to have drowned on the night, in 1717, when *Whydah* was wrecked on Cape Cod.

BEVINS

Robert BEVINS. Joined Captain Bartholomew ROBERTS' ship *Royal Fortune* from the prize galley *Cornwall* at Calabar in Oct 1721. Captured by *HMS Swallow* off the West African coast. Tried at Cape Corso Castle on 28 Mar 1722, found guilty and sentenced to death. No record of his execution, He may have died of wounds or sickness in custody.

BILL

Phillip BILL. (Gave his home as St Thomas, W.I.)b. 1694/5. Joined Captain Bartholomew ROBERTS' ship *Royal Fortune* from the prize *Onslow*. Captured off the West African coast by *HMS Swallow* on 10 Feb 1722. Tried at Cape Corso Castle on 28 Mar. BILL was found guilty and hanged.

BIRTSON (or BIRDSON)

Robert BIRTSON. b. Cornwall, 1692. Sailed with Captain Howard DAVIS. Later he was a crewman to Captain James SKYRM on *Ranger*. Captured off West African coast on 1 Feb 1722 by *HMS Swallow*. Tried at Cape Corso Castle in Mar 1722. BIRTSON was found guilty and hanged.

BISHOP

Captain Richard BISHOP. An English pirate captain in the early 17th century. He joined John WARD's fleet of pirates at Sallee in 1604. He left Tunis in 1608 and sailed the Atlantic in company with Captains John JENNINGS and James HARRIS. In 1609 he visited Southwest Ireland with 11 ships and 1000 men. His own ship of 240 tons carried 27 guns. In 1611 BISHOP surrendered to the authorities in Ireland and settled in Schull, Co. Cork. 17 years after his retirement, almost 60 years old, he was sheltering a pirate captain who was found and arrested in his house.

BISHOP

? BISHOP. An Irishman. Chief Mate to the pirate Captain COBHAM.

BISHOP

William BISHOP. Crewman to Captain John AVERY. Hanged at Execution Dock, Wapping in 1691.

BLACKBEARD

(See Captain Edward TEACH)

BLACKBURNE

Lancelot BLACKBURNE. b. England. 1659. In his youth BLACKBURNE was a chaplain-gunner on an English privateer. In 1724 he was made Archbishop of York.

BLADS (or BLADES)

William BLADS. b. Rhode Island, 1674/5. Crewman to Captain Charles HARRIS on his *Ranger*. Captured by *HMS Greyhound*. Tried at Newport R.I. in Jul 1723. Found guilty of piracy and hanged near Newport on 19 Jul 1723.

BLAKE

Benjamin BLAKE. A Boston lad. Taken prisoner with Captain Thomas POUND's crew at Tarpaulin Cove, 1689.

BLAKE

James BLAKE. Crewman to BLACKBEARD. Wounded and captured at the battle at Ocracoke Inlet on 1 Dec 1718. BLAKE was tried, found guilty of piracy and hanged.

BLANCO

Captain Augustine BLANCO. The leader of a band of pirates who sailed the Bahamas in small craft. In 1725 they took the sloop *Snapper* near Ragged Island. They then raided property ashore on a neighbouring island.

BLAND

Robert BLAND, Crewman to Captain CORNELIUS on *Morning Star*.

BLAZE

John BLAZE. A crewman to Captain Edward LOW. BLAZE was given command of a prize log-wood schooner in the bay of Honduras. He and his prize-crew of 4 were sent off with the ship, presumably to sell it.

BLEWFIELDS (or BLUEFIELDS or BLAUFELDT)

Captain ? BLEWFIELDS. A Caribbean buccaneer. He seems to have gone from buccaneer to logwood cutter to privateer, then pirate. A man of great influence and reputation, though little fact is known. The town of Bluefields in Nicaragua is obviously named after him. He treated the natives well on the Spanish Main and in return got much help from them. In 1649 he brought a prize vessel into Newport R.I. and in 1663 he was living among the Indians at Cape Gratia de Dios on the Spanish Main.

BLOT

Captain ? BLOT. A French Filibuster. In 1684 he commanded *La Quagone*, a vessel of eight guns and ninety men.

BOGGS

Captain Eli BOGGS. An American pirate, active in the 1850s.

BOLIVAR

Lieutenant ? BOLIVAR. A Portugese pirate. On 17 Dec 1821 he took the Boston schooner *Exertion* at Twelve Leagues Key. A huge man with a swarthy complexion and a very loud voice.

BONITON

Captain Peter BONITON. A Cornish pirate captain in the early 17th century. Based in Southwest Ireland, he took vessels in the Straits of Gibraltar. He was finally captured off Faro in 1609 by a French galleon after a gallant fight. He was taken to Marseilles and executed.

BONNET

Major Stede BONNET. b. Barbados, 1689. Of English plantation-owning family, BONNET had no experience of the sea when he decided to become a pirate. He purchased a sloop and named it *Revenge*, fitted it out and took on a crew. When he announced that he was to become a pirate, the crew were given the choice of becoming pirates or 'governors of the next deserted island we find'. He was heartless and cruel, even by pirate standards. He invented 'walking the plank' and is thought to be the only pirate to use that technique. He met BLACKBEARD at sea off the Carolinas. BLACKBEARD made fun of BONNET's hopeless seamanship but took him aboard, got him very drunk and persuaded BONNET's crew to vote a Lieutenant Turner as their captain. BONNET became a joke among the pirate brethren. Eventually BLACKBEARD returned 'Revenge' to him and told him to seek a pardon from Governor EDEN of Bath Town. BLACKBEARD promised to follow him into port if all was well. BONNET obtained his pardon, but of course BLACK-BEARD didn't enter harbour. BONNET sailed again under the name of Captain Thomas, with *Revenge* renamed *Royal James*. He put ashore at Cape Fear River to career with two prizes. Colonel RHETT, who was hunting the pirate Charles VANE, heard that there were pirates in the river and captured BONNET and his crew. He was tried and found guilty. Unlike most pirates he had to be dragged to the gallows crying and pleading. He was hanged on 12 Nov 1718.

BONNY

Anne BONNY (nee CORMAC). Born at the families Black River plantation, Carolina, she had flaming red hair. She married James BONNY, a sometime pirate and sailed to Providence, Bahamas, where James BONNY made a sort of living by handing in pirates to the Governor. She met Captain John (Calico Jack) RACKHAM and they fell in love. She sailed off with RACKHAM in a stolen sloop. One of RACKHAM's crew is reported to have made advances to her, she soundly beat him. They put into Cuba while she delivered a child. Leaving the infant there, they sailed again. She discovered that one of the crew was Mary Read, the other famous lady pirate. When their vessel was captured off Jamaica, only Anne BONNY and Mary READ and one crewman remained on deck to fight. The crew and RACKHAM, who hid below deck were shamed by their bravery. RACKHAM was hanged in Jamaica. Anne BONNY and Mary READ were both sentenced to death but pleaded that they were with child. Anne's sentence was postponed until after she had given birth. She seems to have been sentenced and reprieved twice more before the matter was over. She later (still under twenty years of age) became mistress of Robert FENWICK of Fenwick Castle, near Charleston, Carolina. She ran away from FENWICK with a young lover but FENWICK caught them and made her help him to hang the lover. She promised not to run away again.

BONNY

James BONNY. Husband of Anne BONNY. A pirate crewman who took Woodes ROGERS pardon at Providence and was working as a fisherman when he met Anne. He complained to Woodes ROGERS when Anne had an earlier affair and then again when she was seen about Providence with RACKHAM. BONNY seems to have made a living by turning in his old colleagues and reporting on their activities to WOODES ROGERS. After Anne's departure, BONNY went back to fishing.

BOOTH

Captain George BOOTH. A gunner on the pirate ship *Dolphin*.

Whilst ashore in Madagascar, he and others took over the vessel of a Captain FOURGETTE. They met up with Captain Thomas White and cruised the Indian Ocean in his company for some time. BOOTH was killed in the assault on a Arabian fortress on Zanzibar.

BOOTH

? BOOTH. A reluctant crewman on the galley *George*, taken by Captain John SMITH's *Revenge* on 3 Nov 1724. He escaped to the mainland of Scotland when *Revenge* went aground in the Orkneys. BOOTH alerted the local magistrates, which led to SMITH and his crew being arrested and tried.

BOOTH

Samuel BOOTH. Of Charleston, Carolina. A crewman to Major Stede BONNET. Captured with BONNET at Cape Fear River. Tried at Charleston, Carolina and hanged on 8 Nov 1718.

BOOTMAN

John BOOTMAN. One of a large number of reluctant crewmen taken by Captain William PHILLIPS. This group eventually overpowered the pirates and sailed the vessel to Boston. BOOTMAN was tried for piracy on 12 May 1722 and acquitted.

BOREMAN

Lieutenant ? BOREMAN. b. Isle of Wight. He had been a Naval Lieutenant on a man-of-war. BOREMAN joined the merchant service and was on a vessel taken by Captain Thomas WHITE. BOREMAN gradually became a crew member, though he never commanded a pirate vessel. My guess is that he was probably kept by WHITE for his skills in navigation.

BOURNANO (or De BERNANOS or BERNANO)

Captain ? BOURNANO. A French Filibuster. He was one of the buccaneer Captains who assembled for Captain Bartholomew SHARP's expedition to the Pacific in 1680. BOURNANO would have been useful to the expedition because of his influence with the Darien Indians. However, his French crew argued with the English buccaneers and they did not sail with SHARP's fleet. BOURNANO died on 15 July 1695 at the age of 47, when English and Spanish forces landed to plunder the town of Port de Paix.

BOWEN

Captain John BOWEN. b. Bermuda. First went to sea on the merchantman *Carolina* He studied navigation and rose to command. He was captured by

French pirates and held as a navigator in the West Indies and Guinea Coast. He seems to have become a pirate gradually and risen to command of his own ship. BOWEN built a small town on the East coast of Madagascar. He settled there and took raiding trips into the Indian Ocean between long spells ashore. He sailed off the Malabar coast in company with Captain HOWARD for some time. BOWEN died ashore in the Marascenas Islands.

BOWMAN

William BOWMAN. A buccaneer. He crossed the Isthmus of Darien with Captain Bartholomew SHARP's expedition in 1681. BOWMAN re-crossed the Isthmus on foot. Lionel WAFER said that he was a weakly man, a tailor by trade. He was carried away by the current when crossing one river and nearly drowned. The weight of 400 pieces-of-eight in his satchel didn't help. BOWMAN, with SPRATLIN, eventually caught up with the main party on the Caribbean coast.

BOYD

Robert BOYD. Of Bath Town, Carolina. A crewman to Major Stede BONNET. Captured with BONNET 27 Sep 1718 at Cape Fear River. Tried at Charleston and hanged on 8 Nov 1718.

BOYZA (or BOYGA)

Manuel BOYZA. A Colombian. Crewman to Captain GILBERT on *Panda*. He was tried and hanged in Boston on 11 Mar 1835. BOYZA was hanged behind the Leverett Street Jail. On the night before his execution he managed to cut himself severely with a piece of tin and was so weak from loss of blood that he had to be hanged sitting in a chair. A distinction of sorts, I suppose.

BRADENHAM

Robert BRADENHAM. Ship's surgeon to Captain William KIDD. He agreed to give evidence against KIDD at his trial. BRADENHAM was given immunity from prosecution in exchange for his evidence.

BRADISH

Captain Joseph BRADISH. b. Cambridge, Mass. 28 Nov 1672. In Mar 1689 he shipped out of London on *Adventure* for Borneo. In Sep 1698, when the officers and passengers were ashore on the Island of Polonais, he cut the anchor cable and sailed off with the ship and 3,700 Spanish dollars. Arriving at Long Island on 19 Mar 1699, the crew sank the ship and dispersed. BRADISH was caught and gaoled at Boston, but Caleb RAY, the gaolkeeper, was a kinsman and allowed him to escape. A reward of £200 got him back and he was shipped to London on the same vessel as Captain KIDD. He was tried, found guilty and hanged in chains at Hope Dock, London.

BRADLEY

George BRADLEY. Sailing Master to Captain John FENN on *Morning Star*. Wrecked on the Cayman Islands in Aug 1722. He surrendered to a Bermuda sloop and was taken to Bermuda.

BRADLEY

Samuel BRADLEY. Crewman and brother-in-law of Captain William KIDD. Bradley had a long running disagreement with KIDD which was only resolved when KIDD marooned him on the island of St Thomas in the West Indies. He survived to give evidence against KIDD at his trial.

BRATTLE

Nicholas BRATTLE. A ship's Fiddler. Taken in the prize galley *Cornwall* in Oct 1721 at Calabar by Captain Bartholomew ROBERTS' ship *Royal Fortune*. Captured by *HMS Swallow* off the West African coast on 10 Feb 1722. Tried at Cape Corso Castle on 28 Mar 1722 and found not guilty of piracy.

BRAZILIANO

Captain Rok BRAZILIANO. A Dutch-born buccaneer. BRAZI-LIANO (obviously not his real name) sailed with L'OLLONAIS' punitive expeditions against the Spanish Main in 1666-67. After the Treaty of Breda L'OLLO-NAIS sold BRAZILIANO a captured Spanish brig of 80 tons, bearing 12 guns. BRAZILIANO continued buccaneering on his own account thereafter.

BREAKES

Captain Hiram BREAKES. Son of a Councillor on the Dutch island of Saba, WestIndies. In 1764 he shipped to Amsterdam. 19 years old, tall and handsome, he fell in love with a Mrs SNYDE. He was given command of a small ship which traded between Schiedam and Lisbon. While in Amsterdam, he and Mrs SNYDE murdered her husband, were tried and acquitted. BREAKES stole the vessel from the owner and turned pirate. He took a vessel in Vigo harbour that carried 200,000 small gold bars, sailed to the Mediterranean and purchased a privateers licence from the Governor of Gibraltar. He hunted around the Balearic Islands. He and his crew took 'a wife each' from a nunnery at Minorca. He eventually retired to Amsterdam to find that Mrs SNYDE had been hanged for the murder of their son. He committed suicide by jumping into a canal.

BRECK

John BRECK. A crewman to Captain John QUELCH on his

brig *Charles*. Tried and sentenced to death at Boston in 1704. BRECK was later freed 'to join the Queen's service'.

BRENNINGHAM

Captain ? BRENNINGHAM. A buccaneer Captain who frequented Jamaica and Tortuga. In 1663 he commanded a frigate of 60 guns and 70 men.

BRIERLY

John (Timberhead) BRIERLY, of Bath Town, Carolina. A crewman to Major Stede BONNET. Captured with BONNET on 27 Sep 1718 at Cape Fear River. Tried at Charleston and hanged on 8 May 1718.

BRIGHT

John BRIGHT. b. 1698/9. A crewman to Captain Charles HARRIS. Captured by *HMS Greyhound*. BRIGHT was tried at Newport R.I. He was found guilty and hanged on 19 Jul 1723.

BRINKLY

James BRINKLEY. b. Suffolk, 1695/6. A crewman to Captain Charles HARRIS on *Ranger*. Captured by *HMS Greyhound*. Tried at Newport R.I. BRINKLEY was found guilty and hanged on 19 Jul 1723.

BRISBAU

Max BRISBAU. A crewman to Captain William KIDD. Nothing more known.

BRODELY

Captain Joseph BRODELY. A buccaneer Captain. He was with Henry MORGAN at the sacking of Chagre and Panama. BRODELY was chosen by MORGAN as his Vice Admiral. He had earlier served with MANSFELT at the taking of St Catherine's Island (Old Providence).

BROOKER

Thomas BROOKER. A ship's carpenter from Rochester in Kent. He was the accomplice of Henry STAKES. They took the *Golden Cock* at Orford Ness in 1613 and sold the plunder at St Bartholomew's Fair in London. They were brought to trial. STAKES and BROOKER were Thames pirates, not deep-sea men.

BROOKS

Joseph BROOKS (Senior). Crewman to BLACKBEARD. Killed in the battle at Ocracoke Inlet on 22 Nov 1718, when BLACKBEARD was also killed.

BROOKS

Joseph BROOKS (Junior). Crewman to BLACKBEARD. Captured at the battle at Ocracoke

Inlet, when BLACKBEARD was killed. He was tried and hanged in Virginia.

BROUS

Joseph BROUS (real name Joseph La ROCHE). One of the crewmen on the schooner 'Eliza' which left Philadelphia for St Thomas in Aug 1799. Some of the crew mutinied and took the vessel. 9 days later Captain Wheland and his bulldog regained control of the ship. BROUS was tried in Philadelphia and hanged at Smith's Island on 9 May 1800.

BROWN

Captain? BROWN. A notorious pirate who cruised the Eastern coasts of Central America in the early 19th century.

BROWN

Captain? BROWN. Commanded the *Blessing* with 10 guns and 70 men. He sailed from Jamaica on 24 Jul 1702 with Edward DAVIS aboard to sack the town of Tolu on the Spanish Main. The town was taken, but BROWN was shot in the head and killed.

BROWN

Captain Israel BROWN. b. Titchfield, Hants. England. BROWN was appointed Captain of *Mary Ann* which sailed from Portsmouth in Aug 1700 on a slaving voyage. At Boutrou, West Africa, the black slave dealers stole a quantity of brass pans, pewter pots and beads, which BROWN had landed as payment for slaves. This seems to have determined BROWN to break all the existing rules of the trade. He took two local canoes and broke them up for firewood. At Cape Mesurado he went ashore and stole 8 slaves from an African dealer. When the Royal African Company representative boarded *Mary Ann* to protest, BROWN had him clapped in irons and demanded a ransom. The Company paid the ransom in gold, ivory and rice. Further along the coast he imprisoned slave dealers who came aboard to trade with him, intending to sell them in the Caribbean. To compound his 'crime', he demanded a ransom for these dealers, then kept both the ransom goods and the people who delivered them. On BROWN's return to Britain, after further adventures, he was charged with piracy and imprisoned in the Marshalsea for two years while the charge was investigated. An 'out of court' deal was made and BROWN was released. Almost 20 years later he is recorded as selling 327 slaves from the London vessel *Wright Galley* in Barbados.

BROWN

John BROWN (The Taller). b. County Durham, 1694/5. Crewman to Captain Charles HARRIS on *Ranger*. Captured by *HMS Greyhound*. Tried at Newport R.I. BROWN was found guilty and hanged on 19 Jul 1723.

Note: These two John BROWNs were both crewmen to HARRIS and were identified on the ship and later in court as The Taller and The Shorter.

BROWN

John BROWN (The Shorter). b. Liverpool, 1705/6. Crewman to Captain Charles HARRIS. He was captured with the rest of the crew at Newport R.I. and found guilty. Because of his youth he was recommended to the King's favour and a stay of execution for one year was granted.

BROWN

John BROWN. Of Jamaica. A crewman to Captain Samuel BELLAMY. BROWN was captured on Cape Cod on the day after BELLAMY's ship *Whydah* was wrecked there. He was tried at Boston and hanged there on 15 Nov 1717.

BROWN

Captain Nicholas BROWN. One of the pirates who accepted a pardon from the Governor of the Bahamas in 1717. He turned pirate again and cruised off Jamaica's coasts. BROWN was killed in 1727 and his head was taken to Jamaica so that the

£500 reward could be claimed from the Governor.

BROWN

? BROWN. Crewman to Captain Thomas GREEN on *Worcester*. Falsely imprisoned, tried, sentenced and hanged at Leith, Scotland in Apr 1705.

BROWN

William BROWN. b. Ireland, 1779. Active in the 1850s.

BROWNE

Captain James BROWNE. He commanded a mixed crew of English, Dutch and French pirates. He took a Dutch slaver off the Spanish Main in 1677. Lord VAUGHAN, Governor of Jamaica, sent a frigate to capture BROWNE. He was tried and sentenced to death in Jamaica. The Island Council, under the influence of Henry MORGAN, wanted him released, VAUGHAN had BROWNE hanged quickly and secretly to prevent any further dissent.

BROWNE

Edward BROWNE. Of York River, Virginia. Crewman to Captain Thomas POUND. Wounded at Tarpaulin Cove in 1689.

BROWNE

John BROWNE (alias MAMME). An English sailor who joined the

Barbary pirates at Algiers and turned Mohammedan. He was captured aboard the *Exchange* in 1622 and taken to Plymouth.

BROWNE

Richard BROWNE. Surgeon-General to Henry MORGAN's fleet which sacked the Spanish Main in 1669. He was one of the few who survived the explosion on the frigate *Oxford*. BROWNE, who didn't care much for MORGAN, gave him credit for his humane treatment of prisoners and women.

BROWNRIGG

? BROWNRIGG. A crewman aboard the *Vineyard* which was taken in a mutiny by Charles GIBBS. BROWNRIGG claimed to have been a reluctant pirate and gave evidence against the others, thereby escaping trial.

BRUBAKER

King John BRUBAKER. Established the Kingdom of Bokelia at Charlotte harbour, Florida, with the assistance of his associate Captain Jose GASPAR.

BRUCKLEY

? BRUCKLEY. Crewman to Captain Thomas GREEN on *Worcester*. Falsely imprisoned, tried, sentenced and hanged at Leith, Scotland in Apr 1705.

BUCK

Eleazer BUCK. A crewman to Captain Thomas POUND. Tried at Boston in 1689 and found guilty of piracy. Pardoned on payment of a fine of 20 marks.

BULL

Captain Dixey BULL. b. London. Of a respectable family, BULL went to Boston in 1631, where he traded for beaver pelts. His vessel and goods were seized by a Frenchman in Penobscot Bay in 1632. BULL collected a small crew and turned pirate. He took several vessels off the New England coast. He is rumoured to have returned to England and settled down to a respectable life.

BULL

Mr ? BULL. A buccaneer who sailed (and marched) with Captain Bartholomew SHARPE's expedition to the Pacific in 1680. BULL was killed at Chepillo on the Pacific coast of Panama on 22 Apr 1680.

Note: RINGROSE calls him Mr BULL, which implies that he was not a common seaman.

BULLOCK

? BULLOCK. A surgeon. Sailed with Captain Bartholomew SHARP's expedition to plunder the Pacific coasts of America in 1680/81. BULLOCK was captured during SHARP's second unsuccessful attempt on the town of Arica. A prisoner who escaped later said that he had seen BULLOCK alive some time after his capture.

BUNCE

Charles BUNCE. b. Ottery St Mary, Devon. 1695/6. Joined Captain Bartholomew ROBERTS *Royal Fortune* from a Dutch prize galley in Apr 1722. Captured by *HMS Swallow* off the West African coast on 10 Feb 1722. Tried at Cape Corso Castle. Found guilty and hanged.

BUNCE

Phinneas BUNCE. (Close kin to the BUNCE above, I would guess) Took WOODES ROGERS pardon in 1718 at Providence Island. Was later crewman and Quarter-master to Calico Jack RACKHAM.

BURKE

Jeremy BURKE. b. Ireland. BURKE was a Bosun, or Bosun's Mate, to Captain Samuel BEL-LAMY on *Whydah*. BURKE is believed to have drowned on the night that their vessel foundered on Cape Cod in 1717.

BURDEN

William BURDEN. Mayor of Dover, Kent. An unlikely pirate, but in 1563 he captured 600 French vessels and a large number of others. He also annoyed the King of Spain, with whom England was at peace, by taking 61 Spanish vessels.

BURGEN

Hans BURGEN. b. Denmark. A retired Indian Ocean pirate who, with John PLANTAIN and James ADAIR, established a stockaded fortress at Ranter Bay, Madagascar. They lived in great style, each with an exotic harem. John PLANTAIN, the leader, was known as "The King of the Pirates" and their stopping place grew rich on trade with pirates and passing commercial vessels. Their settlement dispersed in about 1720, as naval forces in the area became more established.

BURGESS

One of the pirates who took Woodes ROGERS pardon in Providence in 1718.

BURGESS

Captain Thomas BURGESS. Another BURGESS who took Woodes ROGERS pardon in the Bahamas. BURGESS and his crew were amongst the 300 pirates who formed a 'guard of honour' when WOODES ROGERS stepped ashore at New Providence. He later sailed on a legitimate voyage for Woodes ROGERS but died on the journey.

BURGESS

Captain Samuel BURGESS. b. New York. "A well-set man and bandy legged". Sailed on three voyages for New York masters, trading with pirates and local rulers in Madagascar. On the next voyage he was bringing back 20 pirates who were taking LITTLETON's offer of pardon. While taking on supplies at Cape of Good Hope an East Indiaman's crew recognised some of the pirates and took their vessel, despite BURGESS protests. Brought to London and tried, he was pardoned. He then returned to the Indian Ocean as a pirate captain. He made several successful cruises of the Indian Ocean and settled ashore in Madagascar. He seems to have outlasted all his contemporaries and died at a ripe old age.

BURK

Captain ? BURK. An Irishman. Was a very active pirate off the Newfoundland coast in the late 17th century. He was drowned in a hurricane in the Atlantic in 1699, according to a letter from Lord BELLOMONT in Nov 1699.

BURRIDGE

? BURRIDGE. He was Mate of the prize vessel *Jolly Bachelor* taken by Captain Francis SPRIGGS on 22 May 1724. BURRIDGE signed pirate articles and the vessel was allowed to proceed. SPRIGGS captured the same vessel 6 days later and was about to kill the crew in his anger. BURRIDGE begged for the life of Captain HAWKINS, his former commander. SPRIGGS spared HAWKINS life, after making him eat a dish of candles. I know nothing more of BURRIDGE.

BURRILL

? BURRILL. A crewman to Captain John PHILLIPS. On 17 Apr 1724 the captives on PHILLIPS' ship, who outnumbered the pirates, overpowered the pirates and sailed the vessel to Boston. PHILLIPS and BURRILL were both killed in the fight. Their heads were brought to Boston pickled in a barrel as evidence.

CACHEMAREE

Captain ? CACHEMAREE. A French filibuster. He commanded the vessel *St Joseph*, a ship of 6 guns and 70 men. In 1684 his headquarters was at San Domingo.

CAESAR

Captain ? CAESAR. A pirate captain in Jose GASPAR's fleet which hunted the Gulf of Mexico until 1821. The tightening pressure of the US Government decided them to disperse. They shared 30,000,000 dollars before they split up.

CAESAR

Black CAESAR. Legend and fact are mixed as regards this black pirate captain. North of Key Largo, Florida, Caesar's Channel and Caesar's Rock are named on charts. CAESAR certainly based himself in that area and captured passing shipping sailing North in the Gulf Stream waters. Legend claims CAESAR to have been an African Chief lured onto a slaving ship, escaping with the Mate of the vessel and burying much treasure on Elliott Key. Legend normally stems from fact. What is a fact is that CAESAR joined the famous pirate BLACKBEARD and fought with him against the navy at Ocracoke Inlet in 1718. BLACKBEARD died in the battle. CAESAR was taken prisoner while trying to blow up their vessel's powder magazine, he was later tried and hanged.

CALLICE (or CALLES or CALLIS)

Captain John CALLICE. b. Tintern, Cornwall. A notorious pirate off the Welsh coasts and in the English Channel in the reign of Elizabeth I CALLICE sailed often in company with Captain HICKS and they considered themselves safe from arrest because of their business connections in Dorset, where they disposed of their goods. They were both arrested in 1577 and CALLICE used his connections to obtain a pardon. HICKS was hanged. CALLICE was captured again some time later. He was eventually hanged at Wapping, London. Before his death he wrote a long, begging letter to Lord WALSINGHAM, but to no avail.

CAMMOCK

William CAMMOCK. A Buccaneer on Captain Bartholomew SHARP's expedition to plunder the Pacific. He died as a result of too much drink ashore at La Serena (which they had just plundered and burned) causing a malignant fever and hiccough. Buried at sea on 14 Dec 1680 at Lat 30 deg 30 Min South.

CANDOR

Ralph CANDOR. Taken prisoner by Captain George LOWTHER's *Ranger*. Captured at Blanquilla by the sloop *HMS Eagle*. Tried at St Christopher (St Kitts) on 11 Mar 1724. Found not guilty and acquitted.

CANE

John CANE. He was taken from the prize *Charlton* by Captain Bartholomew ROBERTS' ship *Royal Fortune* in Feb 1722. Captured by *HMS Swallow* off West African coast. Tried at Cape Corso Castle and found not guilty.

CARACCIOLI

Father CARACCIOLI. A priest in Rome. He became the mentor of the French pirate Captain MISSON and remained as friend, spiritual and political adviser, and able lieutenant throughout their lives. CARACCIOLI preached a form of socialismand was the idealist behind the setting up of the city state of Libertalia. He was Secretary-General of the state and was instrumental in making its laws. He lost a leg in battle with a Portugese ship in the Mozambique River. He was eventually killed by natives in Madagascar.

CARMAN

Thomas CARMAN. b. Maidstone, Kent. A crewman to Major Stede BONNET. Captured with BONNET on 27 Sep 1718 at Cape Fear River. Tried at Charleston and hanged on 8 Nov 1718.

CARNES

John CARNES. Crewman to BLACKBEARD. CARNES was wounded and captured at Ocracoke Inlet on 1 Dec 1718. Tried and hanged.

CARR

John CARR. A Massachusetts pirate. A crewman to Captain HORE. CARR was found hiding in Rhode Island in 1699, by which time he must have been quite elderly.

CARTER

⌐Dennis CARTER. A crewman to Captain John QUELCH. Tried at the Star Tavern in Boston in Jun 1704.

CARTER

Thomas CARTER. One of the pirates who surrendered to Woodes ROGERS pardon at Providence Island in 1718.

CARTY

Patrick CARTY. A crewman to Captain Calico Jack RACKHAM. He was captured with RACKHAM off Jamaica on 1 Nov 1720. Tried at St Jago de la Vega, Jamaica and found guilty.

CARTY was hanged at Kingston on 17 Nov 1720.

CASTEN

Captain Jan CASTEN. A Fleming. One of John WARD's pirate captains in his Mediterranean fleet. CASTEN was killed in action on 21 Mar 1608 when two of WARD's men-of-war and a prize were taken by Venetian galleys. A rare occurrence.

CASTILLO

? CASTILLO. A Colombian. Crewman on the *Panda*. Tried in Boston and hanged on 11 Mar 1835 behind the Leverett Street Jail.

CAVERLEY

Richard CAVERLEY. b. Rhode Island. CAVERLEY was a Sailing Master to Captain Samuel BELLAMY on *Whydah*. He is believed to have drowned on the night, in 1717, when *Whydah* was wrecked on Cape Cod.

CHAMPNIES

William CHAMPNIES. Taken from the prize galley *Lloyd* by Captain Bartholomew ROBERTS' ship *Royal Fortune*. Captured by *HMS Swallow* on 10 Feb 1722. Tried at Cape Corso Castle on 28 Mar 1722. Found not guilty of piracy and acquitted.

CHANDLER

Henry CHANDLER. A Devon seaman. Probably captured by Turkish Corsairs in the Mediterranean. Turned Mohammedan (with little option, I guess) and rose to prominence as a corsair shipbuilder. As a Devon man, he may well have grown up in the trade. He appointed GOODALL, an English slave as Master of a corsair ship *Exchange*. RAWLINS, another English slave, sailed in her with CHANDLER. The slaves seized the ship and sailed her to Plymouth. CHANDLER was hanged, probably for turning to Islam.

CHAPELLE

? CHAPELLE. A crewman on Captain Edward BENNETT's *Relampagos*. Captured by the corvette *Espiegle* near Buena Ventura, Mexico. He was tried and claimed to have only become a pirate to save his life. Transported to Tasmania as a prisoner. He may later have sailed to San Francisco.

CHAPPELL

James CHAPPELL. A Quartermaster on Captain Bartholomew SHARP's ship which cruised the Pacific coasts of America in 1680/81. He fought a duel ashore with Basil RINGROSE, the ship's pilot, on 12 Aug 1681. Both seem to have survived and finished the cruise the next year.

CHARLES

Snivelling CHARLES. (Obviously a nick-name, based on the man's character) CHARLES was from West Lulworth, Dorset. He was gunner to Captains HICKS and CALLICE on their ship, the *Elephant*.

CHEESEMAN

Edward CHEESEMAN. Taken aboard Captain John PHILLIPS pirate ship from the prize *Dolphin* on Newfoundland Banks in 1724. He was one of the party of prisoners who overpowered the pirates and sailed the ship to Boston.

CHEVALLE

Daniel CHEVALLE. Crewman to Captain John QUELCH. Captured with QUELCH and tried at BOSTON in the Star Tavern in 1704.

CHILD

Thomas CHILD. b. 1708/9. A crewman on Captain Charles HARRIS *Ranger*. Captured by *HMS Greyhound*. Tried at Newport R.I. in Jul 1723. CHILD was found not guilty, probably because he was only 15 years old.

CHILD

William CHILD. Taken from the prize galley *Mercy* at Calabar in

Oct 1721 by Captain Bartholomew ROBERTS' ship *Royal Fortune*. Captured off the West African coast by *HMS Swallow* on 10 Feb 1722. Tried at Cape Corso Castle and found not guilty of piracy.

CHRISTIAN

Captain ? CHRISTIAN. A buccaneer. He spent many years living among the Darien Indians. CHRISTIAN sailed with Captain BROWN on *Blessing* in 1702 to take the town of Tolu on the Spanish Main. BROWN was killed in the action, CHRISTIAN was elected commander in his stead.

CHUI-APOO

CHUI-APOO of Wang-na-kok, Hong Kong. He was the admiral of a huge fleet of pirates off the coasts of Southwest China in the mid-19th century. His fleet was engaged by HMS Columbine and the steam sloop HMS Fury. The naval vessels sank 27 pirate junks, killing hundreds of pirates. CHUI-APOO was injured but escaped. Royal Marines landed and captured the pirate village. They found vessels under construction and huge stores of guns and munitions. (A sketch by the ship's surgeon, Edward CREE, was printed in the Illustrated London News on 2 Feb 1850.

CHULY

Daniel CHULY. Tried for piracy in Boston in 1706.

CHURCH

Charles CHURCH. b. St Margarets, London, 1702/3. Crewman on Captain Charles HARRIS *Ranger*. Captured by *HMS Greyhound*. Tried at Newport R.I. CHURCH was found guilty and hanged on 19 Jul 1723.

CHURCH

Edward CHURCH. Crewman on *Vineyard*. Plotted with Charles GIBBS and took over the vessel. They killed the Master and Mate. They were drowned off Rhode Island in 1831.

CHURCH

William CHURCH. Taken from the prize vessel *Gertruycht* of Holland by Captain James SKYRM's *Ranger* in Jan 1722. Captured by *HMS Swallow* on 1 Feb 1722 off the West African coast. Tried at Cape Corso Castle and acquitted.

CHURCHILL

John CHURCHILL. Crewman to Captain George LOWTHER on *Ranger*. Captured by the sloop *HMS Eagle* at Blanquilla in Oct 1723. Tried at St Christopher (St Kitts) on 11 Mar 1724. CHURCHILL was found guilty and hanged.

CHURCHILL

Nicholas CHURCHILL. Crewman to Captain William KIDD

on *Adventure*. Surrendered to pardon at New York. He found that the pardon did not extend to KIDD and his crew. He was shipped to London and tried at the Old Bailey in May 1701. Found guilty and hanged at Execution Dock.

CLARKE

Jonathan CLARKE of Charleston. Crewman to Major Stede BONNET. Captured with BONNET on 27 Sep 1718 at Capr Fear River. Tried at Charleston and found not guilty because he had not received any share of the prizes taken.

CLARKE

Captain William CLARKE. Ex Bosun's Mate in the English Channel Squadron. He became an English pirate in the early 17th century. With Captain James GENTLEMAN he raided the Westmann Isles off Iceland in 1614. His headquarters seem to have been in Algeria. In Jun 1615 he was one of 5 English captains in a fleet of 6 Algerian ships that attacked *Susan Constance*, of London, off Cadiz. He was a well-known leader of the pirate community at Marmora, Morocco.

CLARKE

Richard CLARKE (alias JAFAR). An English seaman who turned Mohammedan and became chief gunner on a Barbary corsair ship. Captured on *Exchange* and brought to Plymouth. He was hanged. (see CHANDLER).

CLEMENTS

James CLEMENTS. b. Bristol, 1701/2. Joined Captain Bartholomew ROBERTS' ship *Royal Fortune* from the prize sloop *Success* in Jul 1720. Captured by *HMS Swallow* on 10 Feb 1722 off the West African coast. Tried at Cape Corso Castle on 28 Mar 1722. Found guilty and hanged.

CLEPHEN

Thomas CLEPHEN. Taken from the prize vessel *Tarlton* in Jan 1722 by Captain James SKRYM's *Ranger*. Captured off the West African coast on 1 Feb 1722 by *HMS Swallow*. Tried at Cape Corso Castle on 28 Mar 1722. Found not guilty of piracy.

CLIFFORD

John CLIFFORD. A New Englander. Seaman on Captain John QUELCH's *Charles*. He gave the principal evidence against QUELCH at his trial in Boston in 1704. CLIFFORD was granted immunity from prosecution in exchange for the evidence.

COBHAM

Captain ? COBHAM. b. Poole, Dorset. At 18 years old COBHAM began smuggling and was most successful. He once smuggled 10,000 gallons of brandy into Poole. His smuggling vessel was taken by a King's cutter. COBHAM bought a cutter of his own and turned pirate. He took an Indiamanin the River Mersey with £40,000 aboard, then sank the ship and drowned the crew. In Portsmouth he met MARIA and took her aboard. His crew did not like that, but accepted it because they were married. They crossed the Atlantic and took vessels between Cape Breton and Prince Edward Island. On taking one vessel, he put the crew into sacks and dumped them overboard. MARIA seems to have been no kinder. She once stabbed a Liverpool captain in the heart. On another occasion she had a captain and two mates lashed to a windlass and then shot them with her pistol. She always wore naval uniform. COBHAM wanted to retire but MARIA had her heart set on buying Mapleton Hall, near Poole. Having amassed a huge fortune the couple eventually bought a large estate near Le Havre. The estate had its own harbour where they kept a pleasure yacht. Once, out sailing in the yacht, they came upon a becalmed brig and went to visit the captain. On board the brig they seem to have given way to temptation. COBHAM shot the captain while MARIA and the yacht crew killed the rest of the brig's crew. They sold the brig in Bordeaux for a good price. COBHAM was made a magistrate. MARIA killed herself with poison, but COBHAM lived to a good age. They left many descendants in the area, and as late as the last century they were still influential people in Le Havre.

COBHAM

Maria COBHAM. The notorious pirate wife of the above COBHAM.

COCKLYN

Thomas COCKLYN. One of the pirates who accepted a pardon from the Governor of the Bahamas in 1717. A year later he was with DAVIS and La BUSE in a ship of 24 guns off Sierra Leone. He was eventually hanged.

CONFRECINA

Captain ? CONFRECINA. A Spanish-American pirate. Active in the South Atlantic in the early 19th century. He was eventually captured by the US Navy at the island of St Thomas. He was executed in Porto Rico in the Spanish way, by garotting.

COLE

John COLE. A crewman to Captain Calico Jack RACKHAM. He had joined the vessel at Negril Point, Jamaica on the very day of its capture. He was tried at St Jago de la Vega on 16 Nov 1720 with the rest of the

crew. The case against him was adjourned for want of evidence until 24 Jan 1721. No further evidence was found but he was still found guilty and hanged at Kingston on 18 Feb.

COLE

Samuel COLE. Crewman to Captain William FLY on *Elizabeth*. The father of 7 children, COLE was captured with FLY and brought to trial with him at Boston. He was sentenced to death and hanged on 12 Jul 1726. COLE's body was taken to Nix Mate Island for burial.

COLEMAN

John COLEMAN. b. Wales, 1697/8. Joined Captain Bartholomew ROBERTS' ship *Royal Fortune* from the prize sloop *Adventure* in Apr 1721. Captured off the West African coast by *HMS Swallow* on 10 Feb 1722. Tried at Cape Corso Castle. He was found guilty and hanged.

COLLINS

Tom COLLINS. A Welshman. A seaman on the pirate vessel *Charming Morning* from Barbados. He became a crewman to Captain George BOOTH in Madagascar.

COMBS

John COMBS. The Master of a vessel taken captive by Captain

William PHILLIPS. He was forced to be a crewman on the pirate vessel. COMBS was one of the group who overpowered the pirates and sailed the ship to Boston. Tried on 12 Apr 1724 and acquitted of piracy.

COMRY

A surgeon by trade. Taken from the prize sloop *Elizabeth* by Captain James SKRYM's *Ranger* in Jan 1722. Captured by *HMS Swallow* off the West African coast on 1 Feb 1722. Tried at Cape Corso Castle on 28 Mar 1722. COMRY was found not guilty of piracy and acquitted.

CONDELL

Captain ? CONDELL. An Indian Ocean pirate captain. CONDELL commanded the ship *Dragon*. In 1720 he was known to have been at Madagascar, where he traded plundered gold for a boatload of brandy from a merchant captain.

CONDENT

Captain ? CONDENT. b. Plymouth. One of the pirates who took Woodes ROGERS offer of pardon at Providence in 1718. Later he was the Quartermaster of a New York sloop trading to Madeira and the Cape Verde Islands. They seized a vessel and crossed the Atlantic to South America, taking vessels off Brazil. Sailing then to Madagascar, they took aboard some of Captain John HALSEY's pirates who were ashore there. After cruising the Indian Ocean he petitioned the Governor of the Marascenas Islands for a pardon. The Governor agreed on condition that he burned his vessels. He did so, settled there and married the Governor's sister-in-law. They returned to Europe later and settled at St Malo, where he became a respectable merchant.

Note: I suspect that CONDENT and CONDELL might be the same man. The name CONDELL was given by word-of-mouth in evidence against the merchant captain who traded with him.

CONDICK

George CONDICK. A crewman to Captain William FLY. The pirates were overpowered by the number of prisoners they had taken. The prisoners sailed them to Boston. CONDICK was tried in Boston and pardoned because it was decided that he was little more than a drunken ship's cook.

COOK

George COOK (alias RAMEDAN). An Englishman among the Barbary corsairs of Algiers. Was gunner's mate when captured on *Exchange*. He was brought to Plymouth and hanged. (see CHANDLER)

COOK

William COOK. Servant to Captain Edmund COOK on SHARP's expedition to plunder the Pacific. On 7 Jan 1681 he was found to have a list of the buccaneers names in his possession. It was suspected that he might be preparing to pass the names to one of the Spanish prisoners, for later vengeance.

Note: None of the diarists on that voyage named pirates, except for the commanders who were already well-known, or those that died. The fear of reprisal or conviction for piracy was always present.

COOK

Captain John COOK. A Creole (maybe) from St Kitts. COOK was a member of SHARPE's expedition to the Pacific in 1681. After that expedition COOK was Quartermaster to Captain YANKEY in the Caribbean. COOK gained command of a Spanish prize vessel, but YANKEY took it from him. On 23 Aug 1683 he set sail from the Carolinas with his own command. With him were many of the survivors of SHARPE's pirates, among them DAMPIER, COWLEY, WAFER and COPPINGER. In West Africa they captured a Dutch vessel loaded with Danish silver and 60 black girls. They renamed the vessel *Bachelor's Delight* and took her to Cape Verde and then South America. Rounding Cape Horn, they fell in with Capt Charles SWAN and *Cygnet* in the Pacific. They made attempts on several towns in Central America, with only limited success. COOK became ill in April 1684. He died in June at Galapagos and was buried there.

COOKE

Captain Edmund COOKE. A buccaneer captain in the Caribbean. COOKE took his ship of 35 tons and 43 men on SHARPE's great expedition to the Pacific Coasts of the Americas in 1681. Throughout the expedition there was some uneasiness between COOKE and his crew. It was only explained when William COOK (see above) was questioned about his list of names. COOKE's servant William revealed that his master had sodomised him on a fairly regular basis and against his will. Edmund COOKE was held in irons for some time for the offence. This seems to give a lie to the current view that buggery was a common sport among the 'brethren of the coasts'. At the first opportunity COOKE left SHARP's command and led 50 buccaneers back across the Isthmus of Darien on foot.

COOPER

Captain ? COOPER. He commanded the pirate sloop *Night Rambler*. COOPER took the galley *Perry* off Barbados on 14 Nov 1725. The next day he took a French sloop. They sailed to Aruba where they divided the spoils and left the crews of both prizes on the beach.

COOPER

Captain? COOPER. A buccaneer, He commanded a frigate of 10 Guns and 80men. On 19 Oct 1663 he brought two Spanish prize vessels into Port Royal, Jamaica. One of the vessels was loaded with mercury for the Mexican mines and also several Spanish friars.

COPPINGER

Herman COPPINGER. He was second-surgeon on the *Bachelor' Delight* under Captain John COOK. Lionel WAFER (the diarist) was the other second-surgeon. The chief-surgeon (name unknown) was given a woman by the King at the mouth of the Sherbro River in West Africa, caught a fever and died. After COOK's death at Galapagos, COPPINGER and many others joined Captain SWAN on *Cygnet*. By Feb 1687 he had become so disillusioned with SWAN that he attempted to run away at Pulo Condore, in the Philippines. He was caught and brought back. He managed to leave *Cygnet* at Coromandel. William DAMPIER met him in May 1689 at Pulo Verero. He was surgeon on a Danish ship then.

CORBET

Captain ? CORBET. Sailed with Captain HEIDON from Bantry Bay, Ireland in 1564. They were looking for a vessel to steal for CORBET to go a'pirating in. Their ship was wrecked on Alderney, Channel Isles, and they were all arrested. CORBET and several others escaped in a small boat

CORNELIUS

Captain? CORNELIUS. Basically a slaver. He started slaving on the Guinea Coast then sailed to Madagascar and agreed to go to war for a local ruler in exchange for two shiploads of slaves. He completed one run from there to the Americas. On the second run a crewman, Joseph WILLIAMS, took over command of the vessel, fearing that CORNELIUS's laxity would allow the slaves to take over the vessel.

CORNER

Richard CORNER. Quartermaster to Captain Calico Jack RACKHAM. Captured with RACKHAM off Jamaica on 1 Nov 1720. Tried at St Jago de la Vega and found guilty. Hanged at Port Royal on 17 Nov 1720. His body was hung in chains at Gun Key as a warning to other seafarers.

CORP

Robert CORP. A seaman on the merchant ship *Prince's Galley*. On 15 Sep 1723 *Prince's Galley* was taken by Captain George

LOWTHER. CORP was one of the crew who volunteered to join the pirates.

COSINS

James COSINS. Joined Captain James SKYRM's vessel *Ranger* in Jan 1722. Captured by *HMS Swallow* on 1 Feb 1722 off the West African coast. He was probably a deserter from a man-of-war because he was referred to the Marshalsea for trial in London. I don't know the outcome of the trial.

COWARD

Captain ? COWARD. An English pirate captain in the early 17th century. He was based at one time in Bantry Bay, Ireland, but probably worked the Atlantic coast as far south as Morocco.

COWARD

William COWARD. In Nov 1689 he rowed out to the ketch *Elinor* in Boston Harbour with 3 other men and a boy. They took the ketch (not difficult because the crew were all sick with smallpox) and sailed her to Cape Cod. There they were all caught and held in the new stone gaol at Boston. COWARD was hanged on 27 Jan 1690.

COWLEY

Captain William Ambrose COWLEY MA Cantab. On 23 AUG 1683 he shipped out of Cape Charles, Virginia as Sailing Master on *Revenge*, with DAMPIER, under Captain John COOK. They turned pirate as soon as they left land and sailed to Sierra Leone, where they took a Danish ship with 60 black girls aboard and renamed her *Bathers' Delight*, then to Brazil and round Cape Horn. They met up with Captains SWAN and TOWNLEY in Central America. COWLEY joined Captain John EATON's crew on *Nicholas* after John COOK's death at Galapagos. They sailed on across the Pacific to Guam and the Ladrones Isles. In Apr 1685 they re-fitted at Canton. COWLEY and about 20 others left EATON at Timor and made their way home by way of Cheribon (Java) and Batavia. He and two others arrived back in London on 12 Oct 1686. COWLEY was a dubious navigator and an unreliable diarist. His journal was published 13 years after his return.

COX

Captain John COX. A New England man. He went with Captain Bartholomew SHARP's expedition to plunder the Pacific in 1681. COX started the expedition with the rank of vice-admiral and at different times seems to have commanded a vessel or been a prominent member of raiding parties. COX seems to have been instrumental in having SHARP replaced as leader by

WATLING. He was more an adaptable, tough survivor than a great leader. COX was the Starboard Watchkeeper on SHARP's vessel by the time they rounded Cape Horn on their return to the Caribbean.

COXON

Captain John COXON. He began logwooding with his brother William on Beef Island in 1669. In 1675 he assembled a group of colleagues and obtained a privateers licence from Tortuga. The next year he declared himself a pirate and sailed to Santa Martha with 100 Englishmen under his command. He spent 2 years ashore in Jamaica then sailed again in the company of Captain Richard SAWKINS and Captain Bartholomew SHARP. William DAMPIER joined them. They formed a huge buccaneer army under the command of Captain Peter HARRIS and crossed the Isthmus of Darien to take Santa Maria. COXON had a disagreement with the other captains and returned across the Isthmus. In 1681, at the Mulatas Islands, he met DAMPIER who had just returned from the Isthmus. COXON rejoined the huge buccaneer fleet but it was dispersed by a storm. In 1682 COXON obtained a privateers licence from Sir Thomas LYNCH of Jamaica. He turned pirate again and was taken by LYNCH, but escaped hanging.

For a further ten years he sailed the Mosquito Coast as a slaver and trader.

COYLE

Captain Richard COYLE. b. Exeter, Devon. An honest seaman at first, Mate to Captain Benjamin HARTLEY. On arriving in Ancona with a load of pilchards, a new carpenter, RICHARDSON, joined the vessel. COYLE and RICHARDSON became good friends and agreed to take their vessel over. They threw HARTLEY overboard and sailed for Tunis. There they convinced the British Consul that they were the legitimate owners and obtained money from him. They immediately got drunk and let slip that they were pirates. The Consul had them shipped back to the Marshalsea in London. They were tried at the Old Bailey and hanged at Execution Dock, Wapping on 25 Jan 1738.

CRACKERS

Captain ? CRACKERS. (See John LEADSTONE).

CRANE

James CRANE. Joined Captain James SKYRM's vessel *Ranger* from the prize *Kanning* in Aug 1721. Captured by *HMS Swallow* off the West African coast on 1 Feb 1722. He must have already been a deserter from a man-of-war because he was referred to the Marshalsea for trial in London. The outcome of the trial is not known.

CRISS

Captain John CRISS (alias Jack the Bachelor). b. Lorne, (Larne?) N. Ireland. The son of a fisherman who sold his catches in Londonderry. CRISS was a ladies man from an early age. He first took to smuggling, then bought a French galliot. Sailing from Cork, he took vessels off the French coast, selling them at Cherbourg. He made a habit of drowning his victims. He later cruised the Mediterranean and plundered the Port of Amalfi in Calabria. Calling at Naples, he stayed in the Ferdinand Hotel. The maid found him dead in his bed one morning. In spite of his nickname, it was found after his death that he was married to three women, all at the same time.

CROMBY

James CROMBY. b. Wapping, London. Joined Captain Bartholomew ROBERTS' ship *Royal Fortune* from the prize *Onslow* in May 1721. Captured off the West African coast by *HMS Swallow* on 10 Feb 1722. Tried at Cape Corso Castle on 28 Mar 1722 and found guilty of piracy. Sentenced to 7 years' transportation to the colonies of the Royal African Company.

CROW

Robert CROW. b. Isle of Man, 1677/8. Joined Captain Bartholomew ROBERTS' ship *Royal Fortune* from the prize sloop *Happy Return* in Jul 1720. Captured by *HMS Swallow* off the West African coast on 10 Feb 1722. Tried at Cape Corso Castle on 28 Mar 1722. Found guilty and hanged.

CRUMPSTEY

Captain Andrew CRUMPSTEY. Master of the *Mary Anne* of Dublin? Sailed reluctantly with Captain Samuel BELLAMY's fleet off the Eastern Seaboard. He was probably drowned when BELLAMY's ship *Whydah* was wrecked on Cape Cod on 26 Apr 1717, though rumour had it that BELLAMY murdered all his captives that night.

CULLEN

Pierce CULLEN. b. Cork. Brother of Andrew CULLEN. Crewman to Captain Philip ROCHE. No further information.

CULLEN

Andrew CULLEN. b. Cork. Brother of Pierce CULLEN. Crewman to Captain Philip ROCHE. No further information.

CULLIFORD

Captain Robert CULLIFORD. One of a group of mutineers who

took over the East Indiaman *Mocha*. He became a pirate captain in the Indian Ocean. CULLIFORD sailed in company with Captain William KIDD from 1699. Many of KIDD's crew stayed with CULLIFORD when KIDD sailed to New York to surrender. He was tried and convicted of being a Madagascar pirate in 1702, but was pardoned, along with Captain Samuel BURGESS.

CUMBERLAND

George, Third Earl of CUMBERLAND. 1558-1605. MA Trinity College, Cambridge. He left Cambridge and studied Geography at Oxford. CUMBERLAND sailed in 1586 on the first of 12 self-financed buccaneering voyages to the Spanish Main. He was a great favourite of Queen Elizabeth. He always wore in his hat, a glove that she had given him.

CUNDON

Maurice CUNDON. Crewman to Captain William FLY on *Elizabeth*. CUNDON was one of the original members of the crew. When the captives overpowered the pirates and sailed the ship to Boston, CUNDON was tried but acquitted.

CUNNINGHAM

Patrick CUNNINGHAM. b. 1688/9. Crewman on Captain Charles HARRIS *Ranger*. Captured by *HMS Greyhound* Tried at Newport R.I. in Jul 1723. Found guilty, but the sentence was respited for one year and he was recommended to the King's favour.

CUNNINGHAM

William CUNNINGHAM. Gunner on BLACKBEARD's *Adventure*. He later accepted Woodes ROGERS pardon at Providence. Later still he was a crewman to Captain John AUGER. He was taken prisoner when AUGER's sloop went aground on Long Island W.I. CUNNINGHAM was tried and hanged at Providence.

CURTICE

Joseph CURTICE. Crewman To BLACKBEARD. He died in the battle at Ocracoke Inlet on 1 Dec 1718, when BLACKBEARD was also killed in the action.

DAMPIER

William DAMPIER. b. East Coker, Somerset. 1651/2. His parents died while DAMPIER was at school and his guardians agreed to apprentice him to the Master of a Weymouth vessel. DAMPIER left the vessel in the West Indies. In 1675/6 he worked on a vessel transporting logwood between Campeachy Bay and Jamaica. In 1680 he joined the huge buccaneer fleet that assembled under SAWKINS at Negril Point, Jamaica. They crossed the Isthmus of Darien on foot, capturing vessels in the Pacific. When SAWKINS was killed, DAMPIER re-crossed the Isthmus on foot with 43 others. In 1683 he joined Captain Edmund COOK on *Revenge* at Chesapeake for a long voyage. The crew included Lionel WAFER (another diarist) and Captain John DAVIS. They sailed first to West Africa where they took a slaver with many young female slaves aboard. They renamed their vessel *Bachelors' Delight* and set off for the Pacific. COOK died at Galapagos in 1684. The remainder of the crew sailed on across the Pacific, most of them completing a circumnavigation.

The remarkable thing about DAMPIER was that throughout his adventures and travels, he maintained his diaries. A meticulous recorder of places and events. His observations led him to be the first to identify the great ocean currents, not just as a local phenomenon, but as part of a world-wide geographical system.

DAN

Joseph DAN. A crewman to Captain Henry AVERY. He turned King's witness at his trial in 1696, thus escaping hanging.

DANGERFIELD

Robert DANGERFIELD. A crewman on a pirate vessel which operated off the coast of West Africa in 1684. DANGERFIELD joined the pirates from Jamaica (reluctantly he said) and voyaged with them to Boston, then West Africa and back to North America. They took a Dutch and a French merchant ship off the African coast and sold the cargo which included slaves to the local English Governor. They voyage ended in a shipwreck in the Carolinas, just south of the Ashly River. DANGERFIELD wrote an account of his time with the pirates.

DANIEL

Captain ? DANIEL. A French filibuster. A man as well-known for his blood-thirstiness as for his religious piety. When he was purchasing supplies on the Isles des Saintes, he invited the local priest aboard to celebrate mass. One of the crew showed insufficient respect for the ceremony, so DANIEL shot him through the head. He said to the priest, "Do not be troubled, Father. I have punished him to teach him better." I suppose it did, in a way.

DANIEL

Stephen DANIEL. Crewman to BLACKBEARD. He was wounded and captured in the battle at Ocracoke Inlet on 1 Dec 1718. Later, he was tried and hanged.

DANIELS

James DANIELS. A crewman to Captain Thomas POUND. DANIELS was killed in the battle at Tarpaulin Cove in Oct 1689, when POUND's ship was captured.

DANZIGER

Captain Simon DANZIGER (or DANSKER or DANSEKER). A Fleming. He was a privateer and pirate in the Mediterranean in the early 17th century. DANZIGER worked out of Marseille, probably under a French licence. Later he took service with the Dey of Tunis and sailed under John WARD as one of the commanders in his huge Corsair fleet. He refused to convert to Islam though he was known in the fleet as DALI RAIS (Captain Devil). In 1608 he attempted to negotiate a return to France, where his wife

and children lived. He seems to have been unsuccessful then, but his next great prize, a Spanish galleon, he took into Marseille. This gained him a pardon from King Henry IV of France, and the enmity of the Dey of Tunis. DANZIGER served the Duke of Guise for the next three years. Unwisely, he returned to Tunis in 1611 to negotiate the ransom of several French vessels. He was captured and hanged.

DANSON

George DANSON. Taken from the prize galley *Lloyd* by Captain Bartholomew ROBERTS *Royal Fortune* in May 1721. Captured by *HMS Swallow* on 10 Feb 1722. Tried at Cape Corso Castle on 28 Mar 1722. He was found guilty but for some reason was acquitted.

DANZY

Robert DANZY. b. Britain. DANZY was a crewman to Captain Samuel BELLAMY on *Whydah*. He is believed to have drowned on the night, in 1717, when *Whydah* was wrecked on Cape Cod.

DARBY

John DARBY. From Marblehead. Joined Captain Thomas POUND from the vessel *Mary*. DARBY went ashore at Falmouth, Maine to arrange the supply of water, lead and a doctor. While ashore he persuaded English soldiers from the local fort to join the pirate crew. DARBY was killed in the battle at Tarpaulin Cove in Oct 1689, when POUND's ship was captured.

DARLING

William DARLING. Taken from the prize vessel *Jeremiah and Anne* by Captain Bartholomew ROBERTS' ship *Royal Fortune* in Apr 1721. Captured by *HMS Swallow* on 10 Feb 1722. Tried at Cape Corso Castle on 28 Mar 1722. Found not guilty of piracy and acquitted.

DAVIS

Arthur DAVIS. One of the pirates who surrendered to Woodes ROGERS offer of pardon at Providence, Bahamas in 1718.

DAVIS

Captain Edward DAVIS. Quartermaster to Captain John COOK on *Bachelors' Delight*. DAVIS took command of the vessel and the rest of the fleet on COOK's death at Galapagos in 1684. They sailed the coasts of Chile and Peru, sacking towns and villages. On 28 May 1685 they met with a Spanish Fleet in the Bay of Panama and were lucky to escape from the disastrous battle alive. DAVIS return to Jamaica by way of Cape Horn, with 50,000 pieces of eight as well as much plate and jewels. He retired to Cape Comfort, Virginia, only to take up piracy again in 1702. He sailed with Captain BROWN on *Blessing* to take the town of Tolu on the Spanish Main. Later they took Porto Bello, but got little plunder for their efforts. Davis' main claim to fame must be that he held a pirate crew under his command for longer than anyone except Bartholomew ROBERTS, which says much for his leadership.

DAVIS

Captain Howell DAVIS. b. Milford, South Wales. Was Mate of the Bristol snow *Cadogan*. The vessel was captured by Captain Edward ENGLAND. ENGLAND took some of the cargo, gave DAVIS command of the vessel, with sealed orders to be opened when they reached a certain latitude. The orders gave DAVIS very dubious title to the vessel and suggested that he sell the cargo in Brazil. DAVIS sailed instead to Barbados, which had been the vessel's original first port-of-call. The authorities there gaoled him for three months before they believed his story. With such a question mark hanging over him, there was little chance of his finding a post as a ship's officer. DAVIS sailed to Providence, Bahamas, where Woodes ROGERS was still encouraging pirates to accept pardons. He accepted a sloop and a commission as a privateer from Woodes ROGERS but sailed to the Azores and Cape Verde Islands as a pirate. He took many vessels and cargoes. The Portugese Governor of the Island of Mayo accepted DAVIS and his men as guests, they sacked and captured his fortress. At Gambia Castle, West Africa they tricked the Governor into believing that they were a British man-of-war. DAVIS put a pistol to the man's head and they took the castle without injury on either side. They met with the French pirate La BOUCHE and captured him a better vessel than the one he had. They later fell in with the pirate Captain COCKLYN. The three ships cruised together off the Guinea Coast and took many vessels. They decided to try tricking a Governor again, as they had at Gambia. The Governor of the Isle of Princes, however, had heard what had happened to his colleague in Gambia and was prepared. DAVIS was shot in the stomach in an ambush and died minutes later. Probably in Mar 1720.

DAVIS

John DAVIS. A crewman to Captain Calico Jack RACKHAM. Captured with RACKHAM off Jamaica on 1 Nov 1720. He was tried at St Jago de la Vega, Jamaica. Found guilty and

hanged at Gallows Point, Port Royal on 17 Nov 1720.

DAVIS

Gabriel DAVIS. Tried for piracy at the Star Tavern in Boston in 1704.

DAVIS

John DAVIS. Taken from the prize vessel *Tarlton* by Captain James SKYRM's *Ranger* in Jan 1722. Captured less than a month later by *HMS Swallow* off the West African coast. He was tried at Cape Corso Castle on 28 Mar 1722. Found not guilty and acquitted.

DAVIS

Thomas DAVIS. b. Carmarthenshire, Wales. Carpenter and crewman to both Captain Benjamin HORNIGOLD and Captain Samuel BELLAMY. He survived the wreck of BELLAMY's *Whydah* on Cape Cod. DAVIS was tried for piracy but probably proved that he had been held for his skills as a carpenter because he was acquitted. He said that BELLAMY was "a more decent man than most".

DAVIS

Thomas DAVIS. Taken from the prize galley *Cornwall* by Captain Bartholomew ROBERTS' ship *Royal Fortune* in Oct 1721. Captured by *HMS Swallow* off the

West African coast on 10 Feb 1722. Tried at Cape Corso Castle on 28 Mar 1722 and found not guilty of piracy.

DAVIS

William DAVIS. b. Wales, 1699. He joined Captain James SKYRM's *Ranger* at Sierra Leone in Jul 1721. Captured by *HMS Swallow* on 1 Feb 1722 off the West African coast. Tried at Cape Corso Castle. Some of the evidence against DAVIS was that he had deserted from the galley *Ann* at Sierra Leone after fighting with, and beating, the mate. He lived among the natives, from whom he received a wife, but sold her one night for punch to quench his thirst. Her relatives and friends pursued him and he handed himself over to the Governor, Mr PLUNKET for protection. Mr PLUNKET handed him to his wife's relatives who considered chopping off his head, instead they sold him to Seignior JOSSEE, 'a Christian black and native of that place' who bound DAVIS to two years work in repayment. In the meantime, SKYRM and ROBERTS sailed into the harbour and DAVIS stole away with them. DAVIS was found guilty and hanged.

DAWES

? DAWES. b. Saltash, Cornwall. He served for at least 8 years as a crewman on a Barbary corsair ship, from 1684 onwards.

DAWES was probably captured from a Christian vessel in the Mediterranean. As a deep-sea sailor he would have been given the choice of slavery ashore or sailing as a corsair.

DAWES

Robert DAWES. One of the mutineers on the brig *Vineyard* in 1830. It was DAWES confession that brought about the conviction and hanging of Charles GIBBS.

DAWSON

Henry DAWSON. Taken from the prize sloop *Whydah* at Jaquin in Jan 1722 by Captain James SKYRM's vessel *Ranger*. Captured off the West African coast by *HMS Swallow* on 1 Feb 1722. Tried at Cape Corso Castle on 28 Mar 1722 and found not guilty of piracy.

DAWSON

Joseph DAWSON. A crewman to Captain Henry AVERY. Tried at the Old Bailey in 1696. Found guilty and hanged at Execution Dock, Wapping.

DEAL

Captain Robert DEAL. Was Mate to Captain Charles VANE. In Nov 1718, between Cape Meise and Cape Nicholas, they fired on what appeared to be a merchantman. It turned out to be a French man-of-war. VANE and DEAL were all for running away. Most of the crew, led by Calico Jack RACKHAM, wanted to fight. They did run away, but the next day VANE cast DEAL and some others off in a small boat. VANE's sloop was soon taken by a British man-of-war. DEAL was later tried and hanged in Jamaica.

DEANE

Captain John DEANE. A Buccaneer who commanded the vessel *St David*. DEANE was accused by the Governor of Jamaica of robbing the *John Adventure* of several pipes of wine, and cable worth £100, and taking the vessel to Jamaica. He was also accused of flying Dutch, French and Spanish colours. He was tried and condemned to death, but after much argument he was reprieved.

DEATH

Captain William DEATH. Privateer. In October 1756 Captain DEATH ran an advertisement for two weeks in the London Daily Advertiser which read, "To cruise against the French, the *Terrible*, Captain William DEATH, all gentleman sailors, and able bodied landmen, who are inclined to try their fortune, as well as serve their King and Country, are desired to repair on board the said ship." The *Terrible*

sailed from Execution Dock, Wapping, in Nov 1756. Off St Malo she fell in with the French privateer *Vengeance*. After a ferocious, three-hour battle in choppy seas, the Frenchman captured *Terrible*. *Vengeance* lost her Captain, Mate and two-thirds of her crew. Aboard *Terrible* 150 of the crew were killed. Captain DEATH and all of his officers except one died. 17 survivors were taken prisoner.

De GRAAF

Captain Laurens Cornelis Boudewijn De GRAAF. A Dutchman who served for 3 years as a gunner in the Spanish navy before deserting in the Antilles. By 1667 De GRAAF had become the leader of a very wild bunch of buccaneers at Samana Bay, he "never wanted to take out a commission from anyone, nor put into the port of any nation." De GRAAF captured vessels of increasing size until by 1679 he had a Spanish galleon of 28 guns, the *Tigre*. His adventures were so daring and successful that by 1682 Henry MORGAN, then acting governor of Jamaica, called him 'a great and mischievous pirate'. De GRAAF is said to have been tall, blonde and handsome, with a small, pointed beard. In July 1682 he took a 30 gun Spanish treasure ship off Puerto Rico which gave his men shares of 700 pieces of eight per man. In May 1683, with Van HOORN and GRAMMONT, he captured the city of Veracruz and held its 6000 inhabitants to ransom. His audacity increased with the size of his fleet and the scale of his piracy until 1685, when he appears to have retired. He probably settled in French North America. De GRAAF became a French citizen and Governor of the town of Cap Francois (now Cap Haitien, Haiti). The town was attacked by the Spanish on 21 January 1691 but De GRAAF escaped into the hills. He continued to lead French filibuster forces against the Spanish and English forces and settlements throughout the next ten years.

De GRAVES

Captain Herbert De GRAVES. A Dutch pirate. His unusual method of piracy was to go ashore and plunder important houses. He worked his way along the South Coast of England from Sussex to Devonshire. In the war between England and Holland he commanded a fireship with great success. He set ablaze the man-of-war *Sandwich*, from which James, Duke of York, later King James II, narrowly escaped. The Earl of Albermarle and most of the crew perished in the fire. After the war he returned to his normal trade, but he wrecked his ship near Walmer Castle in Kent. De GRAVES and the few of his crew that survived were hanged in a nearby tree.

DEIGLE

Richard DEIGLE. An Elizabethan English pirate. He was shipwrecked in Alderney in the Channel Isles. (see CORBET) He later escaped in a small boat.

DELANDER

Captain ? DELANDER. A Buccaneer. He commanded a chatas (a small coasting craft). Henry MORGAN sent him ahead of the main body of buccaneers in 1671, when they marched from San Lorenzo to attack Panama.

DELIZUFF

Captain ? DELIZUFF. A Barbary corsair. His fleet of 18 vessels joined BARBAROSSA's which they met en route for Constantinople. Soon after the two leaders quarrelled and DELIZUFF was killed. His crews took their vessels and stole away in the night.

DELOE

Jonathan DELOE. A crewman on the schooner *Swift* which was taken by Captain George LOWTHER's ship in Jul 1723. DELOE was forced to become a crewman. No further information on him.

De LORMES

Viscount De LORMES. (An assumed name and title). In 1617, when the Mediterranean corsairs were all seeking pardons and an easier way of life, De LORMES made approaches to several governments, representing himself as the leader of a huge and fabulously wealthy pirate fleet. He claimed to be seeking a safe place for his captains and men to settle. He continued this tactic for five years, fooling the governments of Venice, Tuscany, France and England.

DELVE

Jonathan DELVE. A crewman to Captain George LOWTHER on *Ranger*. Captured by the sloop *HMS Eagle* at Blanquilla in Oct 1723. He was tried at St Christopher (St Kitts), found guilty and hanged.

De MONT

Francis De MONT. Captured in South Carolina in 1717, he was accused of taking the *Turtle Dove* and several other vessels in Jul 1716. De MONT was tried and hanged at Charleston in Jun 1717.

DEMPSTER

Captain Edward DEMPSTER. An English buccaneer captain in the Caribbean. In 1668 he commanded several vessels and over 300 men. He was one of Henry MORGAN's buccaneer captains on his expedition against the Spanish Main in March 1669.

DENBALL

Captain Sampson DENBALL. b. Dartmouth, Devon. An English pirate in the early 17th century. DENBALL arrived in Tunis with John WARD and sailed on several voyages with him. He then turned Mohammedan and took the name of ALI REIS. DENBALL led many expeditions and assumed command of the galleons of YOUSSEF, Dey of Tunis. In 1614 he was captured by a fleet of 14 Christian vessels after a six hour sea-battle. DENBALL (alias ALI REIS) who was known to his English crewman as Captain SAMPSON, was condemned to row in a Christian galley for the rest of his life.

DENNIS

Henry DENNIS. b. Bideford, Devon. DENNIS had been a crewman to Captain Howard DAVIS. He was a crewman on Captain James SKYRM's *Ranger* when he was captured by *HMS Swallow* off the West African coast on 1 Feb 1722. He was tried at Cape Corso Castle on 28 Mar 1722 and found guilty. Sentence was 7 years' transportation to the African Colonies.

DERDRAKE

John (Jack of the Baltic) DERDRAKE. A Danish pirate. He was dismissed from the Danish

King's Dockyard in Copenhagen, then sailed as a carpenter on several voyages to London. His parents died, leaving him enough money to buy a fast brig. He traded timber between Norway and London for some time, then sold his vessel to Peter the Great of Russia and returned to work in the dockyard. In a quarrel he slew another worker. His old ship lay in the harbour, so he took it, sailed it to London, sold its cargo and armed the ship with 12 cannon. En route to Norway he met with a Russian man-of-war. He fought it and won. DERDRAKE took the man-of-war as his own and renamed it *Sudden Death*. For a while he took many English and Russian ships in the Baltic and sold their cargoes in Sweden. The Governor of St Petersburg, General SCHEVELLING, sent two ships to capture him. DERDRAKE had just learned of this when he captured a ship with a lady passenger who happened to be the sister of SCHEVELLING. DERDRAKE stabbed her to death. *Sudden Death* was trapped by two Russian men-of-war at Strothing in Sweden and sunk, but DERDRAKE escaped ashore. His crewmen were hanged alive by hooks in their ribs and sent to drift down the River Volga. DERDRAKE lived for 14 years in great luxury at Stralsund, until he went to Stockholm and was recognised by a captain he had robbed at sea. He was arrested and hanged.

DERDRAN

Captain ? DERDRAN. A French filibuster in the Caribbean in the 1660s. He commanded *Chasseur*, a ship of 20 tons and 120 men, based in French Domingo.

DESMARAIS

Captain Jeremie DESMARAIS. A leading French filibuster. He commanded one of the vessels in Captain Edward DAVIS' fleet which fought a squadron of 14 Spanish men-of-war in the Bay of Panama in May 1685. The pirates got the worst of the battle and most were lucky to escape. Later he was commander of the French buccaneer community at Tortuga. He obtained, by deceit, privateer commissions from both England and France simultaneously. He ended his days in the Bastille, Paris, and sold his interests in Tortuga to Jean-Baptiste COLBERT of the French West India Company for 15,000 livres.

De SORES

Captain Jacques De SORES. A French privateer. De SORES was one of those who sailed with Captain Francois Le CLERC when he plundered the seaport of Santiago de Cuba. De SORES sailed on his own account in 1554 and captured Havana, Cuba. He held the town to ransom and burned it to the ground when the ransom was not paid. He also laid waste all the surrounding land and property and burned the ships in the harbour. De SORES seemed to have got little treasure to show for his brutality and pillage.

DE SOTO

Bernardo De SOTO. First Mate to Captain Don Pedro GILBERT on the *Panda*. When brought to trial it was revealed that De SOTO had previously distinguished himself by saving 72 people from a Salem ship wrecked in the Bahamas. Added to this, his wife was from a family of great influence in Spain. Through the services of the Spanish Ambassador he was pardoned. De SOTO later took a berth on a passenger service in the West Indies. Over 30 years later a Captain Nicholas SNELL of Salem met De SOTO, who was then the Captain of a vessel running a service between Havana and Matanzas.

De SOTO

Bonito De SOTO. He led a mutiny aboard the Portugese slaver *Defensor de Pedro* and took command of the vessel. On 21 Feb 1828 he captured the British merchantman *Morning Star*. De SOTO is said to have buried his treasure on the island of Trinidade. He was eventually caught and was tried and hanged at Gibraltar.

De VINE

Peter De VINE (or more probably DEVINE). b. Stepney, London, 1680. Joined Captain James SKYRM's *Ranger* from the prize vessel *King Solomon* off Cape Apollonia in Jan 1722. Captured by *HMS Swallow* on 1 Feb 1722 off the West African coast and tried at Cape Corso Castle. He was found guilty and hanged.

DEW

Captain George DEW. Of Bermuda. He commanded a Bermudan ship that sailed in company with Captain Thomas TEW. The two vessels became involved in a storm en route for Africa. TEW sailed on for Africa, but DEW turned his vessel to head back to Bermuda. Nothing more was ever heard of DEW. Presumably his vessel was lost to the storm.

DIABOLITO

? DIABOLITO. A Central American pirate who was notorious in the Caribbean in the early 19th century. In 1823 he cruised off Cuba in his ship *Catalina*.

DICKERS

Captain Michael DICKERS. Master of *Rupparell*, a Dutch vessel taken by Captain William KIDD. DICKERS and two others of the ship's company joined KIDD as pirates.

DICK

William DICK. One of the buccaneers on SHARP's expedition to the Pacific in 1681. He returned to London with SHARP, RINGROSE and COX on 25 Mar 1682. They lodged at the Anchor Inn on Saltpeter Bank. Their huge wealth made them conspicuous and they were arrested and brought before the High Court of Admiralty. The charges were dropped for lack of any witnesses.

DIGGLES

Thomas DIGGLES. Taken from the prize snow *Christopher* in Apr 1721 by Captain Bartholomew ROBERTS' ship *Royal Fortune*. Captured by *HMS Swallow* off the West African coast on 19 Feb 1722. Tried at Cape Corso Castle on 28 Mar 1722. He was found not guilty of piracy and acquitted.

DIPPER

Henry DIPPER. One of the soldiers who deserted from Fort Loyal, Falmouth, Maine and joined the pirate Captain Thomas POUND. He was killed in the fight at Tarpaulin Cove in 1689.

DOBBIN

James DOBBIN. A crewman to Captain Calico Jack RACKHAM. DOBBIN was captured with RACKHAM and his crew off Jamaica on 1 Nov 1720. He was tried at St Jago de la Vega, Jamaica and hanged on 18 Nov 1720.

DOBSON

Captain Richard DOBSON. An English buccaneer captain in the Caribbean. DOBSON was one of Henry MORGAN's commanders in his expedition against the Spanish Main in March 1669.

DOLE

Francis DOLE. A crewman to Captain HORE. DOLE was an ex-pirate who had married and settled at Charleston, near Boston. The pirate GILLAM was found by a search party when he was hiding at DOLE's home. DOLE was arrested and committed to gaol in Boston. Francis DOLE would have been quite elderly by this time.

DOLZELL

Captain Alexander DOLZELL. b. Scotland. DOLZELL had been a privateer in his younger days, though he was convicted of high treason and served time in Newgate Prison. He obtained a pardon and his release and turned to piracy. DOLZELL and his men took a French ship at Le Havre. They tied up the crew and threw one of them overboard. He was again captured and tried at the Old

Bailey, this time being convicted of piracy. He was hanged in Dec 1715. The Chaplain of Newgate described him as 'a seaman by profession, a pernicious and dangerous person; of a morose, stubborn and ill disposition by nature'.

DOROTHY

John DOROTHY. A crewman to Captain John QUELCH. He was tried for piracy at Boston in Jun 1704. DOROTHY was eventually pardoned.

DOVE

Nicholas DOVE. An apprentice on the vessel *Degreave*, wrecked on the South Coast of Madagascar in 1703. DOVE joined the Madagascar pirates and made many voyages with them before retiring to the mainland of Africa in 1708. He became a slave trader.

DOVER

Doctor Thomas Dover. 1660-1742. Bachelor of Medicine, Caius College, Cambridge. Dover practiced medicine for many years in Bristol, then sailed with Captain Woodes ROGERS as 'Second Captain'. After rounding Cape Horn they sighted Juan Fernandez Island on 1 Feb 1709. They saw a light in the night and the next day DOVER went ashore and found Alexander SELKIRK, the only inhabitant and Daniel Defoe's model for Robinson Crusoe. Sailing North they took a Spanish vessel and DOVER was given command of her. He sacked Guayaquil in Apr 1709. Later he took the *Acapulco* with £1,000,000 in plunder aboard. In 1711 Dover returned to London very rich, after completing a circumnavigation of the world. Giving up piracy, Dover settled to a London medical practice and saw his patients daily at the Jerusalem Coffee House, Cecil Street. Doctor DOVER wrote 'The Ancient Physician's Legacy to His Country' in which he prescribed mercury as the cure for almost everything. He also invented Dover's Powders, which contained ipecacuanha, and were still used well into the 20th century. Dover died at the age of 82. Few men can claim to have commanded a company of marines, invented a useful remedy and prescribed thousands of poisonous ones, to have rescued Robinson Crusoe and been a pirate captain.

DOWLING

William DOWLING. b. 1693? He may have been one of the pirates who took Woodes ROGERS offer of pardon at Providence in 1718. Later he was a crewman to Captain John AUGER. DOWLING was taken prisoner with AUGER when their sloop ran aground on Long Island W.I.. He was tried and hanged at Providence.

DOWNES

Captain John DOWNES. An English pirate captain in the early 17th century. He took the vessel *Royal* in the 1600s. He and his crew tortured the Master and 2 boys by whipping them, then tightening knotted cords around their heads until they disclosed the whereabouts of the gold that DOWNES knew was aboard. They took 6 bags of reals-of-eight worth £400. In 1631, after the main period of English piracy was over, DOWNES was still using the Helford River in Cornwall as a hideout. Soon after that he was captured on the Isle of Man.

DRAGUT

? DRAGUT. A Barbary Corsair. DRAGUT started as a pirate crewman but was put in command of 12 galleys by BARBAROSSA. He pillaged and pirated the Italian coasts. He was once taken prisoner by the younger DORIA and sentenced to 4 years rowing in the galleys, but was ransomed by BARBAROSSA for 3,000 ducats. DRAGUT is said to have been killed in the Siege of Malta in 1565, but most of the Turkish-led corsairs there died of fever because they made their camp in a malarial swamp.

DRAKE

Sir Francis DRAKE. 1540-1596. b. Tavistock, Devon. DRAKE's

hatred of the Spanish seems to stem from an early experience when, as Captain of Sir John HAWKIN's ship *Judith*, part of an English squadron that were almost all destroyed in the Spanish port of San Juan de Lua (Vera Cruz), only *Judith* and one other vessel escaped to bring the survivors home. He sought compensation from Spain but obtained none. His life from then seems to have been dedicated to compensating himself.

DRAKE made voyages to the West Indies in 1570 and 1571, trading despite the Spanish prohibition. In May 1572 he sailed with two ships to Nombres de Dios, fell in with Captain James RAUSE, a privateer, and together they took the town. DRAKE was badly wounded in the thigh and was taken back aboard his vessel, leaving a large treasure ashore.

They took a large Spanish ship at Cartagena and destroyed many others. They burned the town of

Porto Bello and sacked Vera Cruz but gained little in the way of plunder.

On 1 Apr 1573 they captured a mule-train carrying about 30 tons of silver. He arrived back at Plymouth in Aug 1573. While in the Isthmus of Darien DRAKE had seen the Pacific ocean from a high vantage point. He determined that his next voyage would be to that ocean.

He sailed again in Dec 1577 and rounded South America by the passage that Magellan had discovered. They espied the treasure ship *Nuestra Senora de la Concepcion* on 1 Mar 1579. They took great wealth from the Spanish ship, then plundered on along the coast of Central America.

Drake decided to return to England by sailing 'west-about' and completed his circumnavigation on 26 Sep 1580.

For the next few years DRAKE was in effect the 'Admiral of the Narrow Seas', concerned with the maintenance of the queen's peace and the suppression of pirates.

When Spain imposed an embargo on English ships and goods found on Spanish lands, England retaliated by sending DRAKE with 25 ships and 2000 soldiers to avenge this action in the Caribbean. DRAKE sailed from Plymouth in Sep 1585. On the way he plundered 30,000 ducats at Vigo and burned the town of St Iago (Jamaica?), visited Dominica and St Christopher (St Kitts). He landed his men in force on Hispaniola. They took and ransomed the town of San Domingo. At Cartagena they ransomed the town for 110,000 ducats.

Sailing to Florida they plundered the coastline there and then sailed to the colony of Virginia. The plan had been to re-supply the colony but they found the colonists so disheartened that DRAKE agreed to take them back to England. With them he also took the first tobacco and potatoes that England had seen.

On 2 Apr 1587 DRAKE sailed with a strong squadron to Cadiz (though orders were on the way prohibiting him) where he destroyed 33 Spanish ships and captured 4 others. His force continued to raid along the coast and took over 100 vessels captive. They exchanged these vessels with the Moorish corsairs for English captives that the Moors held.

DRAKE's role in opposing the Spanish Armada is well known but it should be said that finishing his game of bowls on Plymouth Hoe was not an act of bravado. DRAKE knew well that if he sailed in the night he could get well to windward of the Spanish and harry them up the Channel, just as he did.

Drake played a part in the 1589 attempts against Corunna and Lisbon, when losses of 16,000 men marred the success of the campaign.

In Aug 1595 DRAKE sailed again with Sir John HAWKINS.

They reached Porto Rico on 11 Nov and HAWKINS died that day of natural causes. The town, though full of treasure, was well defended and DRAKE was driven off. He decided to cross the isthmus to Panama, but his health was failing and he suffered dysentery. He returned to his ship but died four days later, on 28 Jan 1596, off Porto Bello.

Note 1. England regards DRAKE as a national hero for his defence of the realm. Spanish readers will regard DRAKE's activities as brutal piracy. Less biased readers from other lands will see that both of these views are quite right from their own perspective. DRAKE was a man of his age.

Note 2. DRAKE's body, in its leaden coffin, was located recently and there was a suggestion that it be recovered and brought to Plymouth Hoe for burial to coincide with the 300th anniversary of his death. The anniversary came and went and nothing was done.

DRAKE

John DRAKE. Brother of Sir Francis DRAKE. John accompanied his brother Francis to the New World on his first voyage. In July 1572 he led one of the two groups that encircled and captured the town of Nombres de Dios. On 3 Feb the next year John DRAKE was killed during the capture of Porto Bello.

DRAKE

John DRAKE. Nephew of Sir Francis DRAKE. John sailed with Sir Francis on his voyage into the Pacific Ocean. John DRAKE was the lookout who espied the Spanish treasure ship *Nuestra Senora de la Concepcion* on 1 Mar 1579. He was awarded a gold chain for doing so. The Spanish ship held immense treasure.

DRAKE

Joseph DRAKE. Brother of Sir Francis DRAKE. Joseph sailed with Sir Francis on his first voyage to the Caribbean. He took part in the capture of Nombres de Dios, but soon afterwards 'died of a calenture' which carried off 28 of their party.

DRAKE

Thomas DRAKE. Brother of Sir Francis DRAKE. Thomas sailed with Sir Francis on his second voyage to the West Indies in Dec 1577.

DRAKE

? DRAKE. (Not Sir Francis). A crewman to Captain John JENNINGS on pirate cruises in the Mediterranean, the English Channel and the Western Approaches. Drake was one of the crew who rebelled against JENNINGS and handed him over to the Earl of Thomond in 1609 in Ireland.

DROMYOWE

Peter DROMYOWE. A Breton pirate. He was crewman to Captain LAERQUERAC, who took several English vessels in the Bristol Channel in 1537.

DUBOIS

John DUBOIS. Hanged at Execution Dock, Wapping on 23 May 1701. DUBOIS and Peter MANQUINAM were hanged at the same ceremony at Captain KIDD but were not part of the same prosecution.

DUCASSE

Jean-Baptiste DUCASSE. A French naval officer who arrived in the Caribbean with a very junior rank but became Governor of French Saint Domingue. DUCASSE led French filibusters against the English, Spanish and Dutch possessions and ships during the Nine Years War. In 1682, at the age of 42, the ex-slaver led an unsuccessful attempt against Dutch Surinam. In 1684 he took part in the French expedition against St Kitts (then both English and French). DUCASSE and his 120 filibusters laid their artillery against the besieged Fort Charles. His skillful use of the cannon almost won the day, but the Fort was saved by HEWETSON's force which arrived from Nevis. After the Spanish invasion of Saint Domingue and its huge losses, DUCASSE returned to France to report the crisis and obtain reinforcements. He sailed again from La Rochelle in March 1691. At Martinique he learned of the English occupation of Guadalupe and set off with 6 ships, 2 companies of infantry and 600 filibusters. By May 1691 he had regained both Guadalupe and Marie Galante. In June 1694 he played an important part in the French invasion of Jamaica, which had a limited success. He continued to command local French naval forces in the Caribbean for the duration of the Nine Years War, proving to be a talented commander and tactician. Many times he was able to muster large filibuster forces and use them with regular forces in a way that no-one else but De GRAAF could.

DUELL

William DUELL. A pirate who was sentenced to death by the Admiralty Court in 1740. The Court also demanded that DUELL's body be taken to Surgeon's Hall for dissection. Having been washed, ready for dissection at the Surgeon's Hall, it was noticed that he was still breathing. A surgeon bled him and he recovered sufficiently to be returned to Newgate Prison. His sentence was commuted to transportation to the colonies.

DU FROCK

John du FROCK. Joined Captain Bartholomew ROBERTS' *Royal Fortune* from the prize galley *Lloyd* in May 1721. Captured by *HMS Swallow* off the West African coast on 10 Feb 1722. He was probably already a Royal Navy deserter because he was transferred to the Marshalsea for trial in London. The outcome of that trial, if it occurred, is not known.

DU LAERQUERAC.

Captain John du LAERQUERAC. A Breton pirate. He was captured in 1537 by a seaman called John WYNTER. He had been taking vessels on their way to the great fair at St James, Bristol. He denied the charges at first, but later admitted he might have taken a few odds and ends. No record of the outcome.

DUNBAR

Nicholas DUNBAR. A crewman to Captain John QUELCH on the brig *Charles*. Tried for piracy at Boston in Jun 1704.

DUNKIN

George DUNKIN. A crewman to Major Stede BONNET. Captured with BONNET at Cape Fear River on 27 Sep 1718. DUNKIN was tried at Charleston and hanged on 8 Nov 1718.

DUNN

William DUNN. A crewman to Captain Thomas POUND. DUNN was tried with POUND's crew in Boston in 1690. He was found guilty and sentenced to death but his sentence was remitted on payment of 13 pounds and 6 shillings.

DUNTON

Captain ? DUNTON. A London man. He was taken prisoner by the Sallee pirates of Morocco in 1636. Because he was a better navigator and sailing master than his captors, they put him into a Salle ship as pilot and master. His crew was 21 Moors and 5 Flemings. He was ordered to the English Coast to capture prisoners. Off Hurst Castle, in the Solent, his vessel was seized. The crew were taken and tried at Winchester. DUNTON was acquitted, but his 10 year old son was still a slave in Algiers. They never met again.

EARL

Thomas EARL. A crewman to Captain Calico Jack RACK-HAM. EARL was captured with RACKHAM off Jamaica on 1 Nov 1720. He was tried at St Jago de la Vega and hanged at Kingston on 18 Nov 1720.

EASTON

Captain Peter EASTON. A famous pirate leader in the reign of King James 1. EASTON served as crewman on a Dutch privateer in 1607. He gained command of his own vessel and cruised in company with Captain Richard ROBINSON until they quarrelled. By 1611 he had 40 vessels under his command. The next year he plundered vessels on the Newfoundland Banks, taking supplies, crewmen and vessels too. In 1613 he established himself with the English pirates at Marmora, on the Barbary Coast. He retired to Savoy with a fortune estimated at 100,000 crowns and a pension of £4,000 per year. EASTON built himself a palace and lived like a prince.

EATON

Edward EATON. b. Wrexham, Wales, 1685/6. Crewman to Captain Charles HARRIS on *Ranger*. Captured by *HMS Greyhound*. EATON tried at Newport R.I.

He was found guilty and hanged on 19 Nov 1723.

EATON

Captain John EATON. Commander of the pirate ship *Nicholas* out of London. He met COOKE's *Bachelor' Delight* on 19 Mar 1684 off Valsivia, Chile. EATON was able to report to Cooke that he had already encountered SWAN's *Cygnet* en route for the Pacific, but had lost touch in bad weather. EATON and COOKE sailed together and took several Spanish vessels. They left their plunder at Galapagos and sailed to the coast of Costa Rica, there they met with SWAN and Peter HARRIS (the nephew). The four pirate crews together were now strong enough to take larger towns and they attacked Paita in November 1684, then the Lobos Islands, followed by Guayaquil in December. Still too few to take larger cities, they sent to the Caribbean for reinforcements, taking a Spanish 90 ton ship in the meantime. In February 1685 a party of 200 French filibusters and 8 English buccaneers arrived under the command of GROGNIET and L'ES-CAYER. They brought blank commissions from the Governor of Saint Domingue, so the pirates became privateers. The expedition continued to grow as more men crossed the Isthmus of Darien to join them. What became of EATON is unclear.

EATON

John EATON. Crewman to Captain Calico Jack RACKHAM. He joined the vessel at Negril Point, Jamaica on the day of its capture. Nonetheless, he was tried at St Jago de la Vega on 16 Nov 1720. The case against EATON was adjourned until 24 Jan 1721 for want of evidence. No further evidence seems to have been found, but he was still found guilty at the re-trial. He was hanged at Gallows Point, Port Royal on 17 Feb 1721.

ECHLIN

? ECHLIN. An Englishman. In 1730 he was crewman to Captain JOHNSON, the one-armed commander of *Two Brothers*, a Rhode Island built vessel.

EDDY

William EDDY (Neddy). b. Aberdeen, Scotland. Crewman to Major Stede BONNET. Captured with BONNET at Cape Fear River on 27 Sep 1718. Tried at Charleston, South Carolina. He was found guilty and hanged on 8 Nov 1718.

EDWARDS

Captain EDWARDS. One of the false names that Major Stede BONNET used during his piracy.

ELFRITH

Captain Daniel ELFRITH. An English pirate who brought a Spanish prize vessel to Bermuda. The islanders welcomed the cargo until they discovered that the ship was full of rats. The rats left the ship and infested the islands to such an extent that the islanders almost starved. No dates or further information. Folklore?

ELLIOTT

Captain Stephen ELLIOTT. A privateer captain in the Caribbean. ELLIOTT was captured by 2 French vessels while on a smuggling mission from Jamaica to the Spanish Main. He was held prisoner in Saint Domingue, where he heard plans of a French invasion of Jamaica. ELLIOTT escaped and stole a canoe, spending 5 days at sea before reaching Jamaica on 10 June 1694. He stumbled into the dining room of Governor BEESTON and gave him the news. BEESTON was amazed to see ELLIOTT 'in a very mean habit and with a meagre, weather beaten countenance'. The forces on Jamaica were able to repel the French invasion forces with only limited losses.

EL MAJORCAM

Captain El MAJORCAM. A former officer in the Spanish Navy. Later he was a notorious

West Indies pirate, but in about 1824 he retired from the sea, to become a highwayman ashore.

ENGLAND

Captain Edward ENGLAND. Formerly skipper of a merchantman. He sailed in company with Captain le VASSEUR (The Buzzard) and Captain John TAYLOR. They took the Eastindiaman *Cassandra* (Captain James McREA) at Matsumudu Bay. ENGLAND set McREA free with provisions to reach Bombay and the leaking pirate vessel *Fancy*. This angered the other two pirate captains and they put him ashore on Mauritius with a pistol, powder and a keg of water. ENGLAND made a raft and drifted on it to Madagascar. He died there some years later, a penniless beggar.

ERNADOS

Emanuel ERNADOS. A Carolina pirate who was tried and hanged at Charleston in 1717.

ESMIT

Adolf ESMIT. A Dutch Buccaneer. He later became the Governor of the Danish island of St Thomas. The population of the island was almost all English and ESMIT gave sanctuary, help and finance to pirates whenever he could. He used his popularity to expel his brother, who was the lawful Governor of the island.

ESQUEMELING

John ESQUEMELING. A surgeon and a prolific writer. He wrote in detail about the exploits of the buccaneers and pirates of the late 17th century. He had sailed with many of them as a ship's surgeon. His books were written first in Spanish, then Dutch and English. Each edition was written to please its readership, and all conflicted. Sir Henry MORGAN took him to court for libel in London and won the case against him. ESQUEMELING had to pay compensation and re-write the English version. The later versions were more readable, mainly because much of Basil RINGROSE's work was included. ESQUEMELING returned eventually to Holland and studied medicine at Delft. Note: I believe he was a Dutchman called Melling who wished to preserve his identity in case he was charged with piracy.

ESSEX

Captain Cornelius ESSEX. An English Buccaneer. In Dec 1679 he assembled with several other known buccaneers off Point Morant. They sailed to sack Porto Bello on 7 Jan 1680, but were scattered by a storm. Most of the force landed and sacked the town after a four day march along the coast. Each man's share of the plunder was 100 pieces of eight. ESSEX was later taken by a frigate and tried at Port Royal, Jamaica for plundering along the Jamaican coast. He was acquitted, but two of his crew were hanged.

EUCALLA

? EUCALLA. A black pirate. Hanged at Kingston, Jamaica on 7 Feb 1823. He made a moving speech from the gallows, ending with a prayer. Of the ten pirates hanged that day, it is said that he showed the greatest courage.

EUSTACE

EUSTACE the Monk. A Flemish cleric who was reputed to have mystical and magical powers. He was a privateer under licence issued by King John of England. EUSTACE took French shipping in the Channel and the Dover Straits in the 13th century. EUSTACE turned to taking English shipping also and was driven out of English ports. He became a privateer for the French. In 1214 he attempted an invasion of the Kentish Coast. The English ships who repelled his fleet did so by throwing lime to blind his crewmen, then flights of arrows. EUSTACE's flagship was boarded, he was captured and beheaded on the spot.

EVANS

Edward EVANS. Taken from the prize *Porcupine* in Whydar Roads by Captain Bartholomew ROBERTS *Royal Fortune*. Captured by *HMS Swallow* off the West African coast on 10 Feb 1722. Tried at Cape Corso Castle on 28 Mar 1722 and found not guilty of piracy. Acquitted.

EVANS

Captain John EVANS. b. Wales. He was the master of a sloop sailing out of Nevis, West Indies. EVANS lost that employment and sailed as a mate out of Jamaica. He must have been a fairly unpleasant shipmate because that employment dried up as well. In Sep 1722, he and a small gang stole a boat at Port Royal and did house-breaking along the Jamaican coast. They seized a small sloop at Dun's Hole and called her *Scowered*. They took three vessels in the Windward Isles, giving shares of £150 per man. On 11 Jan 1723 they took the prize *Lucretia and Catherine* and sailed with her to Avis (Nevis or Aves?) to careen. They chased another vessel but lost it, and sailed to the Cayman Islands. EVANS had a dispute with his Bosun on the way and the Bosun challenged EVANS to a duel ashore with pistols and cutlasses, as was the custom. When they reached land the Bosun refused to go ashore and fight. Evans beat him with a cane. The Bosun drew a pistol and shot EVANS through the head and killed him. The crew were left without a navigator, except for the Mate of the ***Lucretia and Catherine*** who refused to navigate for them. The crew dispersed through the Cayman Islands eventually.

EVERTSON

Captain Jacob EVERTSON. A Dutch pirate. In 1673 Samuel PEPYS the celebrated diarist noted that 12 vessels of the homecoming Virginia Convoy, which arrived at Plymouth on 21 Sep 1673, had been taken in the Atlantic by EVERTSON. The Dutchman continued his piracy until he was captured by Henry MORGAN's troops in Jan 1681. His crew were nearly all English. He was tried at Port Royal on 14 May 1681, convicted and sentenced to death. The sentence was remitted because the Governor thought that the sight of a row of bodies hanging from the gallows might have discouraged other pirates from seeking a pardon.

EXTON

Captain John EXTON. An English pirate captain in the early 17th century. All I have discovered of him was that he always dressed entirely in green.

FABENS

Lawrence FABENS. A reluctant crewman to Captain Edward LOW. FABENS was taken from a fishing schooner off Cape Cod. He eventually escaped from LOW's ship with Nicholas MERRITT.

FALL

Edward FALL. A shipmate of John WARD when they deserted from the Channel Squadron and stole a vessel at Plymouth. FALL led their party until he was captured. He was executed in May 1604.

FALL

John FALL. A crewman to Captain Bartholomew SHARPE on the expedition to plunder the Pacific in 1680/81. On the death of John HILLIARD, their ship's master, FALL was promoted to lead the Larboard watch.

FARRINGTON

Thomas FARRINGTON. A crewman to Captain John QUELCH on the brig *Charles*. He was tried for piracy at the Star Tavern in Boston in 1704.

FENWICK

Robert FENWICK. Most famous as the man with whom Anne BONNY settled down to live after the execution of Captain Calico Jack RACKHAM. FENWICK had once been a pirate in the Red Sea and had made enough money to retire in style to Charleston, Carolina, where he built Fenwick Castle and lived in great luxury.

FENN

Captain John FENN. Gunner to Captain Thomas ANSTIS on *Buck* in 1718. FENN had lost a hand at some time. ANSTIS gave him command of the prize *Morning Star*, near Bermuda. He lost *Morning Star* in the Cayman Islands and rejoined ANSTIS on *Good Fortune* in Aug 1722. ANSTIS gave him command of another prize, a ship of 24 guns. He beached this vessel with another prize on the island of Tobago, to careen them. *HMS Winchelsea* came upon the beached vessels and ANSTIS *Good Fortune* which was afloat. ANSTIS fled, leaving FENN and many crew on the beach. FENN was caught after a two-day hunt. He was taken to Antigua where he was tried and hanged.

FERNANDO

Lewis FERNANDO. In 1699 FERNANDO captured a sloop belonging to Samuel SALTERS of Bermuda.

FERGUSON

James FERGUSON. A surgeon to Captain Samuel BELLAMY

on **Whydah**. FERGUSON is believed to have drowned on the night, in 1717, when **Whydah** was wrecked on Cape Cod.

FERGUSON

William FERGUSON. A reluctant crewman to Captain William FLY. FERGUSON was taken from the prize vessel **James**. He was captured with FLY's vessel and tried on 4 Jul 1626 at Boston. He was acquitted of piracy.

FERN

Thomas FERN. Carpenter to Captain John PHILLIPS at the start of PHILLIPS' piracy off Newfoundland. FERN was affronted when John Rose ARCHER was promoted above him by PHILLIPS. He tried to make off in a prize vessel that PHILLIPS had put him aboard. He was recaptured but tried again to make off with a prize Jamaican sloop. This time PHILLIPS killed him.

FERNON (or VERNON?)

William FERNON. b. Somerset, 1699/1700. Joined Captain Bartholomew ROBERTS' ship **Royal Fortune** from the prize vessel **Sudbury** in Jun 1720. **Royal Fortune** was captured off the West African coast by **HMS Swallow** on 10 Feb 1722. FERNON was tried at Cape Corso Castle on 28 Mar 1722. He was found guilty and hanged.

FETHERSTONE

George FETHERSTONE. Sailing Master to Captain Calico Jack RACKHAM. Captured with RACKHAM off Jamaica on 1 Nov 1720. He was tried at St Jago de la Vega. FETHERSTONE was found guilty and hanged at Gallows Point, Port Royal on 17 Nov 1720. His body was hanged in chains at Bush Key as an example to other pirates.

FIFE

Captain James FIFE. He was one of the pirates who surrendered to the pardon of the Governor of the Bahamas in 1717. Later he was killed by his own crew.

FILLMORE

John FILLMORE. A fisherman from Ipswich. Taken from the **Dolphin** on the Newfoundland Banks by Captain PHILLIPS in 1724. He was forced to be a pirate crewman. He and several other captives overpowered PHILLIPS and sailed the ship to Boston, where the pirates were tried and hanged. Note: Millard FILLMORE, the 13th President of the United States, was his great-grandson.

FINN

Captain ? FINN. A Caribbean pirate Captain. FINN and four other pirates were tried and hanged at Antigua in 1723. His body was displayed in chains, hanging at Rat Island in the middle of St John's Harbour.

FITZGERALD

John FITZGERALD. An Irishman. FITZGERALD was a crewman to Captain John COOK on *Bachelors' Delight* in the Pacific in 1683, then under Captain Edward DAVIS in the same vessel. He expressed his unhappiness about DAVIS' captaincy to William DAMPIER after an unsuccessful attack against a Spanish town. I assume that he stayed with DAVIS and returned to the Caribbean with him because DAMPIER makes no more mention of him.

FITZGERALD

John FITZGERALD. b. Limerick, Ireland, 1702/3. A crewman to Captain Charles HARRIS on *Ranger*. Captured by *HMS Greyhound*. Tried at Newport R.I. Found guilty and hanged on 19 Jul 1723. In gaol, awaiting execution, FITZGERALD wrote a poem condemning his former occupation.

In youthful blooming years was I, when that I practice took;
Of perpetrating piracy, for filthy gain did look.
To wickedness we all were bent, our lusts for to fulfill;
To rob at sea was our intent, and perpetrate all ill.

I pray the Lord preserve you all and keep you from this end;
O let Fitz-Gerald's great downfall unto your welfare tend.
I to the Lord my soul bequeath, accept therefore I pray,
My body to the earth bequeath, dear friend, adieu for aye.

Fortunately, FITZGERALD was hanged before he could write any more verse.

FLEMING

Captain Thomas FLEMING. It was FLEMING, in his ship *Golden Hind* (50 tons and 30 men) who first spotted the Spanish Armada off the Lizard on 19 Jul 1588. At the time FLEMING was wanted for piracy, having been accused of taking Thomas NICHOLL's 80 ton *Hope* of Newhaven. Despite the danger of his arrest FLEMMING put into port with the news and beacons were lit to spread the warning throughout the country. He later sailed with the English fleet against the Armada. His ship towed the Spanish ship *San Salvadore* into Weymouth harbour as a wreck. His action earned him a pardon and a reward.

FLETCHER

John FLETCHER. b. Jamaica. Fletcher was a Quartermaster to Captain Samuel BELLAMY on *Whydah*. He is believed to have drowned on the night, in 1717, when *Whydah* was wrecked on Cape Cod.

FLETCHER

John FLETCHER. b. 1705/6. A crewman to Captain Charles HARRIS of *Ranger*. Captured by *HMS Greyhound*. He was tried at Newport R.I. in Jul 1723. Found not guilty and acquitted, probably because he was only 17 years old.

FLETCHER

Robert FLETCHER. Joined Captain James SKYRM's vessel *Ranger* from the prize galley *Stanwich*. Captured off the West African coast by *HMS Swallow* on 1 Feb 1722. Fletcher must have already been a deserter from the Royal Navy because he was referred to the Marshalsea for trial in London. The outcome of the trial is not known.

FLETCHER

Samuel FLETCHER. b. Smithfield, London. He joined Captain Bartholomew ROBERTS' ship *Royal Fortune* from the prize vessel *King Solomon* in Jan 1722. Captured by *HMS Swallow* off the West African coast on 10 Feb 1722. Tried at Cape Corso Castle on 28 Mar 1722 and found guilty. FLETCHER was sentenced to 7 years' transportation to the African Colonies.

FLEURY

Captain Jean FLEURY. A French privateer sailing for the Viscount of Dieppe in 1523. FLEURY was the first to capture Spanish treasure ships returning from the New World. Off Cape St Vincent, Portugal, FLEURY took two of three ships that carried treasure that CORTES had plundered in Mexico. The hoard included 500 lbs of gold-dust, 680 lbs of pearls, other jewels and artifacts of precious metals.

FLY

Captain William FLY. b. Bristol. FLY sailed from Bristol in Apr 1726 as Bosun on the snow *Elizabeth*, a slaver. A brutal man, he persuaded some of the crew to mutiny with him and turn pirate. He lasted three months in this trade, having no skill, little intelligence and not much luck. Eventually his captives on the vessel outnumbered the pirates by 5 to 1 and overpowered them. FLY and his crew were sailed to Boston by their recent captives. They were tried and hanged at Boston on 12 Jul 1726.

FOLLET

Edward FOLLET. An English pirate in the early 17th century. In 1606 he obtained a pardon from Sir Richard HAWKINS, son of the Elizabethan sea dog. Sir Richard himself had commanded a ship against the Spanish Armada and was pleased to pardon any pirate whose victims had been Spanish. Sir Richard was vice-admiral of Devon, a suspicious appointment in itself.

FORREST

William FORREST. One of the mutinous crew of the *Antonio*. He was tried and hanged in Boston in 1672.

FORSEITH

Edward FORSEITH. A crewman to Captain Henry AVERY. Hanged at Execution Dock, Wapping in 1696.

FOSTER

? FOSTER. A Buccaneer and a poet. Only two facts are known about FOSTER; the first is that Henry MORGAN (who was no softy with prisoners) admonished FOSTER for his harshness with captives. The second fact is that he wrote sentimental poetry, notably 'Sonneyettes of Love'. You try and work that out, I can't.

FRANCIA

John FRANCIA. Taken from a prize sloop at St Nicholas by Captain Bartholomew ROBERTS' ship *Royal Fortune* in Apr 1721. Captured by *HMS Swallow* off the West African coast. He was tried at Cape Corso Castle on 28 Mar 1722. He was found not guilty of piracy and acquitted.

FRANCKE

Captain Thomas FRANCKE. An English pirate in the early 17th century. FRANCKE was given command of a pirate vessel by the pirate Captain Robert STEPHENSON. He repaid STEPHENSON by giving him the first prize they took. FRANCKE took the *Primrose* of London in 1609. He took 5 French vessels off the Atlantic coast of France in 1611. FRANCKE's vessel was taken by Flemish pirates. They burned the ends of his fingers off and "tormented him otherwise by the privy members". His crew seem to have been treated likewise.

FRANKLIN

Charles FRANKLIN. b. Monmouthshire, Wales. A crewman to Captain Howard DAVIS. FRANKLIN married a local woman in the Cape Verde Islands, left his ship and settled there.

FRANCO

Captain ? FRANCO (or FRANK or FRANKL). FRANCO was probably a Dutchman who operated under a French privateer's licence in the Pacific. FRANCO sailed from New England to the Pacific via West Africa in March 1687. He planned to join privateers and buccaneers already operating there. He discovered that by the time he arrived there, the days of buccaneering were almost over. With a single vessel, and crew of only 41 men. FRANCO did attack one small town, Acaponata,

Mexico, in November 1688, and captured women and some silver. In October the next year he took a Spanish vessel out of Puna. For 4 years he cruised the Pacific, despite Spanish attempts to capture or sink him. He eventually returned to Europe.

FREEBARN

Mathew FREEBARN. A crewman to Captain George LOWTHER on *Ranger*. He was captured by the sloop *HMS Eagle* at Blanquilla in Oct 1723. FREEBARN was tried at St Christopher (St Kitts) on 11 Mar 1724. He was found guilty and hanged.

FROGGE

William FROGGE. A Buccaneer. FROGGE was with Henry MORGAN in his attacks on Porto Bello and Panama. He kept a diary of events and maintained that the Spanish, and not MORGAN, fired the city. He also maintained that MORGAN cheated the rest of the buccaneers on the share-out of the booty. I doubt that.

FRY

Captain ? FRY. In the last days of English piracy from the port of Tunis, in the early 17th century, FRY fled from the harbour in a stolen vessel with 80 English followers. More than half of his crew were master-gunners.

FULLMORE

Simon FULLMORE. A reluctant crewman to Captain Francis SPRIGGS. On 4 Apr 1724 FULLMORE and 5 other reluctant crewmen were marooned on the island of Roatan with a musket, powder and ball to share between them. They were soon rescued by a passing ship and taken to Jamaica.

GARCIA

Angel GARCIA. A crewman to Captain GILBERT on the schooner **Panda**. He was tried and hanged at Boston in Jun 1835.

GARDINER

An ex-pirate who was appointed Deputy Collector at Boston in 1699. He accepted a bribe of stolen gold from the pirate GILLAM, which caused some gossip.

GARRAT

Thomas GARRAT. Taken from the prize vessel **Onslow** aboard Captain Bartholomew ROBERTS' ship **Royal Fortune**. They were captured off the West African coast by **HMS Swallow** on 10 Feb 1722. GARRAT was tried at Cape Corso Castle on 28 Mar 1722. He was found not guilty and acquitted.

GASPAR

Jose GASPAR. (King of the Florida Pirates) Born near Seville to an upper-class Spanish family. In 1755, as a young man, he kidnapped a woman for ransom. When caught and tried he escaped sentence by enlisting into the Spanish Navy. By 1770 he had risen to the rank of Admiral. He was accused of theft by the authorities, took a naval vessel from Cadiz and turned pirate. GASPAR was

reputed to have taken 60 vessels by 1795. He built himself a pirate base which he called Gasparilla Island in Charlotte Harbour, Florida. When Spain ceded Florida to the US in 1812, the USS Enterprise hunted him down and engaged him in battle. Finding that his vessel **Florida Blanca** was losing the battle, GASPAR wrapped chain around himself and dived over the side to escape the hangman.

GATES

Thomas GATES. Crewman to the pirate BLACKBEARD. GATES was wounded and captured at Ocracoke Inlet on 1 Dec 1718. BLACKBEARD was killed in the battle. GATES was tried and hanged.

GAUTIER

Francois GAUTIER (alias George SADWELL). He was a cook aboard the schooner **Jane**. On passage to Brazil he and the mate killed the captain and helmsman and took the ship. They wrecked her on Stornaway in the Outer Hebrides. They were captured and tried at Edinburgh, found guilty and hanged at Leith in Jan 1822. Their bodies were given to Edinburgh University for dissection by medical students.

GAY

Captain ? GAY. An English pirate captain in the early 17th century. In

1611 he sailed in company with Captains ARTHUR, FRANCKE, STEPHENSON and SMITH, in a large Atlantic fleet.

GAYNY

George GAYNY. One of Lionel WAFER's small party of buccaneers who were lost in the jungles of Darien in 1681. While trying to cross a river, GAYNY drowned. The bag of 300 Spanish dollars round his neck would not have helped his swimming. His body was later discovered downstream by SPRATLIN and BOWMAN but they were too exhausted themselves to climb down into the river and recover the gold in GAYNY's satchel.

GENTLEMAN

Captain James GENTLEMAN. An English pirate captain in the early 17th century. In 1614, along with Captain CLARK, he spent two weeks pillaging, raping and robbing in Iceland. An unusual haunt for pirates.

GERRARD

Thomas GERRARD. Of Antigua. A crewman to Major Stede BONNET. He was captured with BONNET on 27 Sep 1718 at Cape Fear River. GERRARD was tried at Charleston and found not guilty of piracy because he had received no share of the plunder.

GERRISTZ

Captain Hendrick GERRISTZ. The leader of a group of Dutch privateers who entered the Laguna de Maracaibo with 4 men-of-war and two sloops on 16 Oct 1641. They landed over 200 men who stripped the outlying plantations of tobacco, cacao and everything else of value that they could carry. After staying 2 weeks in the Laguna they bombarded the City of Maracaibo, then left the area.

GIBBENS

Garret GIBBENS. Bosun to the pirate BLACKBEARD. He died in the final battle at Ocracoke Inlet, alongside BLACKBEARD on 1 Dec 1718.

GIBBONS

William GIBBONS. A Surgeon's Mate on the merchant ship *Princes Galley*. On 15 Sep 1723 *Princes Galley* was taken by Captain George LOWTHER. GIBBONS was reluctant to join the pirates but was probably taken for his medical skills.

GIBBS

Captain Charles GIBBS. b. Providence, Rhode Island, 1794. GIBBS sailed in the sloop *Hornet* against the British in the War of Independence (or the American Revolution, it depends where you went to school). GIBBS next vessel was *Chesapeake*, which was captured by the British. GIBBS was held prisoner in Dartmoor Gaol until his exchange. Later he unsuccessfully ran a grog- shop. Later still, he sailed as a crewman on a privateer out of Buenos Aires. The crew mutinied and voted GIBBS the captain. They put the ship's officers ashore in Florida. GIBBS' voyage brought him 20 prize vessels. All their captives were killed to remove any witnesses, with the exception of a young Dutch girl who was kept and abused for two months. She was in the end offered the choice of poison or a more violent death, she chose the poison. GIBBS was surprised by a British sloop while plundering a vessel in Cuban waters, and made his escape overland with 30,000 dollars. He enlisted in the war between Brazil and Buenos Aires and was commissioned a lieutenant on the vessel *25th of May*. He was captured by the Brazilians but released. Later he served the Dey of Algeria against the French. Back in the US, he served as a crewman on the *Vineyard* out of New Orleans, then took over the ship, murdering the Master and Mate. He was captured, tried and hanged at Rhode Island in Apr 1831.

GIDDENS

Paul GIDDENS. A crewman to Captain John QUELCH. He was tried at Boston in 1704.

GIDDINGS

John GIDDINGS. Of York River, Virginia. A crewman to Captain Thomas POUND. He was wounded and captured at Tarpaulin Cove in 1689.

GIDLEY

George GIDLEY. The cook on *Earl of Sandwich*. Five of the crew, under McKINLEY, took the vessel. They murdered the Captain, passengers and crew and landed in Ireland. They were caught and hanged near Dublin on 19 Dec 1765.

GILBERT

Captain Don Pedro GILBERT. Captain of the yacht *Panda* which took the American vessel *Mexican* of Salem on 19 Sep 1832. The brig carried $20,000 in silver. *HMS Curlew* engaged *Panda* off the West African coast. *Panda* exploded and sank. The pirates were captured and taken to Salem in *HMS Savage*. On arrival there the port could find no Union Jack to fly as a courtesy, so they borrowed one from the ship. The crew of *Panda* were tried in Boston on 11 Nov 1834. GILBERT was found guilty and hanged behind Leverett Street Jail on 11 Mar 1835.

GILES

Henry GILES. A young lad. A reluctant crewman on Captain

William PHILLIPS ship. GILES was one of the group who overpowered the pirates and sailed the ship to Boston. He was tried in Boston on 12 Apr 1724 and found not guilty of piracy.

GILES

Thomas GILES. b. Minehead, Somerset, 1696. GILES joined Captain James SKYRM's *Ranger* from the prize galley *Mercy*, of Bristol, in Oct 1721 at Calabar. Captured by *HMS Swallow* off the West African coast on 1 Feb 1722. GILES was tried at Cape Corso Castle on 28 Mar 1722. He was found guilty and hanged.

GILLAM

Captain James GILLAM. He led a mutiny aboard the *Mocha*, an East Indiaman. GILLAM murdered the captain with his own hands. He returned to New York with Captain William KIDD and his crew under the name of KELLY. When he was caught in 1699, it was said that he had turned Mohammedan and been circumcised. A surgeon and a Jew were summoned to verify the facts.

GILLS

John GILLS. A crewman to BLACKBEARD. He was wounded and captured at Ocracoke Inlet on 1 Dec 1718. GILLS was tried and hanged.

GLANVILLE

Toby GLANVILLE. He was probably one of Captain John WARD's original crew. GLANVILLE sailed as an Algerian corsair and was captured at Sallee in 1613. The Englishman who captured him shipped him back to England for trial. GLANVILLE realised he had little future and leapt to his death from the stern of the ship.

GLASBY

Henry GLASBY. Taken aboard Captain Bartholomew ROBERTS' ship *Royal Fortune* from the prize vessel *Samuel* in Jul 1720. Captured by *HMS Swallow* off the West African coast on 10 Feb 1722. Tried at Cape Corso Castle. The court heard that the pirates held him against his will, that he had twice tried to escape, and that he had stopped the crew of the *Royal Fortune* blowing up the ship when it was captured. Witnesses gave evidence that when the pirates released prize vessels after plundering them, GLASBY had insisted that they had stores and instruments enough to make a passage. He was found not guilty of piracy and acquitted.

GLASS

William GLASS. Taken from the prize sloop *Whydah* at Jaquin in Jan 1722 by Captain James SKYRM's pirate vessel *Ranger*.

Captured off the West African coast by *HMS Swallow* on 1 Feb 1722. He was tried at Cape Corso Castle on 28 Mar 1722. GLASS was found not guilty and acquitted.

GLEN

? GLEN. A crewman to Captain Thomas GREEN on *Worcester*. GLEN was falsely arrested, imprisoned, tried and hanged at Leith, Scotland in Apr 1705.

GODEKINS

Master ? GODEKINS. A Hanseatic pirate. On 1 Jan 1395 he took an English ship laden with salt fish off the Danish coast. He took another vessel while the crew of it were fishing. Later, off Plymouth, he took a Yarmouth barque.

GOFFE

Christopher GOFFE. He was originally one of Captain WOOLERY's pirate crew. GOFFE took a pardon from the Governor of Boston in 1687 and was commissioned by him to cruise in his ship *Swan* to protect the coast from pirates. His part of the coast to protect was from Cape Cod to Cape Ann.

GOLDSMITH

Captain Thomas GOLDSMITH. b. Dartmouth, Devon. A pirate captain during the reign of Queen Anne. His gravestone in Dartmouth graveyard says it all:

Men that are virtuous serve the Lord;
And the Devil's by his friends adored;
And as they merit get a place
Amidst the blessed or Hellish race;
Pray then, ye learned clergy show
Where can this brute, Tom Goldsmith, go?
Whose life was one continual evil,
Striving to cheat God, man and Devil.

GOMEZ

John GOMEZ (alias Panther Key John). Brother-in-law of the famous pirate leader GASPAR. GOMEZ was said to have died on Panther Key, Florida, in 1900, at the age of 120 years.

GOODALE

John GOODALE. A Devon man. A seaman who turned Mohammedan and rose to importance among the Moorish Corsairs of Algeria. In 1621 he bought from the Moors, the British prize vessel *Exchange*.

GOODLY

Captain GOODLY. An English Buccaneer of Jamaica. In 1663 he commanded a vessel described as a 'junk' with 6 guns and 60 men.

GOPSON

Richard GOPSON. A member of SHARPE's expedition to the Pacific in 1681. GOPSON left the Pacific to re-cross the Isthmus of Darien on foot with COOKE's party. Along with Lionel Wafer and John HINGSON, GOPSON fell behind the main party and spent time with the local Indians until they were recovered enough to continue. They eventually rejoined the others at the Caribbean coast.

GORDON

Captain Nathaniel GORDON. Of Portland, Maine. He owned and commanded a small, full-rigged ship *Evie*, which was fitted out as a slaver. He made four slaving runs to West Africa. GORDON was captured on his last voyage with 976 slaves aboard, by the US sloop *Mohican*. He was tried in New York for piracy and sentenced to death. Much pressure was put on President LINCOLN to reprieve him, but he was hanged at New York on 22 Feb 1862.

GORSUCH

Roger GORSUCH. Taken aboard Captain Bartholomew ROBERTS' ship *Royal Fortune* from the prize snow *Martha* in Aug 1721. Captured by *HMS Swallow* on 10 Feb 1722 off the West African coast. GORSUCH was tried at Cape Corso Castle on 28 Mar 1722 and must have proved that he was aboard *Royal Fortune* unwillingly. He was found not guilty of piracy and acquitted.

GOSS

Cuthbert GOSS. b. Plymouth, Devon, 1701. GOSS joined Captain James SKYRM's pirate vessel *Ranger* from the prize galley *Mercy* in Aug 1721. Captured by *HMS Swallow* on 10 Feb 1722 off the West African coast. He was tried at Cape Corso Castle on 28 Mar 1722 and found not guilty of piracy. GOSS was acquitted.

GOW

(See Captain John SMITH).

GRAHAM

Captain ? GRAHAM. In 1685 he commanded a shallop with 14 men. He cruised in company with Captain VEALE along the coasts of Virginia and New England.

GRAMBO

? GRAMBO. He was the 'Boss' of Barataria, the smugglers' stronghold on the Island of Grande Terre, near Louisiana. He was shot by Jean LAFITTE in 1811.

GRAMMONT

Sieur de GRAMMONT. A French Filibuster. b. Paris. He

enlisted in the French Marines. Later he commanded a frigate in the West Indies and captured a Dutch ship near Martinique with a cargo worth £400,000. He took his prize to Hispaniola and lost it at gambling. He realised then that he could not return to France so he became a filibuster. He sailed to Curacao in 1678 with Count D'ESTREE's fleet which was wrecked on a coral reef at the Isle d'Aves. He raided Maracaibo, and in 1680, La Guayra, where he was wounded in the throat. In 1683 he took part in a huge raid on Vera Cruz, taking command when VANHORN died of gangrene. GRAMMONT joined forces with De GRAFF in 1685 and they led 11,000 men to sack Campeachy. His vessel was the *Hardy*. In 1686 he was granted a French commission, but sailed off to have one final voyage as a filibuster before he took it up. He was never heard of again.

GRANGE

Roger GRANGE. Taken aboard Captain George LOWTHER's *Ranger*. Captured by the sloop *HMS Eagle* at Blanquilla in Oct 1723. Tried at St Christopher (St Kitts) on 11 Mar 1724. He was found not guilty of piracy and acquitted.

GRANGER

Christopher GRANGER. Taken from the prize galley *Cornwall* at Calabar by Captain Bartholomew

ROBERTS' ship *Royal Fortune* in Oct 1721. Captured by *HMS Swallow* on 10 Feb 1722 off the West African coast. He was tried at Cape Corso Castle on 28 Mar 1722. Found not guilty of piracy and acquitted.

GRAVES

Henry GRAVES. Joined Captain James SKYRM's ship *Ranger* from the prize vessel *Tarlton* in Jan 1722. Captured by *HMS Swallow* off the West African coast. GRAVES must have already been a deserter from the Royal Navy because he was referred to the Marshalsea for trial in London. The outcome of his trial is not known.

GRAVES

Captain William GRAVES. An English corsair captain in the Mediterranean in the early 17th century. GRAVES was one of John WARD's original crew. He based himself in Tunis, as many did, and was joint commander of a Turkish vessel. GRAVES was captured by a French Squadron in 1609 and taken to Marseilles, where he was probably executed.

GRAVES

William GRAVES. Taken from the prize vessel *King Solomon* off Cape Apollonia in Jan 1722 by Captain James SKYRM's vessel *Ranger*. Captured by *HMS Swallow* off the West African coast on 1 Feb 1722. Tried at Cape Corso Castle on 28 Mar 1722. He was found not guilty of piracy and acquitted.

GREAVES

Captain (Red Legs) GREAVES. b. Barbados. As an indentured servant (slave), he decided to run away from his master. He swam out to a ship in Carlisle Bay. The ship was under the command of Captain HAWKINS, a notoriously bloodthirsty pirate. GREAVES joined the crew and rose to prominence, though he hated HAWKINS for his cruelty. This eventually led to a duel between the two men and GREAVES won. The crew elected him Captain. A successful pirate leader, he captured the Island of Margarita, off Venezuela, taking a Spanish fleet and turning their guns against the forts ashore. He retired to Nevis but was recognised by a seaman and imprisoned. In the great earthquake of 1680, he was one of the island's few survivors and was picked up by a whaler. While serving on the whaler he helped to captured a gang of pirates and was granted a pardon. He retired again to Nevis. GREAVES was well known for his generous gifts to charities and public institutions.

GREEN

Captain Thomas GREEN. He was master of the trading vessel *Worcester*. The vessel was blown off course as it returned to England from the East Indies. It landed at Leith, Scotland, in Jul 1704. The local people asked the crew about a local vessel that was long overdue and had sailed 'out East'. None of the *Worcester* crew had any information, except an Indian who was wounded and the ship's surgeon, Charles MAY (who had not been aboard for the Eastern part of the voyage). These two seem not to have denied suggestions that the *Worcester* was a pirate vessel which had captured the Leith vessel. Captain GREEN and his men were brought to trial and despite there being no evidence against them, they were found guilty of piracy. After the trial (and death sentence) two crew members offered to give evidence in exchange for a pardon. The statements they made were ludicrous and obviously untrue. In the meantime, two crewmen from the missing vessel had returned on another vessel and a stay of execution was granted until they could be questioned. The local people of Leith would accept no delay in the execution and all the crew of the *Worcester* were hanged. Captain GREEN argued their innocence from the gallows. It became known years later that the missing vessel had been taken by the pirate Captain John BOWEN.

Note: The hanging of Thomas GREEN and his crew almost brought war between England

and Scotland. The Edinburgh 'Mob' had threatened to murder the Scottish Privy Council unless he was condemned. The Mob's intention was to undermine the Act of Union between the two kingdoms, which was eventually accomplished in 1707.

GREENHAM

James GREENHAM. b. Marshfield, Gloucester-shire. He joined Captain James SKYRM's pirate ship **Ranger** from the prize galley **Little York** in Jul 1720. Captured by **HMS Swallow** off the West African coast. He was tried at Cape Corso Castle on 28 Mar 1722. GREENHAM was found guilty and sentenced to hang. His sentence was commuted to 7 years' transportation to the African Colonies.

GREENSAIL

Richard GREENSAIL. A crewman to BLACKBEARD. Wounded and captured at Ocracoke Inlet on 1 Dec 1718. GREENSAIL was tried and hanged.

GRENVILLE

Henry GRENVILLE. A crewman to Captain William FLY. They were overpowered by the number of prisoners they had taken. The prisoners sailed them to Boston and handed them over to the authorities. GRENVILLE was tried and hanged at Boston on 12 Jul 1726.

GRIFFIN

Jack GRIFFIN. He was chief mate of a Bristol vessel. He was one of the mutineers on the galley **Bird** off Sierra Leone in 1715.

GRIFFIN

John GRIFFIN. b. Blockwall, Middlesex. A carpenter. GRIFFIN joined Captain Bartholomew ROBERTS' ship **Royal Fortune** from the prize galley **Mercy** in Oct 1721. They were captured off the West African coast by **HMS Swallow** on 10 Feb 1722. He was tried at Cape Corso Castle on 28 Mar 1722. Found guilty and hanged.

GRIFFIN

Richard GRIFFIN. A gunsmith from Boston. A crewman to Captain Thomas POUND. He was severely wounded in the fight at Tarpaulin Cove in 1689. A pistol-ball entered his ear and came out through his eye. There is no record of his having recovered.

GRILLO

Diego GRILLO. A mulatto pirate captain from Cuba. Along with THURSTON and others he continued to take Spanish shipping after the General Amnesty for Privateers in 1675. It was his custom to take his prizes to Tortuga to sell them. GRILLO, with his 15 gun vessel, fought and defeated 3 Spanish vessels in the Bahamas Channel in 1673. He was almost unique in his time because he was Cuban and Spanish-speaking in a period when pirates were normally Dutch, English or French.

GROGNIET

Captain ? GROGNIET. A French Filibuster. In 1683 he sailed in company with L'ESCAYER, with 200 French Filibusters and 80 English Buccaneers. He joined DAVIS and SWAN at Panama in 1685, and in the unsuccessful attempt on the Spanish fleet in May that year. GROGNIET left DAVIS at Quibo and plundered other towns. Returning to Quibo he met a Spanish squadron and lost his ship in the fight. Rescued by TOWNLEY, he went north with him and sacked Granada, Nicaragua. GROGNIET re-crossed the Isthmus of Darien on foot, but the next year he was back in the Pacific, where he was seriously wounded and died.

GUINEYS

William GUINEYS. Taken from the prize vessel *Porcupine* by Captain James SKYRM's pirate ship *Ranger* in Jan 1722. Captured by *HMS Swallow* on 1 Feb 1722. GUINEYS (maybe GUINNESS?) was tried at Cape Corso Castle on 28 Mar 1722. He was found not guilty of piracy and acquitted.

GUITTAR

Captain Lewis GUITTAR. He cruised as a pirate in the West Indies and captured *La Paix*, a well-found Dutch vessel. After taking two other vessels he sailed for Chesapeake, joining other pirates en route. He met *HMS Shoreham*, under the command of Colonel PASSENGER, in Chesapeake Bay and did battle with them for 10 hours. GUITTAR sent a man swimming to *HMS Shoreham* with an offer to surrender. PASSENGER accepted. GUITTAR was shipped in irons to London where he was tried, found guilty and sentenced to death. He was hanged at Execution Dock, Wapping, on 23 Nov 1700.

GULLIMILLIT

Breti GULLIMILLIT. A South American pirate. Captured with others by the sloop *HMS Tyne*. He was tried and hanged at Kingston, Jamaica in 1823.

GUN

Benjamin GUN (or GUNNE). A retired pirate who lived ashore at Rio Pungo in West Africa. Captain Bartholomew ROBERTS spent 6 weeks in 1721 at GUN's establishment, probably working on his two ships. GUN's name was used by the writer R.L. STEPHENSON in the famous pirate novel "Treasure Island'.

GUTTEREZ

Juan GUTTEREZ. Hanged at Kingston, Jamaica on 7 Feb 1723.

GUY

Captain ? GUY. An English Buccaneer. GUY commanded the frigate *James* with 14 guns and 90 men. He sailed the Caribbean and was based in Tortuga in 1663.

GUY

John GUY. One of the original crewmen to Captain Henry AVERY. GUY was the man who cut the cables of *Charles* when AVERY and his men took her away. GUY sailed with AVERY through all his Indian Ocean piracy, but probably didn't return to England with him. In March 1699 William DAMPIER and his crew on *Roebuck* met with GUY in Bahia, Brazil.

HAAK

Philip HAAK. Taken from the prize vessel *Flushingham* by Captain James SKYRM's ship *Ranger* in Jan 1722. Captured by *HMS Swallow* off the West African coast on 1 Feb 1722. Tried at Cape Corso Castle on 28 Mar 1722. HAAK was found not guilty of piracy and acquitted.

HAGGERSTON

Captain James HAGGERSTON. He was almost the last of the Algiers-based English corsair captains. By the year 1617 HAGGERSTON was back in London, having given up his Mediterranean piracy.

HAINES

? HAINES. A crewman to Captain Thomas GREEN on *Worcester*. He was tried and found guilty of piracy at Leith, Scotland in 1704/5. The verdict was very obviously wrong. In exchange for a pardon, HAINES invented tales of piracy about the rest of the 'Worcester's' crew. The rest of the crew were unjustly hanged.

HAINS

Robert HAINS. A crewman to Captain Edward LOW. When LOW took a Portugese prize at St Michael's, in the Azores, he burned their vessel, but let the crew go ashore in their boats. HAINS was drinking punch from his silver tankard by an open port when the idea occurred to him to drop into the boat, hide, and get ashore with them. He did so, then remembered his silver tankard. He climbed back aboard the ship, got his tankard and hid once again in the boat. He had obviously had enough of the pirate life.

HALL

Robert HALL. A crewman to Captain Charles SWAN on *Cygnet*. After their unhappy voyage across the Pacific and the break-up of the ship's company in the Phillipines, HALL (who kept a journal of his travels) with DAMPIER, COPPINGER and others, made their way to Achin. Both HALL and DAMPIER were quite ill. HALL recovered first and shipped with a Captain Weldon to Madras. From there he took passage to England on *Williamson*.

HALSEY

Captain John HALSEY (of Boston). Commander of the brig *Charles*, commissioned by the Governor of New England to capture French and Spanish vessels. He did just that, off Newfoundland, the Canaries and Cape Verde Islands. HALSEY sailed on to Madagascar and into the Red Sea. He then decided to take Moorish vessels as well. His crew decided they should take a Dutch vessel but HALSEY stopped them, probably because the Dutch were fellow-protestants. The crew restrained HALSEY below decks and attacked the Dutchman. They got badly mauled, sailed off and released HALSEY. He cruised the Indian Ocean and the Malacca Straits, then returned to Madagascar, where he died at the age of 46. He was given a huge pirate funeral.

HAMAN (probably HAYMAN)

Captain John HAMAN. He is really only famous because Calico Jack RACKHAM and Anne BONNY stole his 40 ton sloop to continue their piracy. HAMAN lived with his wife and family on an otherwise deserted island in the Bahamas. He seems to have made a living by taking smaller boats of other nationalities, his main tactic being a smart get-away. The saying in the Bahamas was, "There goes Jack HAMAN, catch him if you can." He retired to Providence after RACKHAM took his sloop.

HAMLIN

Captain Jean HAMLIN. A French Filibuster turned pirate. He sailed from Jamaica in 1682 to take a 'wanted' ship. He took it, re-named it *La Trompeuse* and used it for his piracy. He became the scourge of the Jamaican coasts to such an extent that trade with the island was badly affected. Two British ships were sent to find him but he had a secure base on the Danish Island of St Thomas. He slipped away to West Africa in 1683 and disguised as a British man-of-war he took 17 Dutch and English ships. HAMLIN returned to St Thomas in Jul that year and 3 days later *HMS Francis* caught him there and sank *La Trompeuse*. HAMLIN escaped.

HAMMOND

John HAMMOND. He joined the crew of the pirate Captain ? KENNEDY from the captured slaver *Greyhound* of London on 16 Oct 1716.

HANDS

Captain Israel HANDS. A crewman to BLACKBEARD. He took command of *Adventure* in BLACKBEARD's fleet at the siege of Charleston. HANDS was later given command of his own vessel. During a game of cards with BLACKBEARD, HANDS fell asleep. BLACKBEARD decided to wake him up by firing a pistol under the table. HANDS kneecap was blown away. BLACKBEARD had HANDS put ashore in Bath Town as a crippled, but wealthy pirate. He got through his fortune in record time and returned to London. For many years he was a well-known beggar on the streets of Wapping, where Execution Dock stood in the High Street. He probably saw many old colleagues meet their doom.

HANSEL

Captain ? HANSEL. One of Sir Henry MORGAN's buccaneer captains. He took part in the raid on Porto Bello in 1669. HANSEL later led a raid on Comana, near Caracas, with 400 men, the raid was a complete failure.

HANSON

John HANSON, A crewman to Captain Calico Jack RACKHAM. He only joined RACKHAM's vessel at Negril Point, Jamaica, on the day of its capture. He was tried at St Jago de la Vega on 16 Nov 1720. The case was adjourned until Feb 1721 because there seemed little evidence against him and he had served RACKHAM for less than a day. Nevertheless he was found guilty and sentenced to death. I think he was hanged, but can find no written evidence.

HARADEN

Captain Andrew HARADEN. A reluctant crewman to Captain John PHILLIPS. HARADEN commanded the fishing sloop *Squirrel* which was taken by PHILLIPS off the Isles of Shoals on 14 Apr 1724. HARADEN was one of the captives who overpowered PHILLIPS and his pirates. He had some trouble convincing the authorities in Boston of his innocence, but eventually gave evidence against the pirates at their trial.

HARDING

Daniel HARDING. b. Croomsbury, Somerset, 1695/6. Joined Captain Bartholomew ROBERTS' ship *Royal Fortune* from a Dutch prize vessel in Apr 1721. He was captured off the West African coast by *HMS Swallow* on 10 Feb 1722. HARDING was tried at Cape Corso Castle on 28 Mar 1722. He was found guilty of piracy and hanged.

HARDING

Captain Thomas HARDING. In 1653 HARDING took a rich Barbados vessel. He was later tried at Boston.

HARDY

Richard HARDY. b. Wales, 1697. Was Quartermaster of Captain James SKYRM's *Ranger*. HARDY had previously been a crewman to Captain Howard DAVIS. Captured by *HMS Swallow* off the West African coast on 1 Feb 1722. Evidence against him was that he had been 'very busy' when the sloop *Dilligence* was taken and had been 'the very man that scuttled her'. He was found guilty of piracy and sentenced to death. When it was time for him to hang he questioned that they tied his hands behind him. He said he had seen many men hanged, but not with their hands tied.

HARIOT

David HARIOT. Sailing Master of Major Stede BONNET's vessel. BONNET was no sailor himself, having no sea-going background. HARIOT was captured with BONNET at Cape Fear River on 27 Sep 1718. He offered evidence against the rest of the crew in exchange for leniency but escaped from custody with BONNET. HARIOT was shot and killed when BONNET was recaptured on 5 Nov 1718.

HARPER

Abraham HARPER. b. Bristol, 1698/9. A cooper to Captain Bartholomew ROBERTS' ship *Royal Fortune*. Captured by *HMS Swallow* off the West African coast on 10 Feb 1722. He was tried at Cape Corso Castle on 28 Mar 1722. HARPER was found guilty and hanged.

HARTLEY

Robert HARTLEY. b. Liverpool. He joined Captain James SKYRM's vessel *Ranger* from the prize galley *Sandwich* in Aug 1721. Captured by *HMS Swallow* on 1 Feb 1722 off the West African coast. He was tried at Cape Corso Castle on 28 Mar 1722 and found guilty. HARTLEY was sentenced to death but the sentence was commuted to 7 years' transportation to the African Colonies.

Note: I find it odd that two Robert HARTLEYs, both probably from Liverpool were captured on the same pirate vessel. Not impossible, I suppose, but I suspect an error on the part of the recording clerk at the capture or trial.

HARTLEY

Robert HARTLEY. This Robert HARTLEY was taken aboard Captain James SKYRM's *Ranger* from the prize vessel *Robinson* of Liverpool. Captured by *HMS Swallow* off the West African coast on 1 Feb 1722. He was tried at Cape Corso Castle on 28 Mar 1722. He was found not guilty and acquitted.

HARRIS

Captain James HARRIS. A merchant ship's master, captured and sold into slavery by the Barbary Corsairs. He was bought and freed by Captain Richard BISHOP for 2,500 crowns. He commanded his own pirate vessel in the early years of the 17th century. Early in 1609 he based himself in Baltimore, Ireland. Later in 1609 he was in the Marshalsea Prison with Captain John JENNINGS before JENNINGS was hanged.

HARRIS

Captain ? HARRIS. He led 16 other pirates aboard the hoy *Eagle* of Sandwich, Kent. They had stolen the vessel at Leigh-on-Sea (Thames estuary) in May 1616. A week later they took the Zealand pink *Black Dog*. No further information.

HARRIS

Captain Charles HARRIS. Began his piracy as a crewman to Captain Edward LOW. LOW gave him command of a prize vessel. The two ships lost contact during a hurricane but met up again in the Azores. HARRIS and LOW sailed together again until LOW was cast adrift.

HARRIS

Captain Charles HARRIS. This HARRIS was 2nd Mate on the prize sloop *Greyhound* which was captured by Captain George LOWTHER. LOWTHER gave him command of the sloop and HARRIS sailed in LOWTHER's pirate fleet. He was captured by *HMS Greyhound* and tried at Newport R.I. in Jul 1723. HARRIS was found guilty and hanged on 19 Jul 1723.

HARRIS

Hugh HARRIS. b. Corfe Castle, Dorset. He joined Captain James SKYRM's vessel *Ranger*

from the prize *Willing Mind* in Jul 1720. Captured by *HMS Swallow* off the West African coast on 1 Feb 1722. HARRIS was tried at Cape Corso Castle on 28 Mar 1722 and found guilty. He was sentenced to death but the sentence was commuted to 7 years' transportation to the African Colonies.

HARRIS

James HARRIS. He joined Captain Bartholomew ROBERTS' ship *Royal Fortune* from the prize pink *Richard*. Captured by *HMS Swallow* off the West African coast on 10 Feb 1722. He was probably a deserter from the Royal Navy because he was referred to the Marshalea Prison for trial in London. The outcome of his trial is not known.

HARRIS

Captain Peter HARRIS. b. Kent. He commanded a large pirate fleet that crossed the Isthmus of Darien and sacked the Spanish town of Santa Maria. HARRIS was with Sir Henry MORGAN at Panama. Later he took Dutch shipping off Jamaica. In 1679 he was chased off Southern Cuba by the frigate HMS Success. Sailing a sloop, of shallower draught than the frigate, he led her onto the reefs and made his escape. In 1680 he took his ship of 150 tons, 25 guns and 107 men on Captain Bartholomew SHARPE's expedition to plunder the Pacific coasts of America. He was shot through both legs boarding a Spanish ship in the Gulf of Ballona on 23 Apr 1680. He died of his wounds two days later. "A brave man, much lamented." Said RINGROSE.

HARRIS

Captain Peter HARRIS. The nephew of the Peter HARRIS above. Captain HARRIS sailed to the Pacific in company with Captain SWAN and *Cygnet* in 1684. They met with COOKE's *Bachelor' Delight* and were later joined by filibusters and buccaneers under GROGNIET and L'ESCUYER who had crossed the Isthmus of Darien on foot. Now strong enough in number, they plundered along the Pacific coasts for over a year.

HARRIS

Richard HARRIS. b. Sadbury, Devon, 1677. He joined Captain James SKYRM's *Ranger* from the prize vessel *Phoenix* of Bristol in Jun 1720. Captured by *HMS Swallow* off the West African coast on 1 Feb 1722. He was tried at Cape Corso Castle on 28 Mar 1722. Found guilty and hanged.

HARRISON

Captain ? HARRISON. He arrived in Port Royal, Jamaica, with the buccaneer Captains

PRINCE and LEDBURY, after a raid on the Spanish Main. Governor MORDIFORD was angry that they had acted without a commission from him. He sent them to join Sir Henry MORGAN who was assembling a fleet at Isle la Vache.

HARVEY

Captain Phillip HARVEY. An English pirate captain in the early 17th century. He took command of Captain Tibalt SAXBRIDGE's crew after SAXBRIDGE was killed in about 1608. HARVEY sailed the damaged vessel to Brittany where they took another vessel and sailed to the Cape Verde Islands. They failed to take any further vessels and eventually sailed to Ireland, where they surrendered.

HARVEY

Captain ? HARVEY. A pirate captain. He arrived at New London in 1685, in company with another pirate, Captain VEALE. They claimed to be honest merchantmen, but they were recognised as pirates and fled the port in great haste.

HARVEY

William HARVEY. A crewman to Captain John SMITH. He was captured with SMITH in the Orkney Islands. HARVEY was taken to London and tried for piracy, but acquitted.

HARWOOD

A crewman to Captain John QUELCH on his pirate brig *Charles*. He was tried at Boston in June 1704.

HARWOOD

Noah HARWOOD. A crewman to Captain Calico Jack RACK-HAM. Captured with RACK-HAM off Jamaica on 1 Nov 1720. HARWOOD was tried at St Jago de la Vega, Jamaica. He was found guilty and hanged at Kingston on 18 Nov 1720.

HATSELL

Captain ? HATSELL. A Buccaneer Captain. He served under MANSFIELD in his daring capture of the island of Old Providence. When the island was taken and the Spanish Governor captured, HATSELL and 35 of his men were left behind to hold it.

HAWKINS

Captain ? HAWKINS. A most unpleasant pirate captain. He was renowned for his cruelty. He was eventually challenged to a duel by one of his crewmen, Red Legs GREAVES. GREAVES beat him in the duel and was elected Captain in HAWKINS place.

HAWKINS (or HAWKYNS)

Sir John HAWKINS. 1532-1595. b. Plymouth, Devon. In his youth HAWKINS made several trips to the Canaries, where he found that 'negroes were very good merchandise in Hispaniola, and that they might easily be had upon the coasts of Guinea'.

He sailed with 3 ships to West Africa in 1562, took plunder and slaves from the Portugese and traded them at Hispaniola. He loaded two of the ships with hides, while the third he loaded with more valuable cargo and sailed back to England. The ships with hides were despatched to Spain to sell their cargoes, but both ships and cargoes were seized by the Spanish as illegal traders within their colonies. HAWKINS claimed, but failed to get, compensation from Spain and six months later he raised a larger force to trade in the Caribbean.

In Oct 1564 he sailed from Plymouth with the 700 ton *Jesus* (lent by Queen Elizabeth I) and 2 smaller ships. They raided ashore in West Africa to make up a cargo of slaves, took on water at Dominica on 9 Mar 1565. They met with resistance to trade at Burburata and Rio de la Hacha, where they had to put on a display of force to dispose of their cargo. On the return journey HAWKINS put into the St Johns River for water and found a French colony in poor condition. He left them supplies and a boat, then fished on the Newfoundland Banks for enough food for their return to England. He arrived at Padstow in Sep 1565.

HAWKINS intended to sail again the next year, but the protests of the Spanish Ambassador in London had led to a ban on HAWKINS activities for a while. He sailed again in Oct 1567. The Queen again lent him the *Jesus*, but insisted that he was not sailing as a Queen's officer. Again he plundered along the Portugese settlements of West Africa until he had wares and slaves to the value of 70.000 gold pieces. He sailed to Dominica and sold 200 slaves, then traded the remaining slaves and wares along the coast of the Spanish Main, arriving at Vera Cruz on 16 Sep with 57 slaves left.

A Spanish fleet arrived at the harbour and after some days of argument and failed negotiation a battle broke out. HAWKINS lost most of his vessels but escaped on *Minion*, one of the smallest, while DRAKE escaped on *Judith*. The vessels were separated, but both got back to England in the same week in Jan 1569.

HAWKINS attempted to get compensation from Spain, even entering into an intrigue with Mary Queen of Scots and the Spanish Ambassador, eventually obtaining £40,000. He was appointed Member of Parliament for Plymouth, Treasurer and comptroller of the Navy. Over a period he improved navy vessels

by lengthening the hulls and reducing the height of the castles. He may also have made money by 'cooking the books' on timber and cordage supply.

HAWKINS, as a rear-admiral, commanded the inshore squadron against the Spanish Armada in 1588 and was engaged against them off the Isle of Wight and elsewhere.

In 1592 he was involved in building the Sir John Hawkyns Hospital at Chatham, Kent.

In 1595 he sailed again to plunder the Caribbean, but the Spanish had plenty of warning of this voyage by DRAKE and HAWKINS and were prepared. HAWKINS died as they reached Porto Rico on 12 Nov 1595. He had been ill for some weeks and finally died of exhaustion.

HAWKINS, like DRAKE, was one of those characters who became a national hero, did good works in England and improved the country's navy and treasury. In West Africa and the Caribbean, however, HAWKINS plundered, tortured, murdered and burnt.

HAWKINS

William HAWKINS. b. Devon. d. 1595? A nephew of Sir John HAWKINS. He sailed with Sir Francis DRAKE in Dec 1577 on *Golden Hind* on DRAKES' plundering of the Pacific and circumnavigation. Later HAWKINS made a voyage to India and the East during which he had many

116

adventures and married an Armenian lady. He died on the return journey.

HAWKINS

Thomas HAWKINS. Fisherman and boat-owner of Boston. Captain Thomas POUND hired his boat and then turned pirate. HAWKINS went along and gradually became a pirate himself. He left POUND when he went ashore at the James River but was arrested, tried and found guilty of piracy. When POUND was arrested, a petition was raised among the local important people. The result was that HAWKINS sentence was remitted and POUND's was delayed. HAWKINS' vessel *Rose* was given back to POUND and HAWKINS set off with him for England. On the way they encountered a French privateer who engaged them in battle. HAWKINS was killed in the fight.

HAWS

Robert HAWS. b. Yarmouth, Isle of Wight, 1690/1. He joined Captain Bartholomew ROBERTS' ship *Royal Fortune* from the prize vessel *Joceline* in Oct 1721. Captured off the West African coast by *HMS Swallow* on 10 Feb 1722. HAWS was tried at Cape Corso Castle on 28 Mar1722. He was found guilty and hanged.

HAYES

Captain Bully HAYES. A South Seas Pirate Captain. HAYES was arrested in 1870 by the British Consul in Samoa. There was no prison on the island, so the Consul had HAYES ship run aground while they waited for a man-of-war to appear. HAYES enjoyed his time in a round of parties and entertainments where he demonstrated himself a great 'ladies man'. Another pirate, Captain PEASE arrived, the two pirates appeared to violently disagree. This was obviously all a sham, because HAYES sailed away with PEASE one dark night.

HAYS

Robert HAYS. b. Liverpool, 1691/2. HAYS joined Captain Bartholomew ROBERTS' ship *Royal Fortune* in Jan 1722 from the prize vessel *Tarlton*. Captured by *HMS Swallow* off the West African coast on 10 Feb 1722. He was tried at Cape Corso Castle on 28 Mar 1722. HAYS was found guilty and hanged.

HAZELL

Thomas HAZELL. b. 1672/3. A crewman on Captain Charles HARRIS *Ranger*. Captured by *HMS Greyhound*. HAZELL was tried at Newport R.I. He was found guilty of piracy and hanged on 19 Jul 1723.

HEAMAN

Peter HEAMAN. A French pirate. He sailed from Gibraltar in May 1821 as Mate on the schooner *Jane*. She carried a rich cargo for Brazil, including 8 barrels of Spanish dollars. 17 days out, HEAMAN killed the Captain and Helmsman in the night. The cook, Francis GAU-TIER joined him and they shut the crew in the forecastle and tried to suffocate them with smoke. This didn't work, so they swore them to secrecy and sailed for Scotland. In June they landed on the Hebridean island of Barra. GAUTIER went ashore and bought a large boat. They sailed to the island of Storn-away and sank the schooner, but the boat was wrecked on the rocks. The Maltese cabin-boy informed the Customs of their crimes and the Islanders arrested them. They were taken to Edinburgh and tried for piracy and murder. HEAMAN and GAUTIER were hanged at the low-water mark at Leith and their bodies were donated to Dr Alexander MUNRO at Edinburgh University, for his dissection class.

HEATH

Peleg HEATH. A crewman to Captain William COWARD. Tried and sentenced to death in Boston in 1690. He was later reprieved.

HEIDON

Captain ? HEIDON. He was arrested in 1654 for having taken a Flemish vessel. HEIDON manned the vessel with 13 Scotsmen and his own crew, they next took a vessel laden with wine. They took the wine to the island of Bere in Bantry Bay, Ireland, where he fitted out another vessel *John of Sandwich*. HEIDON was shipwrecked on Alderney in the Channel Isles, and arrested there, but he and some of his crew escaped in a small boat.

HENDRICKSZ

Captain Boudewijn HEN-DRICKSZ. A Dutch privateer in the Caribbean. In September 1625 HENDRICKSZ led a fleet consisting of 14 ships, landing over 700 men at San Juan, Puerto Rico. He besieged the Citadel, but was beaten off by the garrison.

HENLEY

Captain ? HENLEY. He sailed from Boston in 1683 to the Red Sea. There he took Arabian and Malabar vessels.

HERAULT

Samuel HERAULT. A Frenchman. Crewman to Captain George BOOTH on his pirate ship in the Indian Ocean. When BOOTH was killed on Zanzibar,

John BOWEN was voted Captain and HERAULT (for his bravery in the action) was voted Quartermaster. He held the same position when BOWEN sailed in company with Captain Thomas HOWARD.

HERDUE

Captain ? HERDUE. A French Filibuster. He commanded a frigate of 4 guns and 40 men. HERDUE was based at Tortuga in 1663.

HERNANDEZ

Augustus HERNANDEZ. In 1823 HERNANDEZ was hanged for piracy at Kingston, Jamaica.

(These two characters may well be one and the same, but reported from different sources.)

HERNANDEZ

Juan HERNANDEZ. He was captured with 9 other pirates by the sloop *HMS Tyne*. He was taken to Jamaica where they were all tried and sentenced. HERNANDEZ was hanged at Kingston on 7 Feb 1823.

HERRIOT see HARIOT

HEWET

William HEWET, of Jamaica. A crewman to Major Stede BONNET. He was captured with BONNET on 27 Sep 1718 at Cape Fear River. HEWET was tried at Charleston, Carolina, and hanged on 8 Nov 1718. Note: This may have been the Captain HEWET under whom William DAMPIER sailed in about 1676. If so, he would have been about 70 years old when he was hanged. Possible, I suppose.

HEWETSON

Captain Thomas HEWETSON. The commander of a small fleet which left England in 1688 to join the Caribbean buccaneers and make their fortunes. One of the ships blew up at anchor in Barbados in July 1689. The remaining adventurers lost heart and were set to go home but news reached them of war with France. The prospect of French plunder led them on, along with a privateers licence from Governor ROBINSON of Barbados. With 3 vessels, one commanded by Captain William KIDD, HEWETSON Landed at Marie Galante and spent 5 days in December 1689 sacking the island. They took their plunder to Nevis, then rushed to rescue Sir Thomas THORNHILL, who was outnumbered in attacking the French island of Saint Martin. HEWETSON's force engaged DUCASSE at sea and drove off the French reinforcements. Many of HEWETSON's crew resented being used as regular naval forces, when they were there to rob and plunder. Some of them deserted, taking Captain KIDD's ship and his share of the treasure. HEWETSON chartered his ship to the Spanish, who were now allies of England, and became a commercial skipper.

HEYN

Captain Pieter Pieterzoon HEYN. Famous in the Caribbean as Piet HEYN, at the age of 51 he captured an entire Spanish Treasure convoy off Matanzas, Cuba in September 1628. His fleet consisted of 31 ships, bearing 679 cannon, manned by 2300 sailors and over 1000 soldiers. The profits from their privateering expedition were worth over 7,000,000 guilders on their return to Holland. HEYN's success had a serious impact on the economies of both Spain and her colonies, it resulted in the Spanish Caribbean becoming even more dependent upon trade with Northern European adventurers.

HEYNES

Captain Stephen HEYNES. A Dorset-based pirate captain in the reign of Queen Elizabeth I. HEYNES was an exotic figure who, like the other Dorset-based pirates, thought he was immune to arrest because of his local business connections. He was arrested once at Corfe Castle, but gave the officer £20 and a parrot for his release. Parrots figure largely in the folklore about HEYNES, he gave them to several Dorset people in return for 'favours' and several respectable ladies would hide their parrot when the vicar came to tea. In 1582 HEYNES was washed overboard from his ship in a storm and drowned.

HICKS

Captain ? HICKS. b. Saltash, Devon. One of the most notorious Dorset-based pirates in the late 16th century. He was eventually captured in the English Channel in 1577. He was tried, found guilty of piracy, and hanged at Execution Dock, Wapping.

HIDE

Daniel HIDE. b. Virginia, 1699/1700. A crewman on Captain Charles HARRIS *Ranger*. Captured by *HMS Greyhound*. Tried at Newport R.I. HIDE was found guilty and hanged on 19 Jul 1723.

HIGGENBERT

Captain Courte HIGGENBERT. A Dorset-based pirate captain in the reign of Queen Elizabeth I. He took French and Dutch vessels in the English Channel, disposing of his cargoes and prizes to the Vice-Admiral of Dorset and other officers of the Crown. HIGGENBERT's ship went aground at Lulworth, Dorset in 1576/7, and its cargo was unloaded for all to see. This led to a Commission of

Enquiry to investigate the connection between pirates and the local gentry. HIGGENBERT and his crew seem to have left the area then, probably to base themselves in Wales or Ireland where discipline was more lax.

HIGGINS

Jeremiah HIGGINS. b. Jamaica. HIGGINS was a Bosun or a Bosun's Mate to Captain Samuel BELLAMY on *Whydah*. HIGGINS is believed to have drowned on the night, in 1717, when *Whydah* was wrecked on Cape Cod.

HILL

Henry HILL. A crewman to Captain William FLY on *Elizabeth*. I have found no record of his being hanged with FLY at Boston in Jul 1726, but I suspect he was.

HILL

Corporal John HILL. The commander of the guard at Fort Loyal, Falmouth, Maine. They all deserted their posts and joined the pirate Captain Thomas POUND. HILL was killed in the fight at Tarpaulin Cove in 1689.

HILLIARD

John HILLIARD. An English Buccaneer. HILLIARD was 'Chief Mate' to Captain Bartholomew SHARPE on his expedition to plunder the Pacific coasts of the Americas. Hilliard died of dropsy on 1 Jan 1681, he was buried ashore on the island of Juan Fernandez with three volleys of small arms fired as a salute.

HILLS

Captain ? HILLS. b. Plymouth, Devon. A pirate captain in the early 17th century. In 1611 HILLS was engaged in battle by 3 Spanish men-of-war. Rather then surrender, HILLS set fire to his ship. He died, and only 12 badly-burned survivors remained of a crew of 45 men.

HILTON

Anthony HILTON. The self-styled 'Governor' of the buccaneer community on the island of Tortuga. On 21 Jan 1634 a Spanish expedition under the command of Captain Francisco Turrillo de YELVA and John MURPHY captured the island. HILTON and 194 other buccaneers were killed by the Spanish, other residents were allowed to flee.

HINCHER

Doctor John HINCHER. b. Nr Edinburgh, 1701/2. He was aboard Captain Charles HARRIS *Ranger* when it was captured by *HMS Greyhound*. He was tried at Newport R.I. in Jul 1723. He was found not guilty and acquitted.

HIND see HYNDE

HINGSON

John HINGSON. One of the buccaneers who went with SHARPE's expedition to the Pacific in 1681. HINGSON left the expedition with COOKE's party, who re-crossed the Isthmus of Darien on foot. With Lionel WAFER and Richard GOPSON, HINGSON fell behind the main party and lived for a while with the local Indians. The Indians looked after them well once WAFER (a surgeon) had cured the chief's wife. They eventually got to the Caribbean coast. In Aug 1683 HINGSON sailed under Captain John COOK from Carolina to the Pacific, by way of West Africa and Cape Horn. After COOK's death at Galapagos, HINGSON remained on *Bachelors' Delight* under Captain Edmund DAVIS. They returned to the Caribbean the following year.

HIPPS

John HIPPS. Bosun of the sloop *Lancaster*. HIPPS surrendered to Woodes ROGERS offer of a pardon for pirates at Nassau in 1718. Later that year he returned to piracy under the command of Captain John AUGER. They were captured at Green Cay on 6 Oct 1718. All the rest of the crew were hanged but HIPPS convinced the court that he had been forced to join them.

HITCHENS

Robert HITCHENS. b. Devon, 1515. He sailed with Captain HEIDON and was wrecked on Alderney in the Channel Isles in 1564. HITCHENS was tried for piracy and hanged in chains at the low-water mark at St Martin's Point, Guernsey.

HOGG

Captain ? HOGG. In Mar 1667 King Charles II found he could no longer pay to keep his navy at sea. They were laid up for the year, despite war with the Dutch. Samuel PEPYS (diarist and Secretary to the Navy Board) Admiral Sir William PENN (member of the Board and father of William PENN the Quaker) and Admiral Sir William BATTEN (also of the Navy Board) together borrowed a warship, *Flying Greyhound*, from the King. They fitted her out and crewed her as a privateer. The idea was to take Dutch prizes, thus aiding the King and making capital for themselves. HOGG sailed in the summer and brought home several prizes, most of them allied shipping. A court case ensued about two Swedish vessels. PEPYS saw it was all going to end in tears, so he sold his share of the venture to PENN. I find no record of HOGG's further adventures but they will certainly have been interesting.

HOLDING

Anthony HOLDING. He was 1st Mate to Captain John QUELCH on *Charles*. HOLDING had been Quartermaster to the previous (legal) captain. He conspired with QUELCH to nail up Captain PLOWMAN in his cabin until the vessel sailed, and then throw him overboard. HOLDING was very much QUELCH's right-hand man in their short but profitable voyage. He left QUELCH at Marblehead on their return voyage to Boston. He retired quietly, with great wealth, and was never heard of again.

HOLLAND

Captain Richard HOLLAND. A crewman on *HMS Suffolk* in the Mediterranean. He deserted from the vessel at Naples by hiding in a convent. Later he served in the Spanish Mediterranean fleet under Admiral CAMMOCK. HOLLAND settled in the Spanish West Indies. He was joint commander of *Guarda del Costa* with Don BENITO (Edward BENNETT?) with a crew of 60 Spanish, 18 French and 18 English. They took several vessels bound for Virginia.

HOPKINS

Mr ? HOPKINS. A Buccaneer and Apothecary. He was first lieutenant to Captain (Doctor) DOVER on the privateer *Dutchess*

of Bristol. An apothecary by profession and no sailor, but it seems his kinship with DOVER had brought him his high rank. They sailed from Bristol on 2 Aug 1708, and returning to England very rich in 1711, after encircling the world.

HOOF

Peter Cornelius HOOF. Of Sweden. A crewman to Captain Samuel BELLAMY. HOOF was captured on Cape Cod on the day after BELLAMY's ship *Whydah* was wrecked there. He was tried at Boston, found guilty and sentenced to death. HOOF was hanged at Boston on 15 Nov 1717.

HOORN

John HOORN. b. St James Parish, London. He joined Captain James SKYRM's *Ranger* from the prize vessel *Onslow* in Jan 1722. Captured off the West African coast on 1 Feb 1722 by *HMS Swallow* HOORN was tried at Cape Corso Castle on 28 Mar 1722. He was found guilty and sentenced to death. The sentence was later commuted to 7 years' transportation to the African Colonies.

HORE

Captain ? HORE. In about 1650 he turned from privateering to piracy. He was very successful in taking vessels between New

York and Newport R.I. From time to time he sailed to Madagascar to take East Indiamen.

HORNIGOLD

Captain Benjamin HORNIGOLD. He was probably most famous as the pirate who taught BLACKBEARD his trade. HORNIGOLD surrendered to the Governor of North Carolina in 1718. Some time later he was amongst a group of castaways on a desert island. He died there but 5 of his crew built a canoe and escaped.

HOUGHLING

John HOUGHLING. A Dutchman. A crewman on Captain Lewis GUITTAR's *La Paix* when it was captured by *HMS Shoreham*. He had a 'tickett' written by Captain Cornelius ISAAC, the legal captain of the vessel. The 'tickett' said, "John Houghling is forced against his will to stay and remain upon the ship *La Paix* under the command of Lewis Guittar and have set our hands to witness it to ye and no body should trouble him or pretend he was there by his own consent. Witness our hands. – Cornelius Isaac."

HOW

James HOW. Crewman to Captain William KIDD on *Adventure*. He surrendered to pardon at New York with KIDD. They found that the pardon did not extend to KIDD's crew. HOW was shipped with KIDD to London and tried at the Old Bailey in May 1701. He was found guilty of piracy and hanged at Execution Dock.

HOW

Thomas HOW. He joined *Ranger* at Newfoundland as a volunteer. HOW was a crewman to Captain James SKYRM when captured by *HMS Swallow* off the West African coast on 1 Feb 1722. He was tried at Cape Corso Castle on 28 Mar 1722. Found guilty and sentenced to hang. No record found of his hanging, he may have died of his wounds or disease while in custody beforehand, some did.

HOWARD

John HOWARD. A crewman to Captain Calico Jack RACKHAM. HOWARD joined RACKHAM at Negril Point, Jamaica, on the day of his capture. He was tried at St Jago de la Vega on 16 Nov 1720. The case against him was adjourned until 24 Jan 1721 for lack of evidence. No further evidence was produced but HOWARD was still found guilty. He was hanged at Kingston on 18 Feb 1721.

HOWARD

Captain Thomas HOWARD. b. London. HOWARD was a

Thames lighterman (bargee). On his father's death he squandered the small inheritance that came to him and went to sea. He left the ship at Jamaica, took a canoe and went turtling with a small crew. They began their piracy by robbing other turtlers. Then they took an Irish brig. HOWARD exchanged the small brig for a sloop, then the sloop for a large, New England brig. He and his crew took several vessels off the Virginia coast. They sailed for Africa and took several vessels on the way. HOWARD based himself in Madagascar, as many pirates did. While he was hunting ashore his crew sailed away, but HOWARD travelled overland and later joined them with the assistance of a local king. He was shot through the arm by ORT VAN TYLE, a Dutchman living in Madagascar. HOWARD formed an alliance with Captain John BOWEN and they hunted Moorish vessels in company with each other. He eventually settled on the coast of India and married a local woman. "Being a morose, ill-natured fellow, he used her ill, and was murdered by her relatives".

HOWARD

Thomas HOWARD. Taken from the prize vessel *Tarlton* in Jan 1722 by Captain James SKYRM's vessel *Ranger*. Captured off the West African coast by *HMS Swallow* on 1 Feb 1722. HOWARD was tried at Cape

Corso Castle on 28 Mar 1722. He was found not guilty of piracy and acquitted.

HOWELL

John HOWELL. A crewman to Captain Calico Jack RACKHAM. Captured with RACKHAM on 1 Nov 1720. He was tried at St Jago de la Vega, Jamaica. HOWELL was found guilty and hanged at Gallows Point, Port Royal on 17 Nov 1720.

HUGGIT

Thomas HUGGIT. b. London, 1693/4. A crewman to Captain Charles HARRIS on *Ranger*. Captured by *HMS Greyhound*. Tried at Newport R.I. Found guilty and hanged at Newport on 19 Jul 1723.

HULL

Captain Edward HULL. He commanded the frigate *Swallow* in which he sailed from Boston in 1653. HULL took several French and Dutch vessels. He appears to have retired and settled in England with his share of the plunder.

HUGHS

Captain William HUGHS. An English pirate captain in the early 17th century. HUGHS commanded a flyboat of 250 tons with 28 cannon and 6 fowling pieces. In 1611 the *William and Ralph*, a merchantman, surrendered to HUGHS rather than fight.

HULL

Captain William HULL. b. Devon. HULL was the son of the Mayor of Exeter, Devon. He went to sea as the Captain of a Topsham ship and plundered French shipping in the Mediterranean. This was in 1602, which makes him one of the first English pirates of that period. He was given (or sold) a pardon by Sir Richard HAWKINS, the Vice-admiral of Devon, and son of the great Elizabethan sea-rover. I think that this man was the Sir William HULL who was later the Vice-admiral of Munster, Ireland, and got in trouble for not prosecuting the local pirates.

HUNKINS

Henry HUNKINS. He joined Captain James SKYRM's ship *Ranger* from the prize sloop *Success*. Captured by *HMS Swallow* off the West African coast on 1 Feb 1722. He was probably a Royal Navy deserter because he was referred to the Marshalsea Prison for trial in London. The outcome of the trial is not known.

HUNTER

Andrew HUNTER. A crewman to Captain George LOWTHER on *Ranger*. Captured by the sloop *HMS Eagle* at Blanquilla in Oct

1723. HUNTER was tried at St Christopher (St Kitts) on 11 Mar 1724. He was found guilty and hanged.

HUNTER

Henry HUNTER. Like Andrew above, Henry was taken by Captain George LOWTHER from the prize vessel *Swift*. It is most likely that they were of the same family. HUNTER's fate is not known, but he may have been killed at Blanquilla.

HUSK

John HUSK. A crewman to BLACKBEARD. HUSK died with BLACKBEARD in the battle at Ocracoke Inlet on 1 Dec 1718.

HUSSEY

Captain Thomas HUSSEY. An English pirate captain in the early 17th century. HUSSEY commanded *Black Raven*, a ship of 200 tons, 28 guns and 50 men. He bought a share of the vessel from Captain Parker in 1610. HUSSEY was killed by Dutch pirates at Marmora, Morocco, in 1611, when Captains PARKER and PLUMLEY were also killed. He left all his goods to Captain William HUGHS.

HUTNOT

Joseph HUTNOT. A crewman to Captain Thomas QUELCH on

his brig *Charles*. He was tried at the Star Tavern in Boston in June 1704.

HUTT (or HOUT)

Captain George HUTT. An English buccaneer who was given command after Captain ? TOWNLEY was killed in a battle with 3 Spanish galleons near Panama in 1686.

HYDE

Captain Adam HYDE. An English pirate who was hanged at Execution Dock, Wapping, for piracy on Wed 28 Mar 1759.

HYNDE

Israel HYNDE. b. Aberdeen, 1692. HYNDE joined Captain James SKYRM's vessel *Ranger* from the prize galley *Mercy* of Bristol in Oct 1721 at Calabar. Captured by *HMS Swallow* off the West Coast of Africa on 1 Feb 1722, HYNDE lost an arm in the battle. He was tried at Cape Corso Castle on 28 Mar 1722. He was found guilty of piracy and hanged.

INGRAM

Gunner William INGRAM. Chief gunner to Captain Thomas ANSTIS in *Good Fortune* when he took and converted the *Morning Star* to his own use. When INGRAM was tried for piracy it was proved that he had joined the pirates of his own free will and was a very resolute, hardened fellow. He was hanged at Execution Dock along with Captain GOW and Captain Brigstock WEAVER, both of whom had begun their piracy under ANSTIS, but graduated to commands of their own.

IRELAND

John IRELAND. "A wicked and ill-disposed person", said the Royal Warrant of King William III, which he granted to "Our truly and dearly beloved Captain William KIDD" in 1695. KIDD's instructions were to go and seize IRELAND and other pirates who were doing great mischief to shipping off the coasts of America.

IRVINE

Captain ? IRVINE. One of the last Atlantic pirates, active in the early 19th century.

ISAAC

Captain Roger ISAAC. An English pirate captain in the early 17th century. ISAAC sailed in company with Captain John JENNINGS from the corsair port of Tunis. They were caught and arrested in Helford, Cornwall in 1607. ISAAC was released but JENNINGS was held until he could raise the 'ransom' demanded by the local authorities.

IVYMAN (or IVEMAY)

Charles IVYMAN. A reluctant crewman aboard Captain William PHILLIPS' pirate vessel. IVYMAN was one of the group who overpowered the pirates and sailed the vessel into Boston. In the struggle, he threw the pirate SPARKS into the sea. He was tried at Boston on 12 May 1723 and acquitted.

JACKMAN

Captain ? JACKMAN. A buccaneer. In 1665 JACKMAN took part, with MORRIS and MORGAN in their raid on the Spanish Main. They sacked Villa de Mosa and Rio Garta, then the island of Raatan, and Truxillo, before plundering their way down the Mosquito Coast. With much help from the native Indians, they took the town of Granada.

JACKSON

Nathaniel JACKSON. A crewman to BLACKBEARD. JACKSON died alongside BLACKBEARD in the battle at Ocracoke Inlet on 1 Dec 1718.

JACKSON

Captain William JACKSON. A buccaneer. In July 1642 he recruited over 500 men from Barbados and over 25 from St Kitts to make up a band of over 1000 buccaneers. They sailed in 3 ships and plundered Maracaibo and Truxillo. On 25 Mar 1643 he landed a force on the then Spanish island of Jamaica and took the town of St Jago de la Vega (Santiago). The Spanish ransomed the town for 200 cattle, 10,000 lbs of bread and 7,000 pieces of eight. JACKSON's English buccaneers so liked the island that in one night alone, 23 of his men deserted from the party to settle there. For three years this band of buccaneers sailed and plundered the Caribbean.

JACOBSON

Agge JACOBSON. b. 1691/2. He shipped out of Bristol, but was probably a Dutchman or Fleming. JACOBSON became a pirate in 1719 and was captured aboard Captain Bartholomew ROBERTS' ship *Royal Fortune* off the West African coast by *HMS Swallow* on 10 Feb 1722. He was tried at Cape Corso Castle on 28 Mar 1722, found guilty of piracy and hanged.

JACOBSON

Peter JACOBSON. He was sailing master to Captain John JENNINGS in the early 17th century. JACOBSON was one of those who betrayed JENNINGS to the Earl of THOMOND, in Ireland.

JAMES

Captain ? JAMES. A buccaneer of Tortuga and Jamaica. In 1663 he commanded a frigate of 6 guns and 70 men.

JAMES

Captain ? JAMES. An English buccaneer. IN 1640 he was temporarily appointed 'President' of the island of Tortuga by the Providence Company. This was whilst the Governor, Captain FLOOD, was sent to London to answer charges made against him by the island's planters. This JAMES may possibly be the same Captain JAMES above.

JAMES

Captain ? JAMES. He was Captain of the pirate brig *Alexander* in 1709. His vessel was stranded in the Bay of Augustin on the Island of Johanna (Indian Ocean). The vessel, crew and guns were rescued by the pirate Captain Thomas WHITE. JAMES later sailed in company with Ort Van TYLE, the New York pirate.

JAMES

Charles JAMES. A crewman to Captain John QUELCH on his brig *Charles*. He had been taken from the galley *Larimore* at Salem. JAMES was tried for piracy at the Star Tavern in Boston in June 1704.

JAMISON

? JAMISON (alias MONACRE NICKOLA). A gentleman, son of a cloth-merchant in Greenock, Scotland. He shipped as sailing master to Captain JONNIA, who took the schooner *Exertion*. JAMISON was responsible for saving the lives of the *Exertion's* captain and crew. Years later he went to live in Boston with Captain LINCOLN (of the *Exertion*). He made a living by mackerel fishing in summer and teaching

navigation in the winters.

JANQUAIS

Captain ? JANQUAIS. A French Filibuster of San Domingo. He commanded *La Dauphine*, a large ship of 30 guns and 130 men.

JANSZ

Captain Jan Jansz. A Dutch privateer in the Mediterranean who turned Barbary corsair. In 1627 he took his corsair crew as far north as Reykjavik, Iceland, and captured 400 local people as slaves. He also stripped the town of salt-fish and hides.

JAYNSON

John JAYNSON. b. Nr Lancaster, England, 1700. He joined Captain James SKYRM's vessel *Ranger* from the prize vessel *Love* in Jul 1720. Captured by *HMS Swallow* off the West African coast on 1 Feb 1722. JAYNSON was tried at Cape Corso Castle on 28 Mar 1722. He was found guilty of piracy and hanged.

JEFFEREYS

Benjamin JEFFEREYS. b. Topsham, Devon, 1700R/01. He joined Captain Bartholomew ROBERTS' ship *Royal Fortune* from the prize galley *Norman* in Apr 1721. Captured off the West African coast by *HMS Swallow* on 10 Feb 1722. JEFFEREYS was tried at Cape Corso Castle on 28 Mar 1722. Witnesses said that he was so drunk when he joined ROBERTS that he could not have known his actions. The next day he refused to work for the pirates and was given 6 lashes by every member of the crew. For a long time after that he was too ill to work, but later he was made a Bosun's mate. JEFFEREYS was found guilty of piracy and hanged.

JENKINS

Thomas JENKINS. Mate to Captain William FLY. JENKINS was tried with FLY at Boston in 1726. They were jointly accused of taking the snow *Elizabeth* and murdering her captain, John GREEN. JENKINS was found guilty and hanged.

JENKINS

William JENKINS. A crewman to Captain William KIDD on *Adventure*. He surrendered with KIDD at New York but found that the pardon on offer to pirates did not extend to KIDD or his crew. He was shipped to London and tried at the Old Bailey in May 1701. He was found not guilty because he was an indentured apprentice, and therefore bound to do whatever his master ordered without question.

JENNINGS

Captain A. JENNINGS. A Welsh pirate. A man of good position and education, well respected by his fellows. When King George offered a pardon to Caribbean pirates in 1717, it was JENNINGS who presided over the meeting of pirates to decide what they should do. JEN-NINGS said that he intended to take the pardon, and some 150 others did the same. Most of them returned to piracy within a short time, thinking that a pardon in their sea-chest might be useful in the future.

JENNINGS

Captain Henry JENNINGS. A Jamaica based English pirate captain. JENNINGS Was a privateer under licence of Governor HAMILTON of Jamaica. In Nov 1715, when 10 ships of the Spanish treasure fleet were beached by a hurricane off the site of the later Fort Pierce, Florida, JENNINGS raided the camp of the Spanish salvage party. Overcoming the guard of 60 Spanish soldiers, he robbed them of 300,000 pieces-of-eight. The Governor of Cuba complained to the Jamaican authorities but the English colony had benefitted too well from the plunder to take any action against JENNINGS. Later JENNINGS took a Jamaican merchant vessel and only then was he regarded as a pirate in his home port. In Jan 1716 JENNINGS again raided the Spanish salvage camp and again stole substantial gold coinage. At the height of

JENNINGS' fame he commanded several vessels and hundreds of men. In Sep 1717 he was one of the pirates who accepted Woodes ROGERS offer of a royal pardon. He is reputed to have retired to live in great style in Bermuda.

JENNINGS

Captain JOHN JENNINGS. b. South Coast, England, 1570. JENNINGS is probably the best known of the early 17th century pirates. He went to sea as a youth and learned seamanship early. Realising that he would never reach command in the Royal or merchants fleets, he resolved to make his own fortune. He stole a ship in Plymouth and secured a safe base in Dunkirk, by paying off the Governor. His earliest prey were Dutch merchantmen in the English Channel. The Dutch complained to the English authorities and he was caught and held at the Marshalsea Prison. JENNINGS' sister pleaded with those that he had robbed to drop their complaints, she also petitioned Queen Elizabeth and obtained his release. One of the merchants he had robbed provided him with a vessel to carry wine and wool. He soon talked the crew into becoming pirates and they took a Spanish vessel off the North African coast. They were seized at Safi and imprisoned by the Dey of Tunis. Eventually they were free, to sail for the Dey on the agreement that the Dey sold all their plunder in Tunis

and kept a share for himself. JENNINGS had another safe base at Baltimore, Southwest Ireland, which was a fairly lawless area at that time. He took shipping in the Western Approaches to the English Channel. Once, at Baltimore, he brought a woman aboard and the crew protested that the compass would not work in her presence. An English man-of-war engaged them off Baltimore and JENNINGS was wounded. They crew rebelled and Gilbert ROOPE took command, locking JENNINGS in the gun-room. ROOPE proved too strict for the crew and they released JENNINGS. JENNINGS was eventually betrayed by some of his crew, who handed him over to the Earl of THOMOND, in Baltimore. He was shipped to London and hanged at Execution Dock, Wapping on 22 Dec 1609.

Note: JENNINGS once careened his vessel at Mevagissey, Cornwall, within 24 hours. Quite a feat to perform with only hand tools and a large vessel.

JESSUP

John JESSUP (1). He joined Captain Bartholomew ROBERTS' ship *Royal Fortune* from the prize vessel *Onslow* in May 1721. Captured off the West African coast by *HMS Swallow* on 10 Feb 1722. JESSUP was tried at Cape Corso Castle on 28 Mar 1722 and found guilty of piracy.

Note: There were 2 John JESSUPs captured on the *Royal*

Fortune. One was twenty years old, from Plymouth, and he was hanged. The other was from Wisbech in Cambridgeshire, and he was transported to the African Colonies for 7 years. See both John JESSUPs and take your pick.

JESSUP

John JESSUP (2). John JESSUP. Joined Captain Bartholomew ROBERTS' ship *Royal Fortune* at some point on the West African coast. Captured by *HMS Swallow* on the same coast on 10 Feb 1722. Tried at Cape Corso Castle on 28 Mar 1722 and found guilty of piracy.

JINGLE

Captain Thomas JINGLE. A privateer in the Caribbean. JINGLE commanded a fleet of 6 vessels and was probably the man who led the raid against St Augustine, Florida, in March 1683. The surprise element of their plan failed, and after a week in the area JINGLE's vessels withdrew. They took with them some Spanish prisoners whom they later released in Georgia.

JOBSON

Richard JOBSON (or COBSON or GOBSON). He was originally a druggist's assistant in London. One of DAMPIER's party who crossed the Isthmus of Darien both ways on foot in 1681. He was also studying divinity whilst buccaneering and always carried a Greek testament, from which he would translate to anyone in earshot. After great sufferings, the party got back to the Caribbean coast to find a buccaneer ship at anchor. On the way out to it, JOBSON was spilled out of the boat and into the sea. He was rescued, but later died of exposure. JOBSON was buried at Le Sound's Cay with buccaneer honours.

JOCARD

Captain ? JOCARD. A French Filibuster. In 1684 he was based in San Domingo. His ship, *Hirondelle* had 18 guns and 120 men.

JOHNSON

Captain Anthony JOHNSON. An English pirate captain in the early 17th century. JOHNSON is one of those pirates who is known to have regularly sent gold home to his wife and family, once by way of the merchant ship *Husband*. He was mate to the pirate Captain MICHAEL when they met and joined up with Captain John WARD's fleet at Sallee, Morocco, in 1604. Captain MICHAEL soon returned to England, leaving command of his vessel to JOHNSON.

JOHNSON

Captain ? JOHNSON. An English pirate of Jamaica. After Sir Thomas LYNCH, Governor of Jamaica, gave a general pardon to all pirates in 1670, JOHNSON left Port Royal and took a Spanish ship of 18 guns, killing the captain and crew. With a large crew, he cruised in Cuban waters. Sailing back, in order to try and make amends with LYNCH, his vessel was blown ashore in Morant Bay. JOHNSON was arrested and LYNCH ordered his deputy, Colonel MODYFORD, to try him. He was tried and acquitted. LYNCH was furious and tried him again, quite illegally, and hanged him immediately afterwards, before any appeal could be made.

JOHNSON

Benjamin JOHNSON. He served in the East Indiaman *Asia* as a midshipman. JOHNSON was stripped of his rank for stealing from the Purser. In 1750 he deserted his ship and took service with the Sultan of Ormus. He eventually became a great pirate Admiral and converted to Brahminism. He gathered a crew of 200 Englishmen, each of whom was allowed a dancing girl from the Temple, when ashore. JOHNSON ruled the Arabian Sea and the Persian Gulf for some years. He is reputed to have plundered at sea and ashore with the most

horrible brutality. On his retirement, he travelled overland to Constantinople with 10 English companions. He settled there, had a long life and a natural death.

JOHNSON

Captain Henry JOHNSON (alias HENRIQUES the Englishman). b. Northern Ireland. He commanded the *Two Brothers*, a Rhode Island built sloop of 18 guns and 90 men (mostly Spanish). On 20 Mar 1730 he took the prize vessel *John and Jane* after a five-hour battle. The Spanish crewmen wanted to hang the prisoners but JOHNSON and another Englishman ECHLIN, prevented this. They also stopped the chief Spaniard, POLEAS, abusing a woman passenger, Mrs GROVES. JOHNSON had only one hand but was an excellent shot. Rewards were offered for JOHNSON and his crew all along the Eastern Seaboard of North America.

JOHNSON

Isaac JOHNSON. A crewman to Captain John Quelch on the pirate brig *Charles*. He was tried at the Star Tavern in Boston in June 1704.

JOHNSON

Jacob JOHNSON. He was taken from the prize vessel *King Solomon* by Captain Bartholomew

ROBERTS' ship *Royal Fortune* in Jan 1722. Captured by *HMS Swallow* off the West African coast on 10 Feb 1722. JOHNSON was tried at Cape Corso Castle on 28 Mar 1722. He was found not guilty of piracy and acquitted.

JOHNSON

Captain John JOHNSON. An English pirate captain in the early 17th century. His crew once thought that he had cheated them and he locked up all the ship's muskets in the bread-room, for his own safety. No other information.

JOHNSON

John JOHNSON. Taken from the prize vessel *King Solomon* off Cape Apollonia in Jan 1722 by Captain James SKYRM's vessel *Ranger*. Captured by *HMS Swallow* off the West African coast on 1 Feb 1722. JOHNSON was tried at Cape Corso Castle and found not guilty of piracy. He was acquitted.

JOHNSON

Lancelot JOHNSON. b. Gala-shiels, Scotland, 1696. He sailed as a 12 year old boy on a Dutch merchantman. JOHNSON was ashore at Gambia and joined Captain George LOWTHER on *Gambia Castle*. He was one of the crew who escaped capture when LOWTHER's ship was taken at Blanquilla in 1723.

JOHNSON returned to legiti-mate seafaring and died off the coast of Brazil some years later. He was buried at sea without ceremony.

JOHNSON

Marcus JOHNSON. b. Smyrna?? 1700. He joined Captain Bartho-lomew ROBERTS' ship *Royal Fortune* from a Dutch vessel in 1718. He was captured off the West African coast by *HMS Swallow*. JOHNSON was tried at Cape Corso Castle on 28 Mar 1722. He was found guilty of piracy and hanged.

JOHNSON

Robert JOHNSON. b. 1689/90. He gave his home as Whydah, West Africa, but that was prob-ably where he boarded *Royal Fortune*. He joined Captain Bartholomew ROBERTS in Apr 1721. Captured by *HMS Swallow* off the West African coast on 10 Feb 1722. Tried at Cape Corso Castle on 28 Mar 1722. His defence was that he was so drunk when he joined the pirates that he had to be lifted aboard their vessel with a block and tackle. He was found guilty and hanged.

JOHNSTONE

Thomas JOHNSTONE. (Known as the Limping Privateer). He was a crewman on the frigate *Rose*. He was also a pirate at one time and an accomplice of Captain Thomas POUND. JOHNSTONE was the only one of POUND's crew to be hanged for his piracy.

JOL

Captain Cornelis Corneliszoon JOL. A one-legged Dutch privateer in the Caribbean, known and fear by the Spanish as Pie de Palo (Wooden leg). Captain YOL (to the English) sailed with van HOORN's fleet to capture the town of Campeche in Aug 1633. They shared their booty and the captured vessels with the mulatto pirate Captain Diego de los REYES before they dispersed. On 3 Mar 1635 he sailed his ship *Otter* in company with Captain Cornelis van UYTGEEST. They sailed into the narrow channel of Santiago de Cuba, both ships flying Spanish colours and with the crewmen dressed as friars. They had a gun-battle with the warships at anchor but the Governor of the town refused to surrender, they captured a frigate on the way out of the narrows. During the rest of that summer JOL took at least 10 other major Spanish vessels, then he sailed for Holland. His ship was taken by Dunkirk privateers in the Dover Strait and JOL was held prisoner in the Spanish Netherlands for 9 months. He was eventually exchanged and returned to the Caribbean late in 1636. He located a Spanish fleet off Cartagena, but there were so many privateers of different nationalities following the fleet that fighting broke out amongst them. JOL died in 1641 while capturing the Portugese slaving station of Sao Tome in West Africa.

JOLIFFE

Captain Edward JOLIFFE. An English pirate captain in the early 17th century. JOLIFFE's ship was once grappled and boarded by a Dutch man-of-war. He threatened to blow his ship's magazines if they did not leave immediately. They left.

JONES

Captain Achen JONES. JONES commanded the galley *Bedford* in the Indian Ocean. He picked up Captain David WILLIAMS, who had been left ashore in Madagascar. WILLIAMS must have been a stranger to him, because anyone who knew WILLIAMS would have left him on the beach.

JONES

Captain Paul JONES. Whether you consider Paul JONES a pirate or not, depends in which country you learned your history. So much has been written about the man over the years that little needs adding here. However, there are some facts that we should not disagree on. Born in Kircudbright, Scotland, in 1728.

JONES

JONES was the son of the head gardener to Lord SELKIRK. He served as a common seaman and rose to Mate on a merchantman, trading in the West Indies. With the outbreak of rebellion in the North American colonies, JONES joined the rebels and was given command of a privateer. He became a terror to English shipping from 1777 onwards. One of his adventures was to sail his ship *Ranger* to his old home and try to kidnap Lord SELKIRK. In 1779 he fought a furious action with an English convoy off Scarborough, Yorkshire. After great bravery and much damage to both sides, the convoy surrendered. When the peace was restored JONES faded into obscurity and poverty. He died in Paris in 1792, at the age of 64.

JONES

? JONES. Bosun to Captain Thomas ANSTIS on the pirate vessel *Good Fortune* in 1718. JONES was probably hanged in Curacao in late 1722 or early 1723.

JONES or JOHNS

Plantain JONES. A Jamaican-born pirate in the 1720s??

JONES

Thomas JONES. A pirate who died in the Marshalsea Gaol in 1724??

JONES

Thomas JONES. A crewman to Captain Thomas TEW. JONES left TEW in Madagascar, when TEW returned to Newport R.I. JONES eventually returned to Rhode Island himself and married Penelope GOULDEN.

JONES

Thomas JONES. b. Flur?, Wales, 1705/6. A crewman on Captain Charles HARRIS *Ranger*. Captured by *HMS Greyhound*. Tried at Newport R.I. in Jul 1723. Found not guilty and acquitted.

JONES

William JONES. b. London, 1695/6. A crewman on Captain Charles HARRIS *Ranger*. Captured by *HMS Greyhound* in Jul 1723. He was tried at Newport R.I. JONES was found guilty of piracy and hanged on 19 Jul 1723.

JONES

William JONES. Tried for piracy at Boston in 1704.

JONNIA

Captain ? JONNIA. A Spaniard. In 1821 he commanded a fast schooner of 20 guns and 40 well-armed men. He took the Boston schooner *Exertion* on 17 Dec 1821. They sailed the prize to Principe in Cuba and marooned the passengers and crew on a mangrove cay. Those marooned were rescued eventually. JONNIA and some of his crew were later captured by an English ship and taken to Kingston, Jamaica. They were tried and hanged.

JORDAN

Edward JORDAN. A passenger, with his wife and 4 children, on the fishing schooner *Eliza*. JORDAN, with some of the crew, took over the vessel. They were eventually captured by HMS Cuttle off Nova Scotia and brought to Halifax. JORDAN was tried and found guilty. He was hanged at Halifax on 20 Nov 1809.

JORDAN

Margaret JORDAN. The wife of Edward JORDAN above. She was arrested with the rest of *Eliza's* pirate crew. It became evident that she knew of her husband's piracy and had enjoyed a physical relationship with several of his crew. The court at Halifax pronounced her not guilty, probably because she had 4 young children.

JOSE

Miguel JOSE. An elderly man, hanged for piracy at Kingston, Jamaica, in Feb 1823. His plea from the gallows was "No he robado, no he matado ningune, muero innocente."

JUDSON

Randall JUDSON. A crewman to Captain RODERIGO. He was tried and sentenced to death at Cambridge, Mass., in Jun 1675. After a lecture on the evil of his ways, by the Rev Increase MATHERS, he was pardoned and fined, but banished from the Colony.

JULIAN

John JULIAN. He was a native American and a psychic. JULIAN came from Cape Cod. He survived the wrecking of Captain Samuel BELLAMY's *Whydah* on that same Cape. JULIAN never came to trial, he was sold into slavery.

KEIGLE

? KEIGLE. A crewman to Captain Thomas GREEN on the vessel *Worcester*. With the rest of the crew, KEIGLE was falsely imprisoned, tried, sentenced and hanged at Leith, Scotland in Apr 1705.

KELLWANTON

? KELLWANTON. A well-known 16th century English pirate. He was captured on the Isle of Man in 1531.

KELLY

John KELLY. Mate on the fishing schooner *Eliza* which was taken over by Edward JORDAN. Kelly joined the conspirators and was active in killing some of the crew. He left *Eliza* in a rowing boat before the pirates were taken and was not heard of again.

KELLY

Captain Thomas KELLY. An English pirate captain in the early 17th century. In Jun 1615, KELLY was one of 5 English captains in a fleet of 6 Algerian-based vessels that attacked the merchantman *Susan Constance* of London, off Cadiz. KELLY was also a prominent leader of the pirate community at Marmora.

KENCATE

Dr John KENCATE. A surgeon on the prize ship *Sycamore Galley* taken by Captain Charles HARRIS. He became the pirates' doctor. KENCATE was captured with HARRIS's crew on 10 Jun 1723. At his trial on 10 Jul 1723, after much discussion, he was acquitted.

KENNEDY

Captain ? KENNEDY. A crewman to Captain John MARTEL in the West Indies in 1716. He was elected to command of the vessel when MARTEL's cruelty revolted the crew. When KENNEDY's gunner, TAFFIER, knocked a captured captain unconscious with the flat of his cutlass, KENNEDY was so angered that he got into his yawl and made as if to sail away. The crew got him to return only by promising that there would be no more unnecessary violence.

KENNEDY

Captain Walter KENNEDY. He was a crewman to both Captain Howell DAVIS and Captain Bartholomew ROBERTS. KENNEDY led the party ashore in the Isle of Princes in Mar 1720, to avenge the death of DAVIS. Later he took command of ROBERTS' ship *Rover* when ROBERTS went after a sloop in the Surinam River. He sailed to Barbados and took another vessel there. KENNEDY narrowly escaped capture in Virginia when some of his crew were caught and hanged. He next took a Boston sloop, and all the hands who would volunteer to follow him, and sailed to Ireland and then Northwest Scotland. They left the sloop at anchor and went ashore, posing as shipwrecked mariners. Those of the crew who divided into small parties seem to have fared well. The main body (without KENNEDY) stayed together, living riotously and throwing their gold about. 17 of them were arrested in Edinburgh, 2 gave evidence against the others and 9 were hanged. KENNEDY made his way to London where he opened a brothel on the Deptford Road. One of his whores indicted him for robbery and he was sent to the Bridewell Gaol. The woman found a former shipmate of his to identify him as a pirate. He was transferred to the Marshalsea, the Admiralty's Gaol. KENNEDY offered to turn informer himself, but he was tried and sentenced. He was hanged at Execution Dock, Wapping on 19 Jul 1721.

KIDD

Captain William KIDD. b. Greenock, Scotland, 1645/6. In 1688 KIDD set out from England with Captain Thomas HEWETSON's small fleet which sailed for the Caribbean to seek their fortunes. KIDD commanded the *Blessed*

William, a 20 gun vessel with about 90 crew. On hearing of the outbreak of war with the French, HEWETSON's force sacked the island of Marie Gallante, winning great treasure. They returned to Nevis and were directed to save THORNHILL's force which was attacking French Saint Martin. On their return to Nevis, KIDD's crew were discontented at being used as regular naval forces, they wanted plunder. On 12 February 1690, KIDD was ashore, his crew mutinied and made off with his ship and his treasure. KIDD chased them in another vessel as far as New York. There he settled and married Sarah OORT, a woman of property. They had two children. He was recommended by Lord BELLAMONT as fit to command a government vessel to sail against the pirates. A group of businessmen, which included the King of England, financed the fitting out of the vessel and its task was to take pirate ships and French merchantmen 'to the profit of the group'. The vessel was commissioned on 15 Dec 1695, took aboard a crew in New York and sailed to Madeira, Cape Verde Islands and Madagascar. Pirates and Frenchmen proved to be too few, so KIDD decided to take whatever vessels came his way. He turned pirate himself. His best prize was the *Queda Merchant* and he kept that vessel for himself after his own *Adventure* became unseaworthy. KIDD sailed in company with Captain CULLIFORD for some time. Hearing of LITTLE-TON's offer of a pardon for pirates, KIDD decided to accept it. Some of the crew stayed and sailed with CULLIFORD. KIDD sailed to New York to accept the pardon, but found that it did not extend to him or to CULLIFORD, or to their crews. He was shipped to London and tried at the Old Bailey in May 1701. KIDD was found guilty of piracy and hanged at Execution Dock, Wapping on 23 May 1701. At the first attempt to hang him the rope broke and they had to start again. After three tides had washed over his body, it was tarred, wrapped in chains and hung at Tilbury Point. For years his remains could be seen by any vessel entering or leaving the River Thames.

KILLING

James KILLING. A crewman to Major Stede BONNET. KILL-ING gave evidence against BONNET at his trial in Boston in 1718.

KING

Charles KING. A crewman to Captain John QUELCH on the brig *Charles*. He attempted to escape on the galley *Larimore*, but was captured and brought to Salem. KING was tried at the Star Tavern in Boston in June 1704. He was found guilty and sentenced to death, but was later reprieved.

KING

Francis KING. A Scot. KING was a crewman to Captain John QUELCH on the brig *Charles* (and possibly a kinsman to the KING above). He was tried at the Star Tavern in Boston. KING was hanged with QUELCH at Boston on 30 Jun 1704.

KING

John KING. b. Shadwell, London. KING joined Captain Bartholomew ROBERTS' ship *Royal Fortune* from the prize vessel *King Solomon* in Jan 1722. Captured by *HMS Swallow* off the West African coast on 10 Feb 1722. He was tried at Cape Corso Castle on 28 Mar 1722. KING was found guilty and sentenced to 7 years' transportation to the African Colonies.

KING

John KING. Here is another KING who was a crewman to Captain John QUELCH on the brig *Charles*. I feel sure that some of them were related. This one was also tried at the Star Tavern in Boston in 1704.

KING

John KING. b. Jamaica. A crewman to Captain Samuel BEL-LAMY on *Whydah*. KING is believed to have drowned on the night, in 1717, when *Whydah* was wrecked on Cape Cod.

KING

Mathew KING. From Jamaica. A crewman to Major Stede BONNET. He was captured with BONNET at Cape Fear River on 27 Sep 1718. KING was tried at Charleston and hanged on 8 Nov 1718.

KITCHEN

? KITCHEN. A crewman to Captain Thomas GREEN on the vessel *Worcester*. KITCHEN was falsely imprisoned with the rest of the crew. He was tried, sentenced and hanged at Leith, Scotland in Apr 1705.

KNEVES or KNEEVES

Peter KNEVES. b. Exeter, Devon, 1690/1. A crewman to Captain Charles HARRIS on *Ranger*. Captured by *HMS Greyhound*. KNEVES was tried at Newport R.I. He was found guilty and hanged on 19 Jul 1723.

KNIGHT

Captain William Knight. One of Captain Edward DAVIS fleet of pirates who cruised the Pacific coast of Mexico. KNIGHT joined the expedition in 1685, along with TOWNLEY, SWAN and many French filibusters. He raided south with DAVIS while the others ranged north. They met with the French again in August 1687 and captured Teluantepec, Mexico. KNIGHT sailed back around Cape Horn and probably settled in Virginia.

KNIGHT

Christopher KNIGHT. A crewman to Captain William COWARD. He was tried for piracy in Boston in Jan 1690 and found guilty. KNIGHT was later reprieved.

KNOT

Captain ? KNOT. A retired pirate captain. He lived in Boston in 1699. His wife gave information to the Governor, the Earl of BELLOMONT, of the whereabouts of the pirate GILLAM, a notorious and wanted man.

KUO-HSING YEH

KUO-HSING YEH. b. 1623. The son of a Chinese pirate, CHENG CHIH-LUNG, and a Japanese mother. He was brought up to hate the Manchus, who had imprisoned, and later executed his father. His pirate raids along the coast became so successful that the Emperor ordered more than 80 seaports to move 10 miles inland and burn their original towns. He later turned his attention to the Dutch. He became the virtual ruler of Formosa, and through him it became part of China. After his death he was officially canonized.

La BOUCHE

Oliver La BOUCHE. One of the pirates who surrendered to the pardon of the Governor of the Bahamas in 1717.

La CATA

La CATA's real name is not known. He was a bloodthirsty pirate and one of the last of the West Indies pirate gangs. In 1824, off the Isle of Pines, his ship was captured after a furious fight. The English cutter that captured him was only half the size of La CATA's vessel. He was taken to Kingston, Jamaica, where he was tried and hanged.

La CROIX

The real name of the pirate PETERSON who was one of the mutinous crew of the schooner *Eliza*.

LACY

Abraham LACY. b. Devon, 1702/3. A crewman to Captain Charles HARRIS on *Ranger*. Captured by *HMS Greyhound*. He was tried at Newport R.I. Found guilty and hanged on 19 Jul 1723.

La FEVER

Peter La FEVER. Taken from the prize vessel *Jeremiah and Anne* in Apr 1720 by Captain James SKYRM's vessel *Ranger*. Captured by *HMS Swallow* off the West African coast on 1 Feb 1722. He was tried at Cape Corso Castle on 28 Mar 1722. La FEVER was found not guilty of piracy and acquitted.

LAFITTE

Jean LAFITTE. Jean and his brother Pierre were first heard of in New Orleans in 1809. Although both were smiths by profession, they took to smuggling pirate booty. The headquarters of this trade was the Island of Grande Terre, in Barataria Bay. Ex-pirates managed the trade under the leadership of GRAMBO, their acknowledged chief, until he was shot by LAFITTE. In 1814 he refused an English commission, preferring to sign on with General JACKSON. LAFITTE's Baratarians served the guns at the Battle of New Orleans and earned distinction for themselves. LAFITTE dropped from sight after the war, until a British sloop-of-war took a pirate ship in 1823, and it was discovered that the ship was commanded by LAFITTE. He had died in the fighting.

LAGARDE

Captain ? LAGARDE. A French Filibuster. He was at San Domingo in 1684, commanding a small ship *La Subtille*, with 2 guns and 30 men.

LAI CHOI SAN

LAI CHOI SAN. (Queen of the Macao Pirates). She operated from the pirate base of Bias Bay, Macao. The head of a huge 'protection' and piracy fleet, she was active in the 1920s.

LAMBERT

? LAMBERT. A crewman to Captain Samuel BELLAMY on *Whydah*.

LAMBERT

John LAMBERT. b. Salem, 1655. A crewman to Captain John QUELCH on his vessel *Charles*. He was captured, tried, sentenced and hanged at Boston in 1704. LAMBERT's body was cut down from the gallows by his relatives the night after the execution and quietly buried at King's Chapel Burial Grounds. The other pirate corpses were taken out to either Bird Island or Nix Mate and displayed there as a warning to passing ships' crews.

LAMBERT

John LAMBERT. b. Newcastle, England. A Sailing Master (one of three) to Captain Samuel BELLAMY on *Whydah*. LAMBERT is believed to have drowned on the night, in 1717, when *Whydah* was wrecked on Cape Cod.

LANDER

Daniel LANDER. A crewman to Captain Thomas POUND. LANDER was captured with POUND's crew and tried at Boston. He was found guilty and sentenced to death, but was eventually released on payment of 13 pounds and 3 shillings.

LANDRESSON

Captain Michael LANDRESSON. (alias BREHA). A French Filibuster. LANDRESSON went with Captain PAIN on his expedition against St Augustine in 1683. He harried the Jamaicans constantly. His ship *La Trompeuse*, should not be confused with the famous ship of the same name commanded by HAMLIN. LANDRESSON continued to dispose of his plunder through the port of Boston, though successive Governors forbade the trade that the city thrived on. In 1684 LANDRESSON was at San Domingo, commanding 'La Fortune', a ship of 14 guns and 100 men. He was captured with several of his crew in 1686 by the Armada de Barlarento. They were all hanged.

LANE

Captain ? LANE. In 1720 LANE was a crewman to Captain Edward ENGLAND when they took the *Mercury* off the coast of West Africa. *Mercury* was refitted as a pirate ship, LANE was given command and re-named her *Queen Anne's Revenge*. He parted company with ENG-LAND and sailed to Brazil where he had much success against the Portugese.

LANE

John LANE. b. Lombard Street, London. LANE joined Captain Bartholomew ROBERTS' ship *Royal Fortune* from the prize vessel *King Solomon* in Jan 1722. Captured off the West African coast by *HMS Swallow* on 10 Feb 1722. He was tried at Cape Corso Castle on 28 Mar 1722 and found guilty of piracy. LANE was sentenced to death, but this was commuted to 7 years' transportation to the African Colonies.

LANG

Christopher LANG. He joined Captain James SKYRM's vessel 'Ranger' from the prize brig 'Thomas' in Sep 1720. Captured by HMS Swallow off the West African coast on 1 Feb 1722. LANG must have been suspected of being a Royal Navy deserter because he was referred to the Marshalsea Gaol for trial in London. The outcome of his trial is not known to me.

LARIMORE

Captain Thomas LARIMORE. In 1704 he owned and com-manded the pirate galley *Lari-more* and sailed in company with

Captain John QUELCH and other pirate captains. They took many vessels, including a Portug-ese ship with much gold aboard. LARIMORE was captured in 1704. He was tried and sentenced in Boston, and hanged on 11 Jun in that year.

La ROCHE (see Joseph BROUS)

LASSEN

Isaac LASSEN. A Frenchman (or a native American, it depends whom you believe). One of three Frenchmen who were reluctant crewmen of Captain William PHILLIPS. PHILLIPS and his pirates were overpowered by their captives, who sailed the vessel to Boston, but were still tried along with the pirates. The trial was on 12 Apr 1724. Thank-fully, the captives were all found not guilty and acquitted.

LAWRENCE

Nicholas (or Richard) LAWR-ENCE. A crewman to Captain John QUELCH on his pirate brig *Charles*. LAWRENCE was tried in Boston in 1704, I think, and was probably one of those who were 'pardoned to join the Queen's service'.

LAWSON

Edward LAWSON. b. Isle of Man, 1702/3. LAWSON was a

crewman on Captain HARRIS *Ranger*. He was captured by *HMS Greyhound* and tried at Newport R.I. He was found guilty of piracy and hanged on 19 Jul 1723.

LEA

George LEA. An early 17th century pirate, crewman to Captain William BAUGHE. BAUGHE accused LEA of assaulting him and wished to execute him on the spot. The crew refused to allow it. Instead they towed LEA in a small boat to the mouth of the harbour and cast him adrift with one oar and some water.

LEADSTONE

John LEADSTONE. (Known as Captain CRACKERS) LEADSTONE was a retired pirate who lived ashore in Sierra Leone in great style in the early 18th century. Captain Bartholomew ROBERTS spent some time as a guest of Captain CRACKERS in 1721. LEADSTONE treated visiting pirates royally and saluted their departure with 3 cannon which stood outside his door.

LEBOUS

Captain Louis LEBOUS. A French pirate captain who sailed in company with Captain Samuel BELLAMY in the Caribbean for some time. He parted company with BELLAMY and nothing more is heard of him.

Le CLERC

Captain Francois Le CLERC. A French privateer in the Caribbean, known as 'Jambe de Bois' because of his wooden leg. Le CLERC was probably inspired by FLEURY's capture of CORTES' treasure from the New World. In 1553 he led a small fleet of French privateers which cruised the coasts of Hispaniola. His force of 300 men sacked the harbour of Santiago de Cuba and spent 30 days looting the town.

LEE

Joshua LEE. b. Liverpool. LEE joined Captain James SKYRM's vessel *Ranger* from the prize snow *Martha*. Captured by *HMS Swallow* off the West African coast on 1 Feb 1722. He was tried at Cape Corso Castle and found guilty. LEE was sentenced to death but his sentence was commuted to 7 years' transportation to the African Colonies.

LEE

William LEE. b. England. LEE was a crewman to Captain Samuel BELLAMY on *Whydah*. LEE is believed to have drowned on the night, in 1717, when *Whydah* was wrecked on Cape Cod.

Le FAGE

? Le FAGE. A lieutenant of LAFITTE. Le FAGE commanded a pirate schooner and was engaged by the US cutter *Alabama* in the Mississippi Delta in 1819. Six of the pirate crew were killed in the action, the remainder were captured and taken to Bayou St John for trial.

LEMMON

Michael LEMMON. He was taken from the prize vessel *Onslow* in Jan 1722 by Captain James SKYRM's vessel *Ranger*. Captured by *HMS Swallow* off the West African coast by *HMS Swallow* on 1 Feb 1722. LEMMON was tried at Cape Corso Castle on 28 Mar 1722. He was found not guilty of piracy and acquitted.

Le PICARD

Captain ? Le PICARD. A Frenchman. One of the captains of the huge Anglo/French fleet that failed to capture Panama in May 1685.

Le SAGE

Captain ? Le SAGE. A French Filibuster. In 1683 he was in a fleet of French and Dutch buccaneers under De GRAAF which took much Spanish shipping in the harbour at Cartagena. In 1684 he was at San Domingo in command of *Tigre*, a ship of 30 guns and 130 men.

L'ESCUYIER

Captain ? L'ESCUYIER. Another French pirate captain of the fleet that faced a Spanish squadron of 14 men-of-war in the Bay of Panama in May 1685.

LESSONE

Captain ? LESSONE. A French Filibuster. In 1680 he joined Captains SHARPE, COXON and other English buccaneers to attack Porto Bello. Putting 300 men ashore in canoes, they landed 60 miles from the city and marched for 4 days with almost no food. In spite of their hardships, they took the city on 17 Feb 1680.

Le TESTU

Captain Guillaume Le TESTU. A French Hugenot refugee. Le TESTU was a skilled navigator and pilot. He met with DRAKE after the Englishman's failed attempt on the 'treasure train' of mules near Venta Cruz in Feb 1573. Le TESTU told DRAKE of the St Bartholomew's Day massacre of 50,000 Protestants in France. Le TESTU and his 70 men joined DRAKE and they took the mule train of bullion just before it reached Nombres de Dios. Le TESTU was wounded in the stomach and before DRAKE's rescue party could reach him, he was taken by the Spanish and probably executed.

Le VASSEUR

Captain Francois Le VASSEUR. One of the leaders of the international buccaneer community on the island of Tortuga in the mid-17th century. In 1650 Le VASSEUR led an expedition to sack the town of Santiago de los Caballeros on San Domingo. In August 1652 he did the same to the port of Juan de los Remedios in Cuba. Later in 1652 Le VASSEUR was assassinated by rival French buccaneers.

Le VASSEUR

Captain Olivier Le VASSEUR. Known as La BUSE (The Bussard). Le VASSEUR sailed in the Indian Ocean in convoy with Captains John TAYLOR and Edward ENGLAND. He and TAYLOR marooned ENGLAND on Reunion Island because they thought him too lenient with his captives. Le VASSEUR and TAYLOR took the Portugese vessel *Virgen de Cabo* at Reunion. Later they captured the fortress of Fort Lagoa in Lorenzo Marques Bay. The two captains then parted company. Le VASSEUR offered to surrender to the authorities on the Island of Reunion, but they first wanted him to hand over his treasure. One piece of his treasure was called The Fiery Cross of Goa, it was made of gold, rubies, emeralds and diamonds and took three men to lift it. Le VASSEUR left Reunion and sailed to the Island of Mahe, in the Seychelles, where he is rumoured to have hidden the treasure. Later he was shipwrecked on the Isle Sainte Marie. Le VASSEUR worked incognito as a pilot in Antongil Bay, Madagascar, until he was recognised in 1728. He sailed again as a pirate captain but was captured after a fierce battle by Captain L'ERMITTE of the French man-of-war *Medusa*. He was taken to St Denis, Reunion for trial. At his hanging, on 17 Jul 1730, Le VASSEUR challenged the crowd from the scaffold to find his treasure.

LEVERCOTT

Samuel LEVERCOTT. A crewman to Captain George LOWTHER on *Ranger*. He was one of those who were captured by the sloop *HMS Eagle* at Blanquilla in Oct 1723. LEVERCOTT was tried at St Christopher (St Kitts) on 11 Mar 1723. He was found guilty of piracy and hanged.

LEVIT

John LEVIT. Of North Carolina. A crewman to Major Stede BONNET. He was captured with BONNET on 27 Sep 1718 at the Cape Fear River. He was tried at Charleston and hanged on 8 Nov 1718.

LEWIS

James LEWIS. LEWIS had been a prisoner in France, but managed to escape to Spain. He was a crewman to Captain Henry AVERY when they took the prize vessel *Charles the Second.* LEWIS was tried for piracy at the Old Bailey in 1696. He was found guilty and hanged.

LEWIS

Nicholas LEWIS. Quartermaster to Captain George LOWTHER on *Ranger.* Captured by the sloop *HMS Eagle* at Blanquilla in Oct 1723. He was tried at St Christopher (St Kitts) on 11 Mar 1724. LEWIS was found guilty and hanged.

LEWIS

William LEWIS. A prize fighter, he was one of the pirates who surrendered to Woodes ROGERS' offer of pardon at Providence, Bahamas. Later he returned to piracy under Captain John AUGER. He was taken prisoner when AUGER's sloop ran aground on Long Island W.I. LEWIS was tried and hanged at Providence on 12 Dec 1718.

LEWIS

Captain William LEWIS. He sailed from Boston at the age of 11 with BANISTER. They were captured by Spanish pirates and LEWIS was put ashore in Havana, probably because of his age. When he was 16 he stole a piragua (an open canoe type of boat) with Darby McCAFFREY and 8 others. They took progressively

larger vessels until they had the 90 foot long *Morning Star.* By this time they were a crew of 80 men. They took a French 24 gun ship and manned her with a crew of 200 very mixed men. LEWIS maintained command by setting one national faction against another, while he himself grew more irrational and paranoid. Eventually the French faction of the crew murdered him in his bed.

LEYTON

Francis LEYTON. b. New York, 1684/5. A crewman on Captain Charles HARRIS *Ranger.* Captured by HMS Greyhound. LEYTON was tried at Newport R.I. He was found guilty and hanged on 19 Jul 1723.

LIBBEY

Joseph LIBBEY. A crewman on a fishing shallop taken by Captain Edward LOW at Port Roseway on 15 Jun 1722. LIBBEY was at first a reluctant crewman. He later joined the pirate Captain Charles HARRIS and was captured by *HMS Greyhound* in Jun 1723. He was tried and hanged at Newport R.I. on 19 Jul 1723, at the age of 21.

LILBOURN

Robert LILBOURN. Taken from the prize vessel *Jeremiah and Anne* in Apr 1721 by Captain Bartholomew ROBERTS' ship *Royal*

Fortune. Captured off the West African coast by *HMS Swallow* on 10 Feb 1722. LILBOURN was tried at Cape Corso Castle on 28 Mar 1722. He was found not guilty of piracy and acquitted.

LIMA

Manuel LIMA. A Caribbean pirate, captured by the sloop HMS Tyne. Tried and hanged at Kingston, Jamaica in Feb 1823.

LINCH

Captain ? LINCH. An English buccaneer of Port Royal, Jamaica. In 1680 he sailed with Captain Edmund COOK to raid the Spanish Main. This was Lionel WAFER's first buccaneering voyage, well documented by him.

LING

William LING. A crewman to Captain John AUGER. LING had probably already taken a pardon from Woodes ROGERS at Providence, Bahamas. He turned pirate again with AUGER. They were taken prisoner when AUGER's sloop ran aground at Long Island W.I. He was tried and hanged at Providence on 12 Dec 1718.

LINISTER

Thomas LINISTER. b. Lancashire, England, 1702/3. A crewman to Captain Charles HARRIS on

Ranger. Captured by *HMS Greyhound.* Tried at Newport R.I. LINISTER was found guilty and hanged on 19 Jul 1723.

LINSEY

? LINSEY. A crewman on Captain Thomas GREEN's vessel *Worcester.* He was tried and found guilty of piracy at Leith, Scotland in 1704/5. There was no evidence and the verdict was clearly wrong. In exchange for a pardon, LINSEY gave evidence of piracy, and many other things, against the rest of the crew.

LITHGOW

Captain ? LITHGOW. A pirate captain who based himself at Providence in the Bahamas. No further detail or dates, I'm afraid.

LITTLEJOHN

David LITTLEJOHN. b. England. He joined Captain James SKYRM's vessel *Ranger* from the prize vessel *Phoenix* of Bristol in Jun 1720. Captured off the West African coast by *HMS Swallow* on 28 Mar 1722. He was found guilty and sentenced to death, but the sentence was commuted to 7 years transportation to the African Colonies.

LIVERS

William LIVERS, known as Evis. He was a crewman to Major

Stede BONNET. Captured with BONNET at the Cape Fear River. He was tried at Charleston and hanged on 8 Nov 1718.

LIVINGSTON

Robert LIVINGSTON. A business partner of Captain William KIDD. LIVINGSTON was also mate of their ship *Adventure*.

LO

Mrs Hon-Cho LO. She was the widow of a Chinese pirate who was killed in 1921. She took command of her husband's fleet of over 60 ocean-going junks after his death. She was young and pretty, and a merciless pirate and murderer. During the revolution she took sides with General Wong Min-Tong and was granted the rank of Colonel. Afterwards she returned to piracy, afloat and ashore, sometimes taking 50 or 60 girls from a village to sell as slaves. She disappeared from sight quite suddenly, never to be heard of again.

LODGE

Thomas LODGE. A buccaneer, poet and physician. b. 1557. The son of Sir Thomas LODGE, grocer and Lord Mayor of London in 1563. Young Thomas was educated at the Merchant Taylor's School and Trinity College, Oxford. LODGE sailed with Captain CLARKE on several voyages between 1584 and 1590. On 26 Aug 1591 he sailed from Plymouth, Devon with Sir Thomas CAVENDISH in *Desire*, a galleon of 140 tons. They sailed to Brazil and sacked the town of Santa. In Jan 1592 they sailed south, and while stormbound in Patagonia, LODGE wrote his romance "Margerite of America". The vessel arrived, with the ship's company half-starved, in Ireland on 11 Jun 1593. At the age of 40 LODGE took his degree in medicine at Avignon. He published "A Treatise on the Plague" in 1603, and died of it in 1625, at the age of 68.

LOFF

Gabriel LOFF. A crewman on Captain William KIDD's vessel *Adventure*. He surrendered to pardon with KIDD at New York. They found that the pardon did not include KIDD and his crew. LOFF was shipped to London with KIDD and tried at the Old Bailey in May 1701. He was found guilty and hanged at Execution Dock, Wapping.

L'OLLONAIS

Francis L'OLLONAIS (see Captain Jean David NAU).

LONG

Zachariah LONG. A Dutchman. A crewman to Major Stede BONNET. He was captured with BONNET at Cape Fear River on 27 Sep 1718. LONG was tried at Charleston and hanged on 8 Nov 1718.

LONGCASTLE

William LONGCASTLE. He was a noted pirate in the early 17th century. He seems to have purchased his freedom, after capture, by paying £50 to the Lord Admiral.

LOPEZ

John LOPEZ. b. Oporto. A crewman to Major Stede BONNET. He was captured with BONNET at the Cape Fear River on 27 Sep 1718. He was tried at Charleston and hanged on 8 Nov 1718.

LORD

John LORD. A British soldier who deserted with the rest of the guard at Fort Loyal, Falmouth, Maine, to join Captain Thomas POUND's crew. He was killed in the fight at Tarpaulin Cove in 1689.

LOW

Captain Edward LOW. b. Westminster, London. LOW began his murderous career by killing his father in a family brawl. He escaped from London with his brother Ronald, as crewmen on a merchantman bound for Boston. Ronald continued to sail from Boston but Edward got work as a rigger in a shipyard nearby. Edward LOW's foul temper got him into trouble again and he broke his employer's arm in a quarrel. Edward joined Ronald and both brothers boarded a vessel which was commissioned to take Spanish logwood ships in the Caribbean. Inevitably, LOW argued with the Captain and fired a shot at him. The shot missed but the ball struck someone else. Both brothers and some of the others of the crew escaped in a small boat, among them was Charles HARRIS. The next day they seized a small vessel. Shortly afterwards they took another vessel and LOW put HARRIS aboard as Captain. Both vessels were caught in a hurricane and lost contact. LOW sailed for the Azores, refitted and continued his piracy there. He once took 7 vessels at one time without firing a shot. His cruelty was exceptional, even by pirate standards. Once he cut off a man's lips and cooked them in front of him. LOW, in his vessel *Fancy* and Charles HARRIS in *Ranger*, met again in the Windward Islands. The man-of-war *HMS Greyhound* came across both vessels but LOW managed to escape. LOW's behaviour became more irrational, he even murdered his own Quartermaster. The crew finally rose against him and cast him adrift in a boat. He was picked up by a French vessel and tried to convince them that he was the victim of pirates. One man on the French vessel recognised him and he was handed over to the authorities on the island of Martinique. There he was quickly tried and hanged. This was probably in 1723.

LOW

Ronald LOW. b. Westminster, London. The older brother of Captain Edward LOW. Ronald left home with Edward and sailed with him to Boston. Later they sailed together as pirates. Ronald was undoubtedly more pleasant then his brother and nothing is known of him after Edward was cast adrift by his crew.

LOWTHER

Captain George LOWTHER. A Lowland Scot. He sailed from London to Gambia as Second Mate on the merchantman *Gambia Castle*, arriving in May 1721. LOWTHER and the Captain had been in dispute for the whole voyage and the Captain ordered him flogged at Gambia. The men refused to flog LOWTHER and the Captain went ashore. An Army Captain, MASSEY, who had sailed with the vessel, found that conditions ashore were not as they should be. He found that a faction of local traders were ruling the colony, and not the Governor, who was sick. MASSEY and

LOWTHER resolved to bring the Governor aboard and take him back to England. The Governor upset their plans by refusing their offer. This left MASSEY and LOWTHER with the realisation that technically they were pirates. They sailed for the Americas and took a prize in mid-Atlantic. Further prizes fell to them in the West Indies. LOWTHER's vessel was now *Happy Delivery*. He sailed off Honduras and then the Cayman Islands meeting Captain Edward LOW in *Rhode Island* and Captain Charles HARRIS in his sloop *Ranger*. Ashore at Amatique, natives set fire to *Happy Delivery* as she was laid over for careening. LOWTHER took HARRIS's sloop. (HARRIS must have found another vessel and named that vessel *Ranger*.) In early May 1722 they took a brig off Deseada and another vessel on 28 May. LOWTHER and LOW parted company. In Jun 1722 LOWTHER took 3 vessels off New York. *Ranger* ran aground after an engagement in South Carolina and LOWTHER spent all winter there re-fitting. In Spring 1723 he was off Newfoundland and soon after he was back in the Caribbean. He put in to the Island of Blanca (Blanquilla) to careen. The sloop *HMS Eagle* found them there with guns ashore and the vessel on its beam-ends. *Ranger* and many of the crew were captured but LOWTHER and 12 men escaped overland. The captured crewmen were tried at St Christopher (St Kitts) on 11 May 1723. LOWTHER is said to have shot himself on the island. Some of the survivors of his crew say that they found him dead with his pistol in his hand. I have my doubts.

Note: The Journal of the Royal African Company gives a different account of LOWTHER's adventures. It states that while Captain Charles RUSSELL, commander of *Gambia Castle* a Company ship, was ashore negotiating with the King of Barra for the purchase of slaves, the ship sailed away. There were bitter disputes between the sailors and the Company's soldiers on the way across the Atlantic. The ship was burned in Montego Bay, Jamaica, the following year and none of those responsible were apprehended.

LUDBURY

Captain ? LUDBURY. A English buccaneer. LUDBURY sailed with Captains PRINCE and HARRISON in Oct 1670. They sailed up the San Juan River in Nicaragua, with a party of 170 buccaneers, to capture and plunder the city of Granada.

LUKE

Captain Mathew LUKE. An Italian? He commanded a Puerto Rican vessel *Guarda del Costa*. LUKE captured 4 English vessels and murdered their entire crews. His vessel was captured by *HMS Lancestan* in May 1722. LUKE and all but seven of his crew were hanged.

LUMLEY

Robert LUMLEY. A crewman to Captain William KIDD on *Adventure*. LUMLEY surrendered to pardon in New York with KIDD and others. They found that the pardon did not extend to KIDD and his crew. He was shipped to London and tried at the Old Bailey. LUMLEY was found not guilty because he was an indentured apprentice.

LUSHINGHAM

Captain ? LUSHINGHAM. In 1564, this pirate captain was at Berehaven, Bantry Bay, in the West Of Ireland. He had just sold a cargo of plundered Spanish wine to the local Lord O'SULLIVAN, when one of Queen Elizabeth's ships came into the Bay. The pirate ship escaped, with O'SULLIVAN's help, but LUSHINGHAM was killed by a shot from the Queen's ship.

LUSSAN

Le Sieur Raveneau LUSSAN. A French Filibuster. Born into a good family and well educated, LUSSAN wrote an entertaining book, "Journal du Voyage fait a la Mer du Sud avec les Flibustiers de l'Amerique en 1684" which I have not yet found. Pressure from his creditors in Paris drove him to his adventures as a filibuster. LUSSAN seems to have maintained high standards of behaviour as a filibuster and tried to improve the public perception of the buccaneering trade. I am told that his book describes his adventures at sea, as well as many amorous interludes. I look forward to finding an English translation. LUSSAN returned to Paris after his travels, wealthy enough to resume his former lifestyle.

LYNE

Captain Phillip LYNE. A Quartermaster to Captain Francis SPRIGGS. In 1725 LYNE commanded his own pirate vessel with some of SPRIGGS' ex-crewmen. He was eventually captured in Oct 1725 by 2 sloops from Curacao. LYNE and 18 of his crewmen were tried and hanged at Curacao.

McCAFFREY

Darby McCAFFREY. He sailed with William LEWIS from Boston on Captain BANISTER's vessel, when they were both 11 year old boys. McCAFFREY was known as a good ballad singer, a useful and well-appreciated pirate art. He was captured with LEWIS by Spanish pirates and put ashore in Havana. As 16 year-olds, both McCAFFREY and LEWIS went pirating, with great cruelty and success. He was held by the authorities in Trinity Harbour, but LEWIS threatened dreadful reprisals if he was harmed. They released McCAFFREY. He was a constant shipmate and lieutenant to LEWIS, but his end is not known to me.

McCAWLEY

Daniel McCAWLEY. b. Ireland. He was a crewman to Captain John SMITH. When SMITH took over the galley *George* on 7 Nov 1724, it was McCAWLEY who cut the throat of the ship's clerk. He sailed with SMITH to the Orkneys, where they were captured. McCAWLEY was taken to London where he was tried for piracy. He was hanged at Execution Dock on 11 Jun 1725.

McDONALD

Edward McDONALD. A crewman to Captain George LOWTHER on *Ranger*. He was captured with most of *Ranger's* crew at Blanquilla in Oct 1723 by the sloop *HMS Eagle*. McDONALD was tried at St Christopher (St Kitts) on 11 Mar 1724. He was found guilty and hanged.

McKINLEY

Peter McKINLEY. b. Ireland. McKINLEY was the Bosun of a merchant ship *Earl of Sandwich* on passage from the Canaries to England, late in the year of 1765. Three passengers were aboard Captain COCKERAN's ship, they were a Captain GLASS and his family. McKINLEY and 4 other mutineers murdered COCKERAN and the whole GLASS family. They also murdered all the crew, except two cabin-boys. They arrived off Ross, Ireland, on 3 Dec 1765 and loaded the ship's longboat with over 2 tons of gold dollars in sacks which was part of the ship's cargo. They rowed ashore, having murdered the two cabin-boys, and buried all the gold except what they could carry. They scuttled the *Earl of Sandwich*, but she didn't sink. The local Irish people realised what had happened and alerted the authorities. Three of the mutineers were taken in the Black Bull Inn, Thomas Street, Dublin. McKINLEY and another were captured on the road to Cork. All five were hanged in chains on the beach near Dublin on 19 Dec 1765.

MACARTY

Dennis MACARTY. He was one of the pirates who surrendered to Woodes ROGERS' pardon in Providence, Bahamas in 1718. Later he joined Captain Calico Jack RACKHAM. MACARTY was captured with RACKHAM off Jamaica in 1720. He was tried and found guilty in Jamaica. As he was about to be hanged he said, "Some of my friends has said I should die in my shoes. To make 'em liars, I kicks them off." He did, and was hanged.

MACKCONACHY

? MACKCONACHY. A crewman to Captain Samuel BELLAMY. He was arrested as one of the survivors of the wreck of BELLAMY's ship *Whydah* on Cape Cod. MACKCONACHY was released before the other survivors were taken to Boston for trial. He must have convinced the authorities of his innocence.

MACKET

Captain ? MACKET. A Caribbean buccaneer captain. MACKET joined the vessels that were assembling for Captain Bartholomew SHARP's expedition to plunder the Pacific in 1680. He was there with his ship of 14 tons and 20 men. Nothing seems to have been written of him after the fleet assembled at Negril Bay, Jamaica. I doubt that he sailed with them.

MACKINTOSH

William MACKINTOSH. b. Canterbury, Kent. 1701. He joined Captain James SKYRM's vessel *Ranger* in Jul 1720. Captured off the West African coast on 1 Feb 1722 by *HMS Swallow*. MACKINTOSH was tried at Cape Corso Castle on 28 Mar 1722. He was found guilty of piracy and hanged.

MADDER

? MADDER. A crewman to Captain Thomas GREEN on the vessel *Worcester*. MADDER and the rest of the crew were unjustly tried, sentenced and hanged at Leith, Scotland on 11 Apr 1705.

MAER

Michael MAER. b. Ghent, Flanders. 1680/1. MAER sailed in the pirate vessel *Rover* for 5 years before joining Captain Bartholomew ROBERTS' ship *Royal Fortune*. Captured off the coast of West Africa by *HMS Swallow* on 10 Feb 1722. MAER was one of those who plotted to take over *HMS Swallow* en route for Cape Corso Castle where they were tried. At his trial on 28 Mar 1722 he was found guilty and sentenced to death. I have found no record of his hanging. He may have died while awaiting sentence, some did.

MAGNUS

William MAGNUS. b. Mine head, Somerset. 1686/7. A crewman to Captain Bartholomew ROBERTS on *Royal Fortune.* Captured by *HMS Swallow* off the West African coast on 10 Feb 1722. MAGNUS was tried at Cape Corso Castle on 28 Mar 1722. The evidence against him was that he was 'outrageous and emulous in mischief'. He was found guilty and hanged.

MAIN

William MAIN. Bosun to Captain James SKYRM on *Ranger.* MAIN left a brig commanded by a Captain PEET on 6 Jan 1721 to join SKYRM. Captured by *HMS Swallow* off the coast of West Africa. He was severely burned when one of the pirates fired his pistol into a bucket of powder in an attempt to blow up the *Ranger* to avoid its capture. MAIN was tried at Cape Corso Castle on 28 Mar 1722 and found guilty. He was sentenced to death, but no record of his hanging was found. He probably died of his wounds while awaiting sentence.

MAINTENON

Marquis de MAINTENON. A French Filibuster. He arrived in the West Indies in 1676. In 1678 he commanded the frigate *La Soriere*, and cruised off the Spanish Main in company with other Tortuga filibusters. They plundered the Isle of Margarita and also Trinidad, but took little plunder. The fleet was eventually scattered.

MAINWARING

Vice Admiral Sir Henry MAINWARING. b. 1587. The grandson of a Vice-Admiral of Sussex. Awarded a BA at Brasenose College, Oxford in 1602. MAINWARING had a successful military career and was at the siege of Juliens in 1610. In 1611 he was proposed as the Captain of St Andrew's Castle. A year later he bought *Resistance* and sailed, initially as a privateer. He seems to have turned to piracy in the West Indies. He took the *Golden Lion* of Lubeck, and in Aug 1613 the *Gift* of Calais. In Jun 1614 he was on the Newfoundland Banks and took 400 crewmen. He stayed and robbed fishermen until Sep 1614. On Midsummer's Day 1615 he fought a battle with 5 Spanish men-of-war. MAINWARING accepted a pardon in England in 1616. He became Lieutenant of Dover Castle. He was knighted in 1618. He became a Member of Parliament and later one of the Commissioners for the Navy. He died in 1653.

MAIZE

Captain William MAIZE. (See MAZE).

MANQUINAM

Peter MANQUINAM. Hanged at Execution Dock, Wapping, on 23 May 1701. MANQUINAM and John DUBOIS were hanged at the same ceremony as Captain KIDD, but were not part of the same prosecution.

MANSFIELD (or more probably MANSVELDT)

Captain Edward MANSFIELD. A Dutchman. He was a trader, smuggler, privateer and pirate in the Caribbean in the 1650s/60s. MANSFIELD sailed with MYNG and Henry MORGAN against San Francisco de Campeche in 1663.

MANSFIELD

John MANSFIELD. b. Bristol, 1692/3. A crewman to Captain Bartholomew ROBERTS on *Royal Fortune*. Captured by *HMS Swallow* off the West African coast on 10 Feb 1722. MANSFIELD was tried at Cape Corso Castle on 28 Mar 1722. The evidence against him was that he had deserted from the man-of-war *Rose* and had joined the pirates voluntarily, for 'drink rather than gold'. MANSFIELD was so drunk at the time of his capture that he woke hours afterwards shouting "Who shall board the prize?". It took some time to explain to him what had happened. He was found guilty and hanged on 2 Apr 1722.

MARKCOS

Jacobus MARKCOS. A Dutch-born buccaneer who sailed with Captain Bartolomew SHARP's expedition to the Pacific in 1680. SHARP's journal accuses MARKCOS of deserting the buccaneers at the Island of Cavallo on 27 Apr 1681. This was when the expedition was on its way home after almost a year in the Pacific.

MARSHALL

Joseph MARSHALL. A reluctant crewman to Captain William FRY. MARSHALL was taken from the prize vessel *James*. He was captured with FRY and tried at Boston on 4 Jul 1726. He was found not guilty of piracy and acquitted.

MARTEEN

Captain David MARTEEN. A buccaneer, probably a Dutchman. He was based in Jamaica in 1665. This is almost certainly the David MARTIEN below, but from a different source.

MARTEL

Captain John MARTEL. He served in Jamaica, probably as a Militiaman. In Sep 1716 MARTEL began a cruise of the Caribbean in a sloop of 8 guns and 80 men. He took two small vessels then sailed to Calbanas, Cuba, where he took a galley with 20 guns. MARTEL transferred command to the galley and continued his successful cruise for several months. He collected a fleet of 9 vessels, then found a small harbour on the island of St Croix to refit and rest. They were discovered by **HMS Scarborough**, which bombarded them from seaward for several days. MARTEL left his vessel with 20 slaves aboard (all of whom burned to death) and took to the woods with his crew. Neither MARTEL nor his crew were heard of again. Some accounts say that MARTEL had already been deposed for his extreme cruelty, and that an Irishman, KENNEDY had been voted to command in his place.

MARTIEN

Captain David MARTIEN. A Dutch privateer who sailed out of Jamaica with Henry MORGAN's expedition against Villahermosa de Tobasco in February 1663. The expedition went on to sail the coast of the Spanish Main for 7 months, sailing 3000 miles, plundering many settlements and attacking 5 towns. When the expedition returned to Jamaica MARTIEN sailed on to Tortuga on hearing the news that England and the Dutch were at war again.

MARTIN

John MARTIN. A crewman to BLACKBEARD. MARTIN was

wounded and captured in the battle at Ocracoke Inlet on 1 Dec 1718. He was tried and hanged.

MASSEY

Captain (British Army) John MASSEY. MASSEY sailed to Gambia with a small body of troops to reinforce the Colony. He found the Governor ill and being dictated to by a group of local merchants. He resolved to bring the Governor back to England. (See Captain George LOWTHER). MASSEY became a pirate on LOWTHER's vessel, taking 20 soldiers with him. They left Gambia on 13 Jun 1721. MASSEY was never happy at sea and wished to go ashore in the West Indies and capture French settlements. A dispute grew between LOWTHER and MASSEY. Finally MASSEY left with some of the men in a prize sloop. He sailed to Jamaica where he petitioned the Governor for a pardon. The Governor gave him a passage to London. In London MASSEY wrote a sort of confession to the Governor and Directors of the Royal African Company.

He then reported to the Lord Chief Justice's office and asked if there was a warrant for his arrest. There wasn't, so he gave his address in Aldgate Street, in case they should issue one. A warrant was eventually issued and MASSEY was committed to Newgate Prison. He was tried on 5 Jul 1723 and found guilty of piracy. He was hanged 3 weeks later at Execution Dock, Wapping. MASSEY had requested that he might be shot instead.

MAY

William MAY. Taken from the prize vessel *Elizabeth* in Jan 1722 by Captain Bartholomew ROBERTS ship *Royal Fortune*. Captured by *HMS Swallow* of the West African coast on 10 Feb 1722. Tried at Cape Corso Castle on 28 Mar 1722. MAY was found not guilty of piracy and acquitted.

MAYES

Captain William MAYES. The son of a tavern-keeper in Rhode Island. MAYES fitted out a ship and went plundering in the Indian Ocean.

Note: This pirate captain may well be the William MAZE below, I think.

MAZE

Captain William MAZE. A notorious pirate who was mentioned in the Royal Warrant issued to Captain William KIDD, to go and apprehend certain 'wicked and ill-disposed persons'. He arrived in New York in 1699, in a large vessel loaded with plunder from the Red Sea.

MEAD

William MEAD. MEAD joined Captain Bartholomew ROBERTS' ship *Royal Fortune* from the prize vessel *Jeremiah and Anne* in Apr 1721. Captured off the West African coast by *HMS Swallow* on 10 Feb 1722. MEAD was probably already a Royal Navy deserter because he was transferred to the Marshalsea Gaol for trial in London. The outcome of the trial is not known.

MEGHLYM

Hans Van MEGHLYN (or Van Mechelen). A pirate from Antwerp. His 45 ton ship was painted black with pitch. He had a crew of 30 men and cruised the mouth of the River Thames in 1539, preying on shipping entering and leaving the Port of London.

MELVIN

William MELVIN. b. Scotland. A crewman to Captain John SMITH. When they took over the galley *George* on 3 Nov 1724, MELVIN and RAWLINSON cut the throat of the Captain. MELVIN sailed on with SMITH to the Orkneys and was captured there. He was tried in London and hanged at Execution Dock, Wapping on 11 Jun 1725.

MENDOZA

Antonio MENDOZA. A Spanish sailor from San Domingo.

MENDOZA seems to have been the victim of circumstance. A tavern owner and one of his English customers on St Kitts, on 11 Apr 1701, swore that MENDOZA had issued forth horrible curses and threatened everyone, including the King. They also swore that he was a bloodthirsty pirate. MENDOZA was tried and found guilty. His ears were cut off, his tongue burned through with a red-hot iron and he was thrown into a dungeon.

MENZIES

Hugh MENZIES. He was taken from the prize galley *Samuel* by Captain Bartholomew ROBERTS' ship *Royal Fortune* in Jul 1720. Captured off the West African coast by *HMS Swallow* on 10 Feb 1722. He was tried at Cape Corso Castle on 28 Mar 1722. MENZIES was found not guilty of piracy and acquitted.

MERRITT

Nicholas MERRITT, of Marblehead. A reluctant crewman to Captain Edward LOW. MERRITT was taken with 5 others from a fishing schooner. Some time later, MERRITT and a group of other captives escaped from LOW in a captured trading vessel. They called at the Azores, where some of the group were captured. MERRITT escaped again and got back to Marblehead.

MEYEURS

? MEYEURS. An Indian Ocean pirate. He was a crewman to Captain David WILLIAMS. He was killed in a raid against an Arab settlement in Bayu.

MICHAEL

Captain ? MICHAEL. An English pirate captain in the early 17th century. MICHAEL and his crew met up with the successful pirate Captain John WARD in the port of Sallee, Morocco, in 1604. MICHAEL, his first mate Anthony JOHNSON and all their crew joined WARD's fleet with their vessel. MICHAEL soon had enough of pirate life and returned to England. His command passed to Anthony JOHNSON.

MICHEL LE BASQUE

Captain ? MICHEL LE BASQUE. A French Filibuster who sailed in company with L'OLLONAIS and 650 other filibusters. They took the town of Maracaibo in 1667. He was a very successful, but quite ruthless man.

MIGUEL

Captain Don MIGUEL. In 1830 MIGUEL commanded a small group of pirate vessels off the Azores. After seizing a small Sardinian brig off St Michael's, he was captured by a British frigate.

MIGUEL

Francesco MIGUEL. He was hanged for piracy at Kingston, Jamaica, in 1823.

MILLER

John MILLER. A Yorkshireman. MILLER was a crewman on Captain John QUELCH's vessel *Charles*. He was captured, sentenced and hanged with QUELCH at Boston on 30 Jun 1704.

MILLER

Thomas MILLER. Quartermaster to BLACKBEARD. MILLER died alongside BLACKBEARD in the battle at Ocracoke Inlet on 1 Dec 1718.

MILLINGTON

Captain ? MILLINGTON. An English pirate captain in the early 17th century. MILLINGTON cruised in company with Captain WALKER and Captain William BAUGHE. He is known to have given BAUGHE one third of his plunder. This may have been a joint agreement between the three Captains.

MISNIL

Sieur De MISNIL. A French Filibuster. He commanded *La Trompeuse* (yes, another one) of 14 guns and 100 men.

MISSON

Captain ? MISSON. b. Provence, France. MISSON served as an officer aboard a French man-of-war in the Mediterranean, taking Turkish and English vessels. On a trip to Rome, he met CARACCIOLI, a priest who sailed with MISSON from then onwards. MISSON sailed to the West Indies as Mate on the man-of-war *Victoire*. *Victoire* engaged *HMS Winchelsea* in battle off Antigua. Most of the officers on *Victoire* were killed and *HMS Winchelsea* blew up and sank. MISSON took command and talked his men into a sort of commonwealth idea. They took vessels in the Windward Islands, then sailed to Porto Bello and Boca Checa, where they sold their plunder and restocked the ship. After taking further vessels in the West Indies they sailed for West Africa. He took a slaver off the coast and invited the slaves to join his crew, then lectured the crew on the evils of slavery. They careened the ship in the River Lagoa and rebuilt much of it. MISSON took an English vessel at Table Bay, Cape of Good Hope. The crew of the captured vessel (officers excepted) wished to join him, so he now had two vessels. In the Indian Ocean they saved the Queen Regent of the Island of Johanna and her brother from a sinking vessel and returned them to their home, thereby winning valuable friends ashore. Involvement in local politics followed and MISSON and CARACCIOLI were both injured in a fight with a local tribe. They sailed for Zanzibar where they engaged a Portugese ship and CARACCIOLI lost a leg. While CARACCIOLI recovered, MISSON found a place north of Diego Suares where he decided to build a fortified town. They called the town Libertalia and attempted to build a society based on socialist principles. When the town became encumbered by prisoners MISSON released them, giving them cash compensation and a vessel to leave in, if they wished to do so. In the Arabian Sea he took a vessel bound for Jedda with 1600 pilgrims. He took 100 girls for his town of Libertalia and released the others. A Portugese fleet attacked the town but was driven off with much loss of life on both sides. The pirate Captain Thomas TEW joined MISSON. CARACCIOLI was killed in the fighting. TEW and MISSON decided that the town was no longer viable and they split a vast fortune between them and sailed for America in two vessels. MISSON's vessel sank in a storm off southern Africa, within sight of TEW.

MITCHEL

Alexander MITCHEL. A crewman to Captain William FLY on the pirate ship *Elizabeth*. MITCHEL left FLY's ship at Brown's Bank and was never heard of again. At the trial of FLY's crew in Jul 1726, all the blame for piracy was heaped on his head, understandably, because he was absent.

MITCHEL

John MITCHEL. b. Shadwell, London. MITCHEL joined Captain James SKYRM's vessel *Ranger* from the prize galley *Norman* in Oct 1720. Captured by *HMS Swallow* off the West Coast of Africa on 1 Feb 1722. He was tried at Cape Corso Castle on 28 Mar 1722 and found guilty. MITCHEL was sentenced to death, but his sentence was commuted to 7 years' transportation to the African Colonies.

MITCHELL

Captain ? MITCHELL. An English buccaneer. In the year 1663 MITCHELL was the most successful buccaneer based in Jamaica.

MITTON

Thomas MITTON. A crewman to Captain Thomas WARD for a period of 3 years in the early 17th century. MITTON worked with WARD from the port of Tunis. It was MITTON's opinion that CARA OSMAN, the Dey of Tunis, got very much the better part of the deal in disposing of WARD's plunder for him.

MONTBARS

Captain ? MONTBARS (The Exterminator). A filibuster from Languedoc, France. In his youth, MONTBARS read a book about the cruelty of the Spanish towards the natives of the Americas. This inspired a hatred of the Spanish which he maintained throughout his life as a filibuster. MONTBARS' cruelty to Spanish prisoners earned him the nickname 'The Exterminator' amongst all the Spanish Caribbean community. MONTBARS' chosen method of torture was to open his victim's belly, extract one end of his intestine, and nail it to a mast. A blazing torch applied to the victim's bottom made the poor man dance to his death around the mast. He based himself at St Bartholomew, Virgin Islands, and brought all his plunder and prisoners there to be sold.

MONTENEGRO

Juan MONTENEGRO. A Colombian. MONTENEGRO was one of Captain GILBERT's crew on the pirate schooner *Panda*. He was tried and hanged at Boston in 1835.

MONTGOMERY

Robert MONTGOMERY. One of the buccaneers on Captain Bartholomew SHARP's expedition to plunder the Pacific coasts of America. MONTGOMERY was badly injured on 25 Aug 1680 at the Galapagos Island when the buccaneers captured a Spanish vessel which had been sent to capture them. The Spanish vessel was commanded by Don Thomas ORGUNDONNUY, who admitted that he had captured and killed other members of their expedition. MONTGOMERY died of his wounds on 8 Sep 1680.

MOODY

Christopher MOODY. b. 1693/4. MOODY was already an experienced pirate when he served under Captain Howard DAVIS in 1718. He was captured on Captain Bartholomew ROBERTS' vessel *Royal Fortune* off the West African coast on 10 Feb 1722. *HMS Swallow*, the man-of-war that took *Royal Fortune* took all the pirates to Cape Corso Castle for trial. MOODY was found guilty of piracy and hanged.

MOODY

Captain William MOODY. b. London. In 1718 MOODY (according to one, John BROWN) captured a brigantine which was at anchor in the Bay of Caroline. BROWN said that MOODY commanded a vessel called *Rising Sun* which mounted 35 guns and shipped a crew of 130 pirates.

MOON

Edward MOON. b. Ireland. MOON was an ex-privateer who

became a crewman to Captain Samuel BELLAMY on *Whydah*. MOON is believed to have drowned on the night, in 1717, when *Whydah* was wrecked on Cape Cod.

MOONE

Captain Thomas MOONE. Ship's carpenter on Sir Francis DRAKE's *Swan*. On 14 Aug 1572 DRAKE secretly asked MOONE to bore holes in *Swan's* bottom to sink her. MOONE objected because she was a good, new ship. DRAKE convinced him that for success against the Spanish on the coast of Panama, the men must transfer from warships to pinnaces. DRAKE knew that his brother John, who commanded *Swan* would never willingly have left her. MOONE scuttled the ship and the plan succeeded enormously well. On DRAKE's circumnavigation, which began in 1577, MOONE started in command of the 15 ton *Benedict*. Off the coast of Morocco DRAKE captured a Portugese ship and gave the Portugese the *Benedict* to sail home in. MOONE seems to have joined DRAKE on *Pelican* (later the *Golden Hind*). On 5 Dec 1578, in the raid on Valparaiso, MOONE captured a Spanish vessel with only a boat's crew, while DRAKE took the town. He sailed on with DRAKE, around the world and back into Plymouth. In 1585 MOONE sailed again with

DRAKE as captain of *Francis*, in the biggest fleet that had ever sailed against the Spanish Caribbean. He died the next year in an ambush near Cartagena.

MOORE

William MOORE. The Chief Gunner to Captain William KIDD. MOORE made mutinous threats against KIDD on 30 Oct 1696. KIDD threw an iron-bound bucket at him, striking him on the head and breaking his skull. MOORE died and the mutiny was over.

MORE

Joseph MORE. b. Mere, Wiltshire. 1702/3. MORE joined Captain Bartholomew ROBERTS' vessel *Royal Fortune* from the prize sloop *Mayflower* in Feb 1720. Captured off the West Coast of Africa on 10 Feb 1722. He was tried at Cape Corso Castle on 28 Mar 1722, found guilty of piracy and hanged.

MORGAN

Captain ? MORGAN. Not to be confused with Sir Henry MORGAN. Little is known of this Captain MORGAN, other than that he was with HAMLIN on *La Trompeuse* off the coast of West Africa in 1683. He later fell out with the French pirates and left, taking all the English with him in a prize vessel.

MORGAN

Captain ? MORGAN. Another not to confuse with Sir Henry MORGAN. This one was a Welsh pirate in the 17th century. He was a lieutenant to Captain Robert NUTT until NUTT's retirement in 1637. MORGAN then took command of the vessel and continued to plunder shipping off North Wales and in the Irish Sea. MORGAN based himself at Pwllheli, Wales.

MORGAN

Lieutenant Colonel Sir Henry MORGAN, Deputy Governor of Jamaica. Sir Henry was born in Llanrumney, South Wales of a well-to-do farming family. His uncles had served with distinction on both sides in the Civil War. Young Henry followed his uncle, Col Edward MORGAN, to Jamaica, where the family were already plantation owners. Always a charismatic figure and an inspiring talker, Henry soon rose to prominence in the island's Militia, and in local government. When danger of Spanish invasion threatened the island, MORGAN would raise vast hordes of buccaneers and make pre-emptive strikes against Spanish territory and shipping. Jamaica's successive Governors were in a bit of a cleft stick; they welcomed the gold and goods that the buccaneers brought, and they appreciated the peace and prosperity that secure defence provided, but MORGAN was a growing embarrassment in political terms. Finally MORGAN was arrested and shipped to England. He charmed the King and returned to Jamaica as a knight and Deputy Governor. In his later years he devoted more of his time to food, drink, and the expansion of his large estates. His property was left to the sons of his sisters, on the condition that they change their names to MORGAN. It is suggested that he cheated his fellow buccaneers of the fair shares of the plunder, but I doubt that he could have done this and survived. He was also accused of leaving men behind on some of his expeditions. Well, that was fairly common amongst 'the brethren of the coasts'. They were not regular military forces and 'every man for himself' was the order of the day. MORGAN died on 25 Aug 1688, mostly from drink I believe. I strongly recommend Dudley Pope's biography to those who wish to know more about this fascinating and complex Welshman.

MORRICE

Humphrey MORRICE. Of Providence, Bahamas. MORRICE was a pirate who had not accepted Woodes ROGERS' offer of pardon in 1718. He was hanged later that year by his ex-comrades at Providence. From the gallows, he berated them for not rescuing him.

MORRIS

Captain John MORRIS. A Jamaican privateer with MYNGS and MORGAN until 1665, when he became a buccaneer with MANSFIELD. They sacked Vildemo in the Bay of Campeachy, then Truzillo, and later Granada, Nicaragua in Mar 1666.

MORRIS

John MORRIS. A crewman to Captain James SKYRM on *Ranger*. On 1 Feb 1722, when the pirate ship was being captured by *HMS Swallow*, MORRIS fired his pistol into a powder container in an attempt to blow up the ship. He only succeeded in killing himself and badly burning some other pirates.

MORRIS

Captain Thomas MORRIS. One of those who surrendered to Woodes ROGERS' offer of pardon in Providence in 1718. He turned pirate again with Captain John AUGER and was captured when AUGER's sloop ran aground on Long Island W.I. At his hanging he was asked if he wished to repent, he replied, "Yes. I repent that I had not done more mischief, and that we did not cut the throats of them that took us, and I am extremely sorry that you ain't hanged as well as we." He was aged 22 when he was hanged

MORRISON

Captain ? MORRISON. A Scottish pirate captain who lived on Prince Edward Island. See Captain NELSON.

MORRISON

William MORRISON. Of Jamaica. He was a crewman to Major Stede BONNET. MORRISON was captured with BONNET at Cape Fear River on 27 Sep 1718. He was tried in Charleston and hanged on 8 Nov 1718.

MORTON

Israel MORTON. Quartermaster to Major Stede BONNET. Nothing more known.

MORTON

Philip MORTON. Gunner to BLACKBEARD. MORTON died with BLACKBEARD at the battle at Ocracoke Inlet on 1 Dec 1718.

MORWELL

Samuel MORWELL. He was taken from the prize vessel *Porcupine* in Whydah Roads by Captain Bartholomew ROBERTS' ship *Royal Fortune*. Captured by *HMS Swallow* off the West African coast on 10 Feb 1722. MORWELL was found not guilty of piracy and acquitted.

MUDD

John MUDD. A reluctant crewman and carpenter to Captain Charles HARRIS. MUDD gave evidence against HARRIS's crew at their trial at Newport R.I. on 10 Jul 1723.

MULLET

James MULLET (known as Millet). b. London. A crewman to Major Stede BONNET. He was captured with BONNET on 27 Sep 1718 at Cape Fear River. MULLET was tried at Charleston and hanged on 8 Nov 1718.

MULLINS

Darby MULLINS. A crewman to Captain William KIDD. MULLINS surrendered to pardon at New York, but found that it did not extend to KIDD and his crew. He was shipped to London for trial. His defence was that as a common seaman he had to do what his captain ordered for fear of punishment. The prosecution said that may be so, but he was not forced to take a share of the plunder for fear of punishment. He was found guilty at the Old Bailey in May 1701. MULLINS was hanged at Execution Dock, Wapping, on 23 May 1701, at the same time as Captain KIDD.

MUMPER (or MUMFORD)

Thomas MUMPER. b. Martha's Vineyard. MUMPER was a native American, rare for a pirate, I think. He was a crewman on Captain Charles Harris' *Ranger*. Captured by *HMS Greyhound*. He was tried at Newport R.I. in Jul 1723. MUMPER was found not guilty and acquitted.

MUNDON

Stephen MUNDON. b. London. 1702/3. He was a crewman to Captain Charles HARRIS on *Ranger*. Captured by *HMS Greyhound*. He was tried at Newport R.I. MUNDON was found guilty of piracy and hanged.

MUNRO

Captain ? MUNRO. He was the first of the Jamaica privateers to turn pirate and take English ships. MUNRO and his crew were hanged at Gallows Point, Port Royal, Jamaica, on gallows that were newly built for them.

MURPHY

? MURPHY. A carpenter on the galley *George* which was taken by Captain John SMITH on 3 Nov 1724. MURPHY escaped to the mainland of Scotland from the Orkneys and alerted the magistrates, who captured SMITH and his crew.

MURPHY

John MURPHY. An Irish soldier of fortune in Cuba, probably an ex-buccaneer. MURPHY served the Spanish for a long time and rose to become second-in-command of the Militia in Santo Domingo. In December 1653 this Militia mounted an expedition to expel the French buccaneers from the island base of Tortuga. After losing several of their ships on the way, the Spanish took the island in February 1654, capturing over 500 people, 330 of them buccaneers. MURPHY was left in command of the Spanish garrison on the island but was later relieved by a Spanish officer because they were not too sure of his loyalty.

MURRIN

Billy Murrin. Legend in Newfoundland says that an old crewman of Captain KIDD, Billy MURRIN came to spend his last two years in Ladle Cove. The family looked after his every need, expecting to hear the location of KIDD's treasure from him. In his dying minutes, MURRIN called out and the daughter of the house came to his bedside. "Can you keep a secret?" He asked. She nodded. "So can I." He whispered, and died.

MUSTAPHA

A Turkish pirate who sailed with 140 vessels to Minorca in 1558. They besieged the town of Cuidadda, which surrendered. They then slew many of the inhabitants and took the rest away as slaves.

MYAGH

Captain ? MYAGH. An English pirate captain in the early 17th century. MYAGH inherited from the pirate Captain PETERS, all his goods, worth over £6,000.

MYNGS

Commodore Christopher MYNGS. b. 1620. A Royal Navy officer, privateer and buccaneer, MYNGS arrived in the Caribbean on the man-of-war *Marston Moor* in January 1656. He joined Vice-Admiral William GOODSON on several sorties against the Spanish Main. Back in Dover in 1657, MYNGS married, then sailed for the New World again in December. Now the senior British naval officer in the West Indies he repelled an attempted Spanish invasion of Jamaica, then led a revenge assault against Santa Marta and Tolu, returning to Jamaica six weeks later with three Spanish prize vessels. Each prize vessel was bought by men who later became successful buccaneers, Robert SEARLE, Laurens PRINS and John MORRIS. MYNGS sailed again with a host of buccaneers, this time taking Cumana, Puerto Cabello and Coro. He appears to have allowed the buccaneers to do some looting of the captured treasure, because on his return to Jamaica Governor D'OYLEY suspended him and ordered him to England to stand trial for defrauding the state. MYNGS arrived in

England in 1660 to find the country celebrating the restoration of the monarchy. Charges against him were dropped and he was ordered back to the Caribbean. MYNGS sailed again from Jamaica on 1 Oct 1662 with a huge fleet of buccaneers and took Santiago de Cuba on 16 Oct. During his absence from Jamaica he was elected to the governing council of the island. In January 1663 he led an attack on Campeche and was wounded in the face and both thighs. By July that year he had still not properly recovered his health and he sailed to England to do so.

NAU

Captain Jean David NAU (alias L'OLLONAIS). b. Les Sables D'Ollone, France. A French Filibuster. L'OLLONAIS was transported to Dominica as an indentured servant (slave). After completing the term of his service he became a buccaneer on the coasts of Hispaniola. L'OLLONAIS first sailed as a common seaman, but he proved so good that the Governor of Tortuga gave him a ship to command. He took many ships and built up a large crew, but was shipwrecked near Campeachy (Campeche). All of his crew were killed and NAU only survived by pretending to be dead. He escaped with some French slaves and made his was back to Tortuga. There he joined up with MICHEL LE BASQUE and they raided Venezuela, taking 260,000 pieces-of-eight, plate, silver and jewels. By this time L'OLLONAIS was the most famous of the 'Brethren of the Coasts'. He raided Nicaragua with atrocious cruelty, once cutting out a prisoner's still-beating heart and chewing it, to make other prisoners tell where their treasure was hidden. Many of his crew left him and sailed with his second-in- command, Moses Van VIN. L'OLLONAIS' ship was once again wrecked, this time on the coast of Honduras. It took his crew 6 months to build a boat to leave, and half the crew had to be left behind.

L'OLLONAIS was caught by Indians near Cartagena, he was torn apart by them.

NEAL

? NEAL. b. Cork, Ireland. NEAL was a crewman to Captain Philip ROCHE. I have no further information of NEAL after ROCHE left the vessel.

NEFF

William NEFF. b. Havermill, Mass. 1667. NEFF was a soldier. He was one of the guard at Fort Loyal, Falmouth, Maine, who deserted to join Captain Thomas POUND's crew.

NELLEY

James NELLEY. A crewman to Captain Francis SPRIGGS. NELLEY must have been a nuisance to SPRIGGS because he was marooned with several reluctant crewmen on the island of Roatan on 4 Apr 1724. They were picked up a few days later by a vessel that took them to Jamaica.

NELSON

Captain ? NELSON. b. Prince Edward Island. NELSON was a wealthy man, a Member of the Council and a Colonel of Militia. He bought a schooner to transport and sell his farm produce in Halifax, then lost his military commission after drunken antics in the town. He then left his wife to run the farm and, with MORRISON, bought a ship of 10 guns. With a crew of 90 men, they took a merchant ship and sold it in New York. Cruising the West Indies, they took several English and Dutch ships. On St Kitts they raided plantations, murdering owners and slaves. Later they cruised the coast of Brazil. After 3 years NELSON had accrued a fortune of £150,000, MORRISON (being a Scot) had even more. On returning north their ship was wrecked near Prince Edward Island and MORRISON and most of the crew were drowned. NELSON got home safely and lived out his life in peace and luxury.

NEWMAN

Captain John NEWMAN. b. Poole, Dorset. NEWMAN commanded the bark *Mary of Poole* in the late 16th century and was a minor pirate. He was once robbed at sea by the much more exotic pirate Captain Stephen HEYNES. NEWMAN was outraged that a foreigner (not Dorset bred) could deal in such a way with a local man. NEWMAN was with Captain Clinton ATKINSON when he cut down the body of the hanged pirate Captain John PIERS. PIERS was one of the few pirates not to be hanged at Execution Dock in London. He was hanged on the shoreline at Studland Bay, Dorset, in an attempt to discourage other local pirates.

NICHOLAS

Thomas NICHOLAS. b. London. A crewman to Major Stede BONNET. Captured with BONNET on 27 Sep 1718 at Cape Fear River. NICHOLAS was tried at Charleston and found got guilty of piracy because he had not yet received a share of the plunder.

NOEL

See Captain Jacob NOWELL.

NOLAND

Captain Richard NOLAND. He commanded the galley *Anne* which sailed with Captain Samuel Bellamy's fleet of pirates off the Eastern Seaboard of North America.

NONDRE

Pedro NONDRE. He was hanged for piracy at Kingston, Jamaica, in Feb 1823. It was noticed by the crowd at his execution that he was covered with deep wounds, perhaps incurred during his arrest, though I have read nothing of that. NONDRE was immensely heavy and at the first attempt to hang him the rope broke. They succeeded at the second try.

NORMAN

Captain ? NORMAN. One of Henry MORGAN's buccaneer captains on his expedition to the Isthmus of Darien in 1670. After the buccaneers took Chagres, MORGAN left Captain NORMAN and 500 men to hold the town for their return. NORMAN sent two boats out plundering. The boats met a Spanish vessel which fled into the Chagres River where NORMAN was waiting. The provisions on the ship were vital to the survival of the buccaneers in the town.

NORMAN

John NORMAN. An English pirate in the early 17th century. He was a crewman to Captain Robert NUTT, and later to Captain ? MORGAN.

NORTH

Captain Nathaniel NORTH. b. Bermuda. NORTH was the son of a sawyer. He sailed at the age of 17, out of Bermuda, then out of Jamaica. He was a crewman for a while on a man-of-war, but left it when it was ordered to England. He feared the cold climate. NORTH was a strong swimmer (rare in those days, it saved him twice and enabled him to leave the man-of-war) he was a capable seaman, well-liked by his shipmates and captain, and very brave. He seems to have been happy as a crewman, with no ambition to command. NORTH was shipwrecked on Madagascar and picked up by the pirate Captain SHIVERS who made him Quartermaster. He sailed with many of the Madagascar pirates and was well-liked by all of them, and by the local rulers along the coast. NORTH acquired some local wives and got many children. He had an estate with much farmland and was said to have been an honest and able merchant when he wasn't pirating. His good nature enabled him to settle many pirate and native disputes. His contemporaries regarded him as a good man in a crisis, a sound judge, and a man of his word. He died trying to put down a rebellion in Madagascar and was mourned by all who knew him. I have no firm dates for his birth or death, but 1690's in Madagascar would be about right.

NORTON

George NORTON. A crewman to Captain John QUELCH. NORTON was tried for piracy at the Star Tavern in Boston in 1704.

NOSITER

Joseph NOSITER. b. 1695/6. He joined Captain Bartholomew ROBERTS' ship *Royal Fortune* from the prize vessel *Expedition* of Topsham. Captured by *HMS Swallow* off the West African coast on 10 Feb 1722. He was tried at Cape Corso Castle on 28 Mar 1722. He was found guilty and hanged. At his execution he was too overcome to be able to tell his place of birth.

NOTTINGE

Roger NOTTINGE. A London poulterer who went to Ireland to visit his sister in Baltimore. He was invited onto Captain James HARRIS' ship for a drink. He was given far too much to drink and locked in a cabin until they sailed. In the early 17th century it was wise to know who you drank with. No further information.

NOWELL (Probably NOEL)

Captain Jacob NOWELL. In 1700 NOWELL's pirate ship *Neptune* boarded a West Indies sloop off Sestros, West Africa. NOWELL took slaves and other goods from the sloop. According to the authorities ashore there, both vessels were pirate ships.

NUTT

Captain John NUTT. An English pirate captain in the early 17th century. In May 1623 he and his crew took a barque at the entrance to Dungarvan harbour. The dozen or more women aboard were very badly treated.

NUTT

John NUTT. Sailing Master to Captain William Phillips. NUTT sailed with PHILLIPS throughout his West Indies cruise. In April 1724 a group of the captives aboard the vessel got NUTT drunk and threw him overboard. He held on so grimly that they had to chop off his arms with an axe to make him fall into the sea.

NUTT

Captain Robert NUTT. A West Country pirate in the 17 century. In 1631 he and Captain DOWNES were using Helford, Cornwall, as a hideout. They frequented the northwest corner of Wales and the Irish Sea. NUTT continued his piracy until 1633. His lieutenant, MORGAN succeeded him.

OCHALI

A Barbary Corsair. In 1511 OCHALI took a fleet of 22 ships and 1700 men to sack Menorca. They landed at Soller and pillaged the town. The Menorcans, under Miguel ANCELATS, attacked the corsairs rear and routed the whole force, killing 500 of them.

O'DELL

Samuel O'DELL. O'DELL was one of those captured at the battle at Ocracoke Inlet when BLACKBEARD was killed. He claimed to have been captured from a sloop on the night before the battle. Other sources say he was BLACKBEARD's cabinboy. Take your pick.

OGLE

George OGLE. He joined Captain Bartholomew ROBERTS' ship *Royal Fortune* from the prize vessel *Onslow* in May 1721. Captured by *HMS Swallow* off the West African coast on 10 Feb 1722. He was probably a Royal Navy deserter because he was referred to the Marshalea Gaol for trial in London. The outcome of the trial is not known.

OLOARD

Captain Kit OLOARD. An English pirate captain in the early 17th century. He always dressed in black velvet trousers, crimson silk stockings, black felt hat, his white shirt collar was embroidered in black silk. OLOARD was captured when he sailed into the port of Modone, Turkey, with a prize vessel. A local official handed him over to the authorities, he and two other English pirate captains were hanged from the tower of the castle at Zante.

O'MALLEY

Grace O'MALLEY. 1530–1603. b. Connaught, Ireland. Known as GRANUAILLE (the bald one) because her hair was as short as a boy's. Daughter of a local chieftain and ruler of the lands around Clew Bay, Grace was married at 16 to Donal O'FLAHERTY and lived at his castle at Bunowen (about thirty miles away). She had 3 children before he died. Under Irish Law widows had no rights to property, so Grace moved back to her father's home. She took command of her father's fleet of about 20 vessels, engaged in trade, fishing and piracy. Grace seems to have recognised the law when it offered her protection, and flouted it when that was profitable. Several times she engaged the Royal Navy in battle, once driving off a fleet that was sent to apprehend her. At another time she offered her ships and men in support of the Crown. She married again, to Richard BURKE, another local chief, in 1566. In 1577 she was captured and imprisoned at Limerick for 18 months. Her second husband died in 1583, leaving her once more to defend her possessions. Pressure grew from the local Governor and in 1593 she wrote to Queen Elizabeth I, appealing for 'some reasonable maintenance for the little time she had to live'. Her son was arrested and Grace travelled to London for an audience with Queen Elizabeth at Greenwich Palace. As a result of the meeting the Queen ordered Sir Richard BINGHAM to grant her 'some maintenance'. BINGHAM was relieved as Governor by Sir Conyers CLIFFORD in 1597 and things improved for Grace. Her fleet was allowed to sail again. Grace's sons continued their seafaring and one of them, TIBBOT, was created Viscount of MAYO. Grace O'MALLEY died at Rockfield in 1603.

OSBOURNE

William OSBOURNE. A Gunner to Captain Samuel BELLAMY on *Whydah*. OSBOURNE is believed to have drowned on the night, in 1717, when *Whydah* was wrecked on Cape Cod.

OWEN

Captain ? OWEN. An English pirate captain in the early 17th century. He was the brother-in-law of Sir Richard HAWKINS, Vice-Admiral of Devon and son of the Elizabethan sea-dog. OWEN left Plymouth with his ship in 1607 to become a pirate. His career was not long. His crew mutinied and elected another man as Captain.

OWEN

Abel OWEN. A crewman to Captain William KIDD on the galley *Adventure*. OWEN surrendered to pardon at New York with KIDD, but found it did not extend to KIDD and his crew. Shipped to London and tried at the Old Bailey in May 1701. OWEN was found guilty and hanged at Execution Dock, Wapping.

OWEN

Thomas OWEN. b. Bristol. He joined Captain Bartholomew ROBERTS' ship *Royal Fortune* from the prize vessel *York* of Bristol in May 1721. Captured off the West African coast by *HMS Swallow* on 10 Feb 1722. OWEN was tried at Cape Corso Castle. He was found guilty of piracy and sentenced to death, but the sentence was commuted to 7 years' transportation to the African colonies.

OUGHTERLANEY

Thomas OUGHTERLANEY. He joined Captain Bartholomew ROBERTS' ship *Royal Fortune* from the prize galley *Cornwall* at

Calabar in Oct 1721. Captured by *HMS Swallow* of the West African coast on 10 Feb 1722. He was tried at Cape Corso Castle on 28 Mar 1722. The evidence against him from Captain John TRAHERN of *Apollonia* was that ROBERTS put him aboard the *Apollonia* when he captured it, to act as pilot of the prize vessel. OUGHTERLANEY told TRAHERN to steer under the *Royal Fortune's* stern. He also took one of TRAHERN's suits and his new wig. He was found guilty and sentenced to death, the sentence was never carried out. He was shipped back to London 'to await His Majesty's pleasure'. Eventually he was pardoned.

OXENHAM

John OXENHAM. An officer with DRAKE on his 1572 raid on Nombres de Dios. Later, on the same expedition, OXENHAM captured a fast coaster which was used to transport some of their captured treasure back to England. When DRAKE sailed into the Pacific in Sep 1578, OXENHAM had already crossed the Isthmus of Darien on foot and was leading his crew in a captured or built boat. OXENHAM was taken by the Spanish near Panama. In spite of DRAKE's efforts to ransom or exchange him, he was hanged by the Spanish in 1579.

PAIN

Captain ? PAIN. PAIN began as a privateer and then turned pirate. He attacked the town of St Augustine in Florida. After being driven off by the Spanish, he sacked some neighbouring settlements. PAIN became unwelcome in the Bahamas, and later in Rhode Island. He eventually based himself in the Carolinas.

PAINE

Tom PAINE, 1737–1809. Born in Thetford, Norfolk, the son of a Quaker corsetmaker. At the age of 17 PAINE signed on with Captain DEATH on the privateer *Terrible* but his father arrived at the berth at Execution Dock, Wapping and dissuaded him from sailing. Within a month, on 17 Jan 1757, PAINE sailed on the 340 ton privateer *King of Prussia* under Captain Edward MENZIES. During a six-month cruise *King of Prussia* captured several valuable French vessels and PAINE's income for the voyage was probably about 30 pounds. PAINE became history's most influential political writer. His pamphlet 'Common Sense' and subsequent journalism encouraged and influenced the American War of Independence, the Declaration of Independence and the format of the US Government and that nation's constitution. He spent time in France during the French Revolution, was an influential politician there until he was imprisoned. Claiming American citizenship, he was allowed to return to the US. He suggested the Louisiana Purchase as an alternative to war with Napoleon's France. His later works were mostly against formal religions and brought him hatred from many in the new republic, but his earlier works still remain an influence on political thinking. PAINE was undoubtedly the most important political writer of his own or any other age.

PAINTER

Peter PAINTER. An ex-pirate who retired to live in Charleston. PAINTER was recommended for the post of Public Powder Receiver, but was rejected by the Upper House, "Mr Painter having committed piracy, and not having His Majesty's pardon for the same."

PALMER

Benjamin PALMER. A crewman to Captain Calico Jack RACKHAM. He joined RACKHAM's vessel at Negril Point, Jamaica on the day of its capture. Nevertheless he was tried at St Jago de la Vega on 16 Nov 1720. The case against him was adjourned for want of evidence until 24 Jan 1721. No further evidence was found but he was still found guilty and hanged at Kingston on 18 Feb 1721.

PALMER

Joseph PALMER. A crewman to Captain William KIDD on the galley *Adventure*. PALMER deserted from KIDD's vessel at Isle St Marie. He agreed to testify against KIDD at his trial, and in exchange was given immunity from prosecution.

PAR

Benjamin PAR. He was taken from the Prize vessel *Robinson* by Captain Bartholomew ROBERTS' ship *Royal Fortune* in Jan 1722. Captured by *HMS Swallow* off the West African coast on 10 Feb 1722. PAR was tried at Cape Corso Castle on 28 Mar 1722. He was found not guilty of piracy and acquitted.

PARDAL

Captain Manuel Rivero PARDAL. A scourge along the coasts of Jamaica in about 1670. He came ashore and nailed a canvas 'letter' to a tree, in which he listed the crimes that he had committed against the islanders, and those that he planned. This caused much concern and inspired improvements to the militia and island fortifications.

PARKER

Captain William PARKER. An English Buccaneer. Just when the Spanish thought they had made the town of Porto Bello impregnable, by the building of the massive stone fortress of St Jerome, PARKER and 200 buccaneers took the town in a surprise attack. They burned part of the town and made off with great quantities of booty.

PARKER

Captain ? PARKER. An English pirate captain in the early 17th century. He commanded a Flemish-built vessel of 160 tons with 23 guns and a crew of 70 men. They took the prize *Gift of God* in 1611. Thomas HUNT, Master of the prize vessel was charged with betraying his ship to the pirates. He called witnesses to testify how futile it would have been to turn *Gift of God's* three guns against the pirates. PARKER was killed later in 1611, in battle with Dutch pirates at Marmora.

PARKER

John PARKER. b. Winfred, Dorset. 1699/70. PARKER joined Captain Bartholomew ROBERTS' ship *Royal Fortune* from the prize vessel *Willing Mind* of Poole in Jul 1720. Captured by *HMS Swallow* off the West Coast of Africa on 10 Feb 1722. He was tried at Cape Corso Castle on 28 Mar 1722. Found guilty and hanged.

PARKER

Able Seaman PARKER, Royal Navy. b. 1767? PARKER came

of a respectable family joined the navy at the age of 12 and rose to the rank of Acting Lieutenant. He inherited a small estate and left the service. His fortune didn't last him long and soon he was poor. Parker had the ill-luck to be press-ganged and found himself back in the navy. In May 1797 PARKER led a mutiny of the North Sea fleet which was anchored at Sheerness Kent. The mutiny collapsed on 13June 1797. PARKER was taken and charged with piracy and high treason. He was quickly found guilty and hanged from the yard-arm of his ship, HMS Sandwich.

PARKINS

Benjamin PARKINS. A crewman to Captain John QUELCH on the pirate brig *Charles*. He was tried at the Star Tavern, Boston in June 1704.

PARROT

Hugh PARROT. A crewman to Captain William KIDD on the galley *Adventure*. PARROT surrendered to pardon at New York but found that the pardon did not extend to KIDD's crew. He was shipped to London and tried at the Old Bailey in May 1701. PARKER was found guilty and hanged at Execution Dock, Wapping.

PARROT

James PARROT. A crewman to Captain John QUELCH on the pirate brig *Charles*. PARROT was tried at the Star Tavern in Boston in June 1704. PARROT gave evidence against the other crewmen in exchange for a pardon.

PARSONS

John PARSONS. A fisherman who was taken by Captain John PHILLIPS on 5 Sep 1723 and kept as a reluctant crewman. No further information on him after his capture.

PATER

Captain Adriaen Janszoon PATER. A Dutch privateer in the Caribbean. On 16 Feb 1630 PATER seized the port of Santa Marta on the Spanish Main. He held the town for a week, until a ransom of 5,500 reals was paid.

PATERSON

Neal PATERSON. b. Aberdeen, Scotland. A crewman to Major Stede BONNET. He was captured with BONNET on 27 Sep 1718 at Cape Fear River. PATERSON was tried at Charleston and hanged at White Point on 8 Nov 1718.

PATTISON

James PATTISON. Tried for piracy in Boston in 1704. (A crewman to Captain John QUELCH?)

PAYNE

Henry PAYNE. A reluctant crewman to Captain William PHILLIPS. PAYNE was one of the captives who overpowered the pirate crew and sailed the vessel to Boston. He was tried for piracy in Boston on 12 May 1724, found not guilty of piracy and acquitted.

PAYNE

John PAYNE. An English pirate in the early 17th century. He purchased (for £40) a pardon from the Vice-Admiral of Devon, Sir Richard HAWKINS. Sir Richard was the son of Sir John HAWKINS, the Elizabethan sea-dog. Sir Richard had commanded a ship against the Spanish Armada and was happy to sell a pardon to any pirate whose victims included the Spanish.

PEASE

Captain ? PEASE. A pirate of the South Seas. PEASE commanded an armed ship with a Malay crew. In Jun 1870 he rescued the pirate Captain Bully HAYES from the island of Samoa. He delighted the residents there by firing a 21 gun salute to mark the birthday of Queen Victoria. PEASE sailed with his two European wives, who worked together to make his travels comfortable and civilised.

PELL

Ignatious PELL. Bosun to Major Stede BONNET. Captured with BONNET at Cape Fear River on 27 Sep 1718. He gave evidence to the court at Charleston against the rest of BONNET's crew. He was not tried, he seems to have been given a pardon in exchange for his evidence.

PENNANT

Captain Jeffery PENNANT. One of the buccaneer captains on Henry MORGAN's expedition against the Spanish Main in March 1669.

PENNER

Major ? PENNER. One of the pirates who surrendered to the pardon of the Governor of the Bahamas in 1717.

PERKINS

Benjamin PERKINS. A crewman to Captain John QUELCH on the pirate brig *Charles*. PERKINS was captured with QUELCH at Marblehead in 1704.

PERKINS

Captain John PERKINS. An English pirate captain in the early 17th century. PERKINS plundered over a wide area, ranging from the Azores to Norway. He was captured in the Orkneys in 1610 after being chased by 3 Scottish vessels.

PERRY

Daniel PERRY. b. Guernsey, Channel Isles. PERRY was a crewman to Major Stede BONNET. He was captured with BONNET at Cape Fear River on 27 Sep 1718. He was tried at Charleston, found guilty and hanged at White Point on 8 Nov 1718.

PERRY

Mathew PERRY. First Mate of the vessel *Mary and John* which was captured by Captain Francis SPRIGGS in 1724. SPRIGGS put PERRY back on his own ship as sailing-master, under three pirates. PERRY, with 2 loyal seamen, BARLOW and SIMMONS, killed 2 of the pirates. The third pirate surrendered and PERRY sailed the ship back to Newport R.I.

PETERS

An English pirate captain in the early 17th century. PETERS left all his goods, valued at £6000, to Captain MYAGH.

PETERSON

Captain ? PETERSON. Of Newport, Rhode Island. In 1688 PETERSON arrived in Newport with a 'barkalong' (whatever that was) with 10 guns and 70 men. The Governor had him charged with piracy. The Grand Jury, PETERSON's friends and neighbours, dismissed the charges, though there seems little doubt that he was a pirate.

PETERSON

Erasmus PETERSON. b. Sweden. A crewman to Captain John QUELCH on the pirate brig *Charles*. PETERSON was captured, tried and sentenced with QUELCH at Boston. He was hanged there in 1704.

PETERSON

John PETERSON. b. Denmark. A crewman to Captain John SMITH. When they took over the vessel *George* on 3 May 1724, PETERSON cut the throat of Bonadventure JELPHS, the Chief Mate. He was captured in the Orkneys with SMITH. PETERSON was tried in London, found guilty and hanged at Execution Dock, Wapping on 11 Jan 1725.

PETIT

Captain ? PETIT. A French filibuster of San Domingo. He commanded *La Ruze*, a small ship of 4 guns and 40 men.

PETTY

William PETTY. b. Deptford, London. 1692. A sailmaker by trade, PETTY joined Captain James SKYRM's vessel *Ranger* from the prize ship *Onslow* in Jan 1722. Captured by *HMS*

Swallow off the West African coast on 1 Feb 1722. He was tried at Cape Corso Castle on 28 Mar 1722. PETTY was found guilty and hanged.

PHILIPS

? PHILIPS. A carpenter to Captain John FENN on *Morning Star*. No further information.

PHILIPS

James PHILIPS. b. Antigua. 1686/7. PHILIPS was a pirate on *Revenge* in 1717. He was with Captain Bartholomew ROBERTS on *Royal Fortune* when it was captured by *HMS Swallow* off the West African coast on 10 Feb 1722. He was tried at Cape Corso Castle on 28 Mar 1722. PHILIPS was found guilty of piracy and hanged.

PHILIPS

William PHILIPS. b. Lower Shadwell, London. 1692/3. He joined Captain Bartholomew ROBERTS' ship *Royal Fortune* from the prize vessel *King Solomon* in Jan 1722. They were captured off the West African coast by *HMS Swallow* on 10 Feb 1722. PHILIPS was tried at Cape Corso Castle on 28 Mar 1722. The evidence against him was that he assisted the pirates in their capture of his vessel, and that he signed the pirate articles immediately and without coercion. PHILIPS was found guilty of piracy and hanged.

PHILLIPS

Captain John PHILLIPS. b. Devon. PHILLIPS was a carpenter on a West Country vessel which was captured by the pirate Captain Thomas ANSTIS in *Good Fortune*. *Good Fortune* was part of Captain Bartholomew ROBERTS fleet at that time. PHILLIPS remained as the carpenter on *Good Fortune* until the crew dispersed in Tobago. PHILLIPS returned to England in a sloop that ran aground and sank in the Bristol Channel. He got ashore and was staying with friends in Devon when he heard that a hunt was on for the crew of the sunken sloop. They were being rounded up and gaoled at Bristol. PHILLIPS shipped out of Topsham on a fishing vessel bound for Newfoundland. There he worked at fishing until he found a group of like-minded sailors. Six of them seized a vessel on 29 Aug 1723. They took several more vessels, increasing their crew, then headed for the Caribbean. They searched Tobago for any of ANSTIS crew, but found only one black ex-shipmate, who had no wish to sail with them. PHILLIPS sailed again for Newfoundland, hoping to increase the percentage of volunteers in his crew, most of them being captives. On 4 Apr 1724 he took a schooner, then another 10 vessels in 10 days. By this time the pirates in his crew were hopelessly outnumbered by captives. On 14 Apr the captives overpowered the pirates and PHILLIPS was killed in the fighting. The captives sailed the vessel to BOSTON where they handed it over to the authorities.

PHILLIPS

Joseph PHILLIPS. A crewman to BLACKBEARD. PHILLIPS was wounded and captured at Ocracoke Inlet in the battle in which BLACKBEARD was killed. That was on 1 Dec 1718. He was tried and hanged for piracy.

PHILLIPS

William PHILLIPS. A crewman to Captain John PHILLIPS on his cruise of 1723/24. The pirates were overpowered by the captives and reluctant crewmen on 14 Apr 1724. PHILLIPS was brought to trial at Boston in May 1724. He was found guilty but his execution was stayed for one year, pending a plea for the King's mercy. The outcome of the plea is not known.

PHILLIPS

William PHILLIPS. Another William PHILLIPS who was a crewman to Captain John PHIL-LIPS in 1723/4. This one was shot in the leg while taking a prizes now off Tobago. The leg was amputated by the ship's carpenter, using his biggest saw. An axe was heated to cauterise the wound, but the carpenter burned

him severely elsewhere, 'like to mortify him'. His leg healed eventually but he was not with the crew when they were brought to trial at Boston. He may have been put ashore as a cripple or died in the meantime.

PHINNIS

? PHINNIS. A crewman on the galley 'George' which was captured by Captain John SMITH on 3 Nov 1724. He was one of those who escaped from SMITH's ship in the Orkneys and alerted the magistrates in mainland Scotland. This led to the arrest of SMITH's pirate crew.

PHILMORE

John PHILMORE. b. Ipswich, Suffolk. He was a reluctant crewman on Captain John PHIL-LIPS' pirate vessel. PHILMORE was one of the group of captives who overpowered the pirates and sailed the ship to Boston. All were tried there, to determine who was a pirate and who was a captive. The evidence given for PHILMORE was that his spirited wielding of an axe was one of the deciding factors in the captives overpowering the pirates. He was cleared of piracy by the trial on 12 May 1724.

PHIPS

Richard PHIPS. A soldier who deserted from the guard at Fort

Loyal, Falmouth, Maine, to join Captain Thomas POUND's crew. He was severely wounded at the fight at Tarpaulin Cove, where their ship was taken. PHIPS was captured and taken to Boston Gaol, where he died before he could be brought to trial.

PICARD

Captain Pierre Le PICARD. PICARD was one of L'OLLO-NAIS' filibuster captains. He was with L'OLLONAIS at the Laguna de Maracaibo in 1667, but left him when L'OLLONAIS' luck began to run out. In April 1685 PICARD, with ROSE and DESMARAIS crossed the Isthmus of Darien to join DAVIS, SWAN and TOWNLEY in their plundering of the Pacific coasts. In May 1687, when GROG-NIET, the leader of the French contingent of the expedition died of his wounds, PICARD took over his command. When he had plundered enough in the Pacific, PICARD scuttled his ships on 2 January 1688. He led his men in a running battle across Central America to the headwaters of the Coco River. There his men built rafts and rafted down to the Caribbean. A Jamaican ship picked them up and took them to Jamaica. The welcome for them there was suspicious, so they dispersed, mostly going to North America where they settled.

PICKERING

? PICKERING. A crewman to Captain George BOOTH. On the death of BOOTH in Zanzibar, BOWEN was elected Captain in his place and PICKERING was elected sailing Master. He must have been an accomplished seaman to fill such a post.

PIERCE

Captain William PIERCE. An English pirate captain who sailed the Mediterranean in the early 17th century. PIERCE was the son of a rich Plymouth man. He is known to have had a young Turkish wife.

PIERRE

PIERRE of Tortuga. I have read that PIERRE of Tortuga was known as The Pearl Pirate. I know no more.

PIERS

Captain John PIERS. b. Padstow, Cornwall. A Dorset-based pirate in the late 16th century, PIERS was also the son of a Cornish witch and one of the major pirates of his era. He was captured by Thomas WALSH (another pirate) in Studland Bay in 1581. PIERS was imprisoned at Dorchester with WALSH, who had been hoping for a pardon for bringing in PIERS. They both escaped but were recaptured and held at Corfe

Castle. The authorities at that time were desperate to stamp out piracy in Dorset (young vagabonds from all over Britain were travelling to Dorset to become pirates) so a court was set up at Corfe Castle and the Special Sessions condemned PIERS to be hanged on Studland beach. After the hanging, Captains Clinton ATKINSON and John NEWMAN, both local pirates, rowed ashore and cut down PIERS' body. They took it for burial at sea.

PIERS

George PIERS. A crewman to Captain John QUELCH. PIERS was tried at the Star Tavern in Boston in June 1704.

PIKE

Robert PIKE. A crewman to Sir Francis DRAKE. On 11 Feb 1573, DRAKE and the local Cimeroons lay in wait for the Spanish mule-train of treasure for Venta Cruz to pass them. PIKE leapt out before the signal to attack was given, ruining the plan. DRAKE captured only a few provisions from the advance party of mules. Sadly, I think this is PIKE's only mention in recorded history.

PIKE

Samuel PIKE. A reluctant crewman to Captain Francis SPRIGGS. PIKE was marooned on the island of Roatan on 4 Apr 1724 with several other captives. After a few days they were picked up by a passing vessel and taken to Jamaica.

PINEL

Captain ? PINEL. A French filibuster in the Caribbean. In 1694 he took an 18 gun Royal Navy ship off Barbados. His crew dropped grenades made of glass onto the man-of-war, causing dreadful burns and lacerations. The man-of-war surrendered.

PINFOLD

Captain ? PINFOLD. A Dorset-based pirate in the late 16th century. He was probably more smuggler than pirate. PINFOLD once brought a French prize vessel into Lulworth Cove and sold the cargo ashore. The local Customs officer boarded the ship to claim the duty on the goods. The pirates 'mocked him, called him a good fellow, and offered him a drink'. That demonstrates how piracy was an accepted part of the local commerce in those days.

PITMAN

John PITMAN. He was a crewman to Captain John QUELCH. Tried at the Star Tavern in Boston along with the rest of QUELCH's crew, in June 1704.

PLANTAIN

John PLANTAIN. b. Chocolate Hole, Jamaica. PLANTAIN went to sea at the age of 13. By the time he was 20 he was a pirate. He sailed for some years in the Indian Ocean and the Red Sea before retiring to Madagascar. There, with James ADAIR and Hans BURGEN, he built a stockade at Ranter Bay. They kept an exotic harem and traded with passing ships. Ranter Bay became a favoured place for pirates to dispose of their plunder and replenish their vessels. PLANTAIN was known as 'The King of Ranter Bay' until their community was dispersed. 1720 was probably the height of PLANTAIN's reign.

PLUMLEY

Captain ? PLUMLEY. An English pirate captain in the early 17th century. PLUMLEY was killed in a battle with Dutch pirates at Mamora, Morocco, in 1611.

POLEAS

Pedro POLEAS. A Spanish pirate. Joint commander, with Captain JOHNSON, of *Two Brothers*. In 1731 they took *John and Jane* south of Jamaica. A passenger, John COCKBURN, later wrote an account of the *John and Jane* voyage and its capture by pirates, and also his own 240 mile journey on foot on the Spanish Main to escape the pirates.

PORTER

Captain ? PORTER. A pirate captain in the West Indies. He commanded a sloop and sailed in company with another sloop, commanded by Captain TUCKERMAN. They came across Captain Bartholomew ROBERTS at anchor at Bennet's Key, Hispaniola. Both of these captains being beginners at the trade of piracy, they visited ROBERTS, hoping to learn much about the profession from him. He seems to have been flattered by their hero-worship. ROBERTS entertained them for 3 or 4 nights and gave them supplies of arms, powder and other goods. When they left, ROBERTS said he "hoped the Lord would prosper their handy works".

POUND

Captain Thomas POUND. Pilot of the King's frigate *Rose*. The vessel was seized by the townspeople of Boston in their anger against the unpopular Governor ANDROS. POUND escaped from the town in a fishing vessel, the property of Thomas HAWKINS, whom POUND took with him. Through piracy POUND moved on to bigger and better vessels. Eventually he became so successful a pirate, and such a menace to shipping, that the Governor of Boston sent the sloop *Mary*, under Captain Samuel PEASE to find him. PEASE caught him in Tarpaulin Cove, just finishing careening, and a battle ensued. POUND and PEASE were both badly injured in the battle and PEASE died a few days later. POUND was captured and was held in the new Boston Gaol. He was tried and found guilty but a petition was raised by prominent townspeople, including WAITSTILL, WINTHROP and one of the magistrates who had tried POUND. His sentence was remitted and POUND was given command of his old vessel *Rose*. He sailed for England but en route they met with a French privateer of 30 guns and battle ensued. POUND won the day but HAWKINS was killed. He was greeted as a hero in England and given the command of the frigate *Sally Rose*. He was posted to Boston under command of his old patron, Governor ANDROS. POUND eventually retired to Isleworth, London in 1699, with a reputed fortune of £209,000 from his piracy. He died a gentleman in 1703.

POWELL

Captain Michael POWELL. An English pirate captain in the early 17th century. POWELL is known to have had two wives in England, one in Ratcliffe and the other in Plymouth. The local merchants at Mamora, Morocco, gave him a large ship to use as a storehouse and shop in the port. This was probably a beneficial arrangement to both parties.

POWELL

Thomas POWELL junior. b. Connecticut. 1701/2. A gunner to Captain Charles HARRIS on *Ranger*. POWELL had first been a gunner to Captain George LOWTHER, having joined him on the Honduras coast. Later he served Captain Edward LOW as a gunner. Captured by HMS Greyhound. POWELL was tried at Newport R.I., found guilty and hanged on 19 Jul 1723.

POWER

John POWER. A crewman on the slaver *Polly*. While the Captain was ashore in West Africa, the crew sailed the vessel away with their cargo. They turned pirate and elected POWER their Captain. They attempted to sell their human cargo in the West Indies, but suspicion was raised wherever they tried. They sailed on to New York, where the ship's surgeon informed on them. POWER was arrested and shipped to England for trial. He was found guilty and hanged at Execution Dock on 10 Mar 1768.

PRICE

Thomas PRICE. b. Bristol. A crewman to Major Stede BONNET. PRICE was captured with BONNET on 27 Sep 1718 at Cape Fear River. He was tried at Charleston and hanged on 8 Nov 1718.

PRIE

John PRIE. A pirate and murderer, tried by the Admiralty Court in London in 1727. PRIE was hanged at Execution Dock and his body was displayed in chains on the banks of the River Thames across from Woolwich.

PRIMER

Mathew PRIMER. A crewman to Captain John QUELCH on the pirate brig *Charles*. At the trial at the Star Tavern in Boston in 1704, PRIMER turned 'King's evidence' to escape hanging.

PRINCE

Captain Lawrence PRINCE. An English buccaneer. In 1670 he sacked the city of Granada in company with Captains HARRIS and LUDBURY. Later that year, as part of Sir Henry MORGAN's expedition, he led the attack on the city of Panama.

PRO

John PRO. One of the Madagascar based pirates. During his career he sailed under the pirate captains WHITE, WILLIAMS and BURGESS.

PROPHET

James PROPHET. b. Suffolk. PROPHET was a Bosun's Mate in King James' navy aboard the man-of-war *Royal Anne* on the voyage which delivered the King's daughter, Princess Elizabeth, to Flushing for her wedding. He was discharged from the navy on his return and turned pirate. He was arrested in 1613, sentenced to death and held in the Marshalsea Gaol. He escaped and boarded a vessel at King's Lynn, Suffolk. PROPHET eventually arrived at Mamora, Morocco, where a pirate Captain Wilkinson appointed him Sailing Master.

PROWSE

Captain ? PROWSE. A late 16th century English pirate captain. Based at Weymouth, Dorset, PROWSE was unusual in that he and his crew were all local men. Most of the Dorset pirates of that era were from Devon or Cornwall, but based themselves in Dorset because the county authorities were so involved in the trade themselves.

Note: The Captain Prowse above and below might just be the same man. There are about 20 years between the two references.

PROWSE

Captain Lawrence PROWSE. A Devon man. PROWSE was a noted buccaneer and a terror to the Spanish. At the insistence of the King of Spain, King James I imprisoned him for piracy. He was to have been executed, but a huge public outcry forced the King to free him.

PULLING

Captain John PULLING. He commanded the vessel *Fame*, which set out in company with William DAMPIER in *St George*. While lying off the Downs, Kent, the two captains quarrelled and PULLING left to go pirating in the Canaries. DAMPIER kept to the original plan and sailed off to the South Seas.

PURSSER

Captain ? PURSSER. b. Cheshire. A notorious pirate off the coast of Wales and in the English Channel in the late 16th century. PURSSER based himself at Weymouth, Dorset. When Queen Elizabeth decided to rid herself of Dorset pirates, PURSSER and 42 other pirates were taken by the *Bark Talbot* in 1583. He was examined at the Tower of London by the Judge to the High Court of Admiralty (oddly named Julius CAESAR). PURSSER was tried and condemned by the Court. He was hanged at Execution Dock.

PYE

Robert PYE. He was taken from the prize galley *Stanwich*

by Captain James SKYRM's vessel *Ranger* in Aug 1721. Captured by *HMS Swallow* off the West Coast of Africa on 1 Feb 1722. PYE was tried at Cape Corso Castle on 28 Mar 1722. He was found not guilty of piracy and acquitted.

PYMER

Mathew PYMER. b. New England. A crewman to Captain John QUELCH on the brig *Charles*. He claimed to have been forced by QUELCH to become a pirate. PYMER gave principal evidence against QUELCH at his trial. PYMER seems to have been given his freedom in exchange for his evidence.

QUALLS

Robert QUALLS. Local history on St Thomas, Virgin Islands, tells the story of Bob QUALLS. He was a popular young pirate who came ashore off the brig *Lynx* at Freetown, early in the eighteenth century, to spend the night with a creole girl at the Red Fox Inn. The girl cut his throat and boasted to her friends that she had earned a guinea 'without lifting her skirt.' QUALLS' pirate comrades were so outraged at the crime that they nailed up the doors and windows of the inn with the staff inside and set fire to it. Those who tried to escape were shot as they jumped from windows. From then onwards (so legend says) inns on St Thomas were obliged to have two buckets of water in each public room in case of fire.

QUELCH

Captain John QUELCH. b. London, 1666. QUELCH was appointed Lieutenant-Commander of the armed brig *Charles* by the Governor of Boston. His mission was to chase and capture pirates. When the vessel was ready to sail, QUELCH nailed up the Captain, Daniel PLOWMAN, in his cabin. He sailed with the ship and crew as a pirate vessel. QUELCH took 9 vessels during a 9 month cruise, then returned to Boston. The crew spent their plunder rashly and noisily and soon came under suspicion. They were arrested and two of the crew gave evidence against the others, having claimed that they were reluctant pirates. QUELCH was tried, sentenced and hanged in 1704 at Boston.

QUICK

Thomas QUICK. A crewman to Captain Calico Jack RACKHAM. QUICK joined RACKHAM's vessel at Negril Point, Jamaica, on the day of its capture. He was tried at St Jago de la Vega on 16 Nov 1720. The case against him was adjourned until 24 Jan 1721 for lack of evidence. No further evidence was presented, but he was still found guilty and hanged at Gallows Point, Port Royal, on 17 Feb 1721.

QUINTOR

Hendrick QUINTOR. b. Amsterdam, Holland. A black crewman to Captain Samuel BELLAMY on *Whydah*. QUINTOR was taken prisoner the day after BELLAMY's ship was wrecked on Cape Cod. He was tried at Boston and found guilty of piracy. QUINTOR was hanged on 15 Nov 1717.

QUITTANCE

John QUITTANCE. A crewman to Captain John QUELCH on the brig *Charles*. He was tried at the Star Tavern in Boston in Jun 1704.

RACKHAM

Captain John RACKHAM. Known as CALICO JACK because he preferred to wear sensible cotton clothing, rather than the extravagant velvets and silks so beloved of the other pirates. RACKHAM was a crewman for several years to Captain Charles VANE. When VANE captured the prize vessel *Kingston* he gave command of it to RACKHAM. RACKHAM had long despised VANE for his unnecessary cruelty, he ordered VANE to leave his vessel immediately. They parted company. RACKHAM hunted vessels, mostly Spanish, off the coasts of Jamaica. Hearing from the crew of one prize that England and Spain were at war again, RACKHAM sent his crew to Jamaica to see what chance there was of a pardon from the Governor. The Governor sent a squadron of ships after RACKHAM. He and his crew escaped but the *Kingston* was taken. In two small boats RACKHAM took a Spanish vessel off North Cuba, sailed to Providence Island and accepted a pardon from Woodes ROGERS. In Providence, RACKHAM met and fell in love with Anne BONNY, the wife of another pardoned pirate. In order to escape notoriety (and her vengeful husband) they stole the sloop *Curlew* from the harbour, crewed her with ex-pirates and sailed again. They put into Cuba for Anne to be delivered of a child, which they left there, and sailed again. The woman pirate Mary READ was another 'crewman' of RACKHAM's. They were eventually taken off the coast of Jamaica after a battle in which Anne BONNY, Mary READ and one crewman showed great bravery. RACKHAM and the rest of the crew hid below decks during the fighting. RACKHAM was tried and sentenced in Jamaica. Before his execution Anne visited him and told him, "If you had fought like a man you wouldn't be hanged like a dog." She was not hanged because she was expecting another child.

RANCE

Andrew RANCE. He joined Captain James SKYRM's vessel *Ranger* from a Dutch prize ship in Oct 1721. Captured by *HMS Swallow* off the West African coast on 1 Feb 1722. RANCE was probably a Royal Navy deserter because he was referred to the Marshalsea Gaol for trial in London.

RANCE

Captain James RANCE. A Breton. RANCE was an officer with HAWKINS on his expedition against the Spanish American colonies in 1568. RANCE later met with DRAKE's expedition off the coast of Panama in 1572. RANCE then commanded a small vessel and 30 men. He joined DRAKE in the capture of

Nombres de Dios. Their partnership was dissolved after the raid. RANCE was later known to have been a privateer in the English Channel approaches, probably working out of Brittany and Ireland.

RANDALL

Captain William RANDALL. An English pirate captain in the early 17th century. RANDALL took prizes in the Atlantic and the North Sea, from the Azores to Norway. In 1610 three Scottish ships from Leith chased RANDALL to the Orkneys and captured him there.

RANSON

Andrew RANSON. b. England. 1650? RANSON may have begun his career as a buccaneer. He joined Captain Thomas JINGLE's privateer fleet in 1684. This fleet made an attack on the Spanish town of St Augustine, Florida, in which several of the men, including RANSON, were captured. RANSON, as the senior captive, and possibly the captain of one of the vessels, was sentenced to death by the Spanish Governor. As the executioner was carrying out the sentence of garrotting, the rope around RANSON's neck broke. Monks who were attending the execution claimed RANSON's life as an 'act of God'. RANSON remained a prisoner at St Augustine, always under

the threat of death, until the siege of St Augustine by Governor Moore of South Carolina. RANSON aided the Spanish in breaking the siege and was at last given his freedom to return to the British West Indies.

RAPHAELINO

Captain ? RAPHAELINO. A pirate who was much feared in the South Atlantic in the early 19th century. In 1822 he controlled a fleet of pirates in the vicinity of Cape Antonio.

RAU

Gustav RAU. A former Imperial German Navy seaman. RAU signed on the three-masted barque *Veronica* at Ship Island in the Mississippi Delta. The vessel sailed for Montevideo with a crew of 12 and a cargo of timber on 11 Oct 1902. RAU fermented a mutiny among the crew during the voyage and a group of them murdered the ship's officers and some loyal shipmates. The surviving mutineers; RAU, Moses THOMAS, Otto MONSON, Ludwig FLOHR and Willem SMITH then fired the ship and rowed off, leaving it to sink. They were picked up from Cajueira Island by the British steamer *Brunswick*. En route for Liverpool, Moses THOMAS revealed to Captain BROWNE of the *Brunswick* what the mutineers had done. RAU, MONSON and SMITH were tried and convicted of piracy at Liverpool in May 1903. RAU and SMITH were hanged at Walton Gaol on 2 Jun 1905. MONSON's sentence was commuted to penal servitude for life because of his youth.

Note: This act of piracy was strange, in that the pirates made no financial gain at all, they even lost their own possessions when they fired the ship. It seems to have been inspired by national hatred between the German seamen and the Scottish officers.

RAUSE

Captain James RAUSE. An English privateer captain in the Caribbean in the 16th century. RAUSE met with Sir Francis DRAKE in Jul 1572 and with combined crews they took the town of Nombres de Dios.

RAWLINSON

Peter RAWLINSON. A crewman to Captain John SMITH. On taking over the galley *George* RAWLINSON and MELVIN cut the throat of the ship's legitimate Captain. That was on 3 Nov 1724. He was captured in the Orkneys with SMITH. RAWLINSON was tried in London and hanged at Execution Dock, Wapping.

RAYNER

Captain ? RAYNER. William PENN, in a letter to the Lords of Trade in 1701, wrote that several of Captain KIDD's crewmen had settled as planters in Carolina, with RAYNER as their captain.

RAYNOR

William RAYNOR. A crewman to Captain John QUELCH on the pirate brig *Charles*. He was tried at the Star Tavern in Boston in Jun 1704.

READ

Captain John READ, of Bristol. READ was a crewman to Captain John COOK on *Bachelor' Delight*. They sailed from Carolina in Aug 1683, first to West Africa, then to the Pacific by way of Cape Horn. After Cook's death at Galapagos, READ joined Captain SWAN's *Cygnet* along with many others. *Cygnet* meandered across the Pacific taking few prizes, the crew growing very disenchanted with SWAN's captaincy. Many men left the ship in the Far East and READ became Captain, almost by default. In Jan 1688 *Cygnet* was on the Northwest coast of Australia and her crew were the first Englishmen to set foot in that land. READ was deserted by half his crew on the Coromandel coast in mid-1688, but sailed on with the remainder to Madagascar. Most of his crew joined the pirate community there, though *Cygnet* was so rotten that she sank on her mooring. READ is said to have boarded a ship for New York.

READ

Captain ? READ. He commanded a Madagascar-based pirate brig and once rescued the pirate Thomas WHITE. READ later died at sea.

READ

Mary READ. An English girl who escaped an unhappy family life by going to sea dressed as a boy. She seems to have deceived all until she married a crewman on Calico Jack RACKHAM's *Curlew*. Her husband claimed to have been forced into piracy. Mary once fought a duel in her husband's place and won. When their vessel was captured, Mary and Anne BONNY and one crewman fought bravely while the remainder of the crew hid below decks. At her trial she told the court that she was pregnant and her execution was deferred until she bore the child. Mary is reported to have died in prison of white fever.

READ

Robert READ. A crewman to Captain John SMITH on the galley *George*. Captured in the Orkneys with SMITH. READ was tried in London in May 1725. He was found not guilty of piracy and acquitted.

READ

William READ. B. Londonderry. 1678/9. A crewman on Captain

Charles HARRIS *Ranger*. Captured by *HMS Greyhound*. Tried at Newport R.I. READ was found guilty of piracy and hanged on 19 Jul 1723.

READHEAD

Philip READHEAD. A crewman to Captain HEIDON on the pirate ship *John of Sandwich*. He was wrecked on Alderney in the Channel Isles in 1565. READHEAD was hanged at St Martin's Point, Guernsey, later in that year.

REDFIELD

Captain John REDFIELD. According to one version of the legend, REDFIELD went ashore with Captain William KIDD on an island near Charles Towne, Carolina, in May 1699. KIDD gave him a sloop and four volunteers to build a home on the island and guard the treasure they landed there. REDFIELD married a Charles Towne girl who came from Ireland and they settled there comfortably. Max BRISBAU arrived later, saying that KIDD had sent him to collect the treasure. REDFIELD demanded Captain KIDD's seal to prove his authority but he could not produce it, proving that KIDD had not sent him. Mrs REDFIELD helped her husband to overpower BRISBAU and tie him to a chair, but the other four men sided with BRISBAU. The REDFIELDs were put aboard the sloop and BRISBAU promised that if they did not produce the treasure they would have an 'accident'. With the RED-FIELDs still aboard, BRISBAU put into Charles Towne for supplies and the ship was recognised as REDFIELD's. A search of the vessel revealed the REDFIELD couple who told of their kidnapping. BRISBAU and the other men were tried but escaped hanging. The REDFIELDs learned that KIDD had been hanged. They moved into Charles Towne and lived as respected and wealthy citizens.

REDMAN

Richard REDMAN. b. 1772/3. On 21 Sep 1797 the crew of *HMS Hermione*, a 32 gun frigate, mutinied and killed ten of the ship's officers by throwing them overboard to drown. REDMAN, a Quartermaster's mate, was a leading mutineer. He threw the Bosun, William MARTIN overboard and then raped the Bosun's wife, Mrs MARTIN. He was the only mutineer to behave so wickedly. The crew then sailed the vessel to the Spanish port of La Guaira where they handed it over to the authorities and dispersed. REDMAN joined a Spanish merchant ship which was captured by the Royal Navy. He was recognised and shipped to Portsmouth. REDMAN was tried aboard *HMS Gladiator* in March 1799. He was found guilty, sentenced to death and hanged within the hour. *Note*: 1. Mrs MARTIN survived and shipped out of La

Guaira to the United States, a neutral country from which she could return to Britain.
Note: 2. REDMAN was neither a pirate nor a privateer, but I thought a volume on wicked men at sea should include him.

REYES

Captain Diego de los REYES. Also known as Diego the Mulatto or Diego Lucifer. REYES was born a slave in Havana, Cuba, and having lived in Campeche, Mexico at one time. He joined the Dutch freebooter Captain van HOORN in August 1633 to raid the town of Campeche. They captured the town and held it for 2 days, also taking 22 Spanish ships in the harbour. They kept a vessel or two for themselves, sold 4 back to the Spanish and burnt the rest. After Campeche, REYES and van HOORN went separate ways. In 1636 REYES squabbled with Captain JOL and other privateers over the stragglers from a Spanish treasure fleet. At that time he operated under a Dutch licence, so was a privateer and not a pirate. In 1637 he captured the tiny vessel of Thomas GAGE, an English Catholic priest and traveller. GAGE complained to Diego that the pirates were taking all his goods, Diego told him, "Today fortune has been with me, tomorrow it may be with thee." The same year he took a vessel bearing Dona Isabel de Caraveo, recently widowed wife of the Governor of Yucatan. He delivered her safely ashore with all her goods, which confirms his reputation for honour and magnanimity.

RHOADE

Captain John RHOADE. b. Holland. A Boston-based coastal pilot. In 1674 RHOADE was appointed chief pilot of the Curacao privateer *Flying Horse*. They sailed north as far as the St John River taking several small English vessels engaged in trading furs with the native hunters.

RICE

David RICE. b. Bristol. RICE joined Captain Bartholomew ROBERTS' vessel *Royal Fortune* from the prize galley *Cornwall* in Oct 1721. Captured by *HMS Swallow* off the West African Coast on 10 Feb 1722. He was tried at Cape Corso Castle on 28 Mar 1722. RICE was found guilty and sentenced to hang, but sentence was commuted to 7 years' transportation to the African colonies.

RICE

Owen RICE. b. South Wales. 1694/5. RICE was a crewman on Captain Charles HARRIS vessel *Ranger*. Captured by *HMS Greyhound*. He was tried at Newport R.I., found guilty and hanged on 19 Jul 1723.

RICHARDS

Lieutenant ? RICHARDS. Second-in-Command to the famous BLACKBEARD. In 1717, when BLACKBEARD blockaded Charleston Harbour, RICHARDS was sent ashore with a party of crewmen to demand medical supplies (they mostly wanted mercury for the treatment of venereal diseases). Whilst awaiting a reply from the Governor, RICHARDS and his men scandalised the town with their outrageous and swaggering behaviour.

RICHARDS

John RICHARDS. He was taken from the prize vessel *Charlton* in Feb 1722 by Captain Bartholomew ROBERTS' ship *Royal Fortune*. Captured off the West African Coast by *HMS Swallow* on 10 Feb 1722. RICHARDS was tried at Cape Corso Castle on 28 Mar 1722. He was found not guilty of piracy and acquitted.

RICHARDSON

John RICHARDSON. Son of a New York goldsmith. RICHARDSON ran away from his apprenticeship and went to sea. He served for some years on men-of-war and merchantmen. At Ancona, RICHARDSON was taken on as ship's carpenter by a Captain Benjamin HARTLEY. With another crewman, COYLE,

RICHARDSON planned a mutiny. They murdered the Captain and RICHARDSON became mate. Captured later, RICHARDSON was hanged at Execution Dock, Wapping on 25 Jan 1738.

RICHARDSON

Nicholas RICHARDSON. A crewman to Captain John QUELCH on the brig *Charles*. He was tried at the Star Tavern in Boston in Jun 1704.

RIDDLE

Hugh RIDDLE. RIDDLE was taken from the prize vessel *Dilligence* in Jan 1722 by Captain Bartholomew ROBERTS' ship *Royal Fortune*. Captured by *HMS Swallow* off the West African Coast on 10 Feb 1722. He was tried at Cape Corso Castle on 28 Mar 1722. RIDDLE managed to satisfy the court that he had played no part in piracy and was acquitted.

RIDGE

John RIDGE. b. London. A crewman to Major Stede BONNET. RIDGE was captured with BONNET on 27 Sep 1718 at Cape Fear River. He was tried at Charleston and hanged on 8 Nov 1718.

RIMER

John RIMER. He joined Captain James SKYRM's vessel *Ranger*

from the prize vessel *Tarlton* in Jan 1722. Captured by *HMS Swallow* off the West African Coast on 1 Feb 1722. RIMER must have been a Royal Navy deserter because he was sent to the Marshalsea Gaol in London to be tried.

RINGROSE

Basil RINGROSE. An educated man. RINGROSE joined Captain Bartholomew SHARPE's expedition to plunder the Pacific coasts of America in 1680/81. He wrote a very readable diary of the voyage which gives details of his own adventures and mishaps, as well as good descriptions of the places visited. RINGROSE spent the latter part of the expedition as Supercargo and Pilot on SHARP's vessel. He returned to London after the expedition, but was soon back in the Caribbean, serving under Charles SWAN. RINGROSE was killed while on a foraging party ashore that was ambushed by the Spanish, at Sontispac, Mexico, in February 1686. Fifty other buccaneers died with him.

RIVERS

Joseph RIVERS. RIVERS was first known as a pirate off the coast of Virginia in 1701. Later he was a crewman to Captain Samuel BELLAMY on *Whydah*. RIVERS is believed to have drowned on the night, in 1717, when *Whydah* was wrecked on Cape Cod.

ROACH

Peter ROACH. An Irishman. A crewman to Captain John QUELCH on the brig *Charles*. He was captured, sentenced and hanged with QUELCH in Boston on 30 Jun 1704.

ROB

Alexander ROB. A crewman to Captain John SMITH on the galley *Revenge*. He was captured with SMITH in the Orkneys. ROB was tried in London and hanged at Execution Dock, Wapping, in Jun 1725.

ROBBINS

James ROBBINS. A crewman to BLACKBEARD. ROBBINS was wounded and captured in the battle at Ocracoke Inlet on 1 Dec 1718. He was tried and hanged at Boston.

ROBBINS

James ROBBINS. (Nicknamed RATTLE). b. London. A crewman to Major Stede BONNET. He was captured with BONNET on 27 Sep 1718 at Cape Fear River. ROBBINS was tried at Charleston and hanged on 8 Nov 1718.

ROBERTS

Captain Bartholomew ROBERTS. b. Newey Bach, Nr Haverfordwest, Wales. 1682. ROBERTS became a crewman to Captain Howard DAVIS after having been second mate on the slaver *Princess*, bound from London to the Guinea Coast. At first ROBERTS was reluctant to become a pirate, being a man of staunch religious conviction, but eventually he became a useful member of DAVIS' crew. On DAVIS' death ROBERTS was elected to command the vessel. His first act was to burn the fortress and town on the Island of Princes, where the Governor had killed DAVIS. He took 5 vessels along the African coast then the crew voted to sail to Brazil. Off Devil's Island, Surinam, they took a sloop which had information about a fully-laden brig that was nearby. ROBERTS and 40 men were aboard the sloop, leaving the Irish Quartermaster, KENNEDY in charge of ROBERTS' vessel. The vessels lost contact in violent weather. ROBERTS blamed KENNEDY for the loss of contact, he never had an Irish crewman after that incident. ROBERTS and his crew drafted the most comprehensive set of Pirate Articles, which I have copied at the start of this volume. He sailed the Caribbean until Jun 1720, when he left for a cruise to Newfoundland and across the Atlantic. In Trepassi Harbour he found 22 assorted vessels. ROBERTS destroyed most of them before he plundered the harbour itself. A couple of months later he was back in the Caribbean, where he cruised for a while before sailing for Cape Verde Islands. They fell half a mile to leeward of the Islands and the tradewinds took them back across the Atlantic to Brazil. It was a desperate voyage and they had no water at all for the last two days. After another cruise of the West Indies ROBERTS arrived at Sierra Leone in Jun 1721. He was at Calabar in Oct 1721. While careening at Princes Island, he lost over 100 men to the fever. In Jan 1722 ROBERTS was at the Whydah River, the great slaving port. On 10 Feb 1722, off the West African coast, ROBERTS' vessel *Royal Fortune* was sighted by *HMS Swallow*. During a running battle ROBERTS was killed. His vessel and most of her crew were captured. During his career as a pirate ROBERTS took more than 400 vessels captive or sunk. It was Bartholomew ROBERTS' boast that he had never forced any man to become a pirate.

ROBERTS

Owen ROBERTS. Ship's carpenter to the famous BLACK-BEARD. ROBERTS died in the battle at Ocracoke Inlet on 1 Dec 1718, when BLACKBEARD was also killed.

ROBERTS

Thomas ROBERTS. Taken from the prize vessel *Charlton* in Feb 1722 by Captain Bartholomew ROBERTS' ship *Royal Fortune*. Captured by HMS Swallow off the West African coast on 10 Feb 1722. ROBERTS was tried at Cape Corso Castle on 28 Mar 1722. He was found not guilty of piracy and acquitted.

ROBERTSON

Captain Andrew Gordon ROBERTSON. b. Glasgow. 'Of medium height, red hair and a fearsome figure'. ROBERTSON enlisted in the Chilean navy in 1817. He served as a Lieutenant on the man-of-war *Galvarino*. At Concepcion he flogged a Spanish officer by the name of PACHECO. ROBERTSON retired to settle on the Island of MOCHA, 100 miles south of the Bay of Concepcion. Growing restless he joined the Peruvian navy and later was at the siege of Fort Real Phillipe, Callao, as an army Captain. He fell in love with, and was scorned by, Tereza Mendez, a beautiful young widow. On 16 Jul 1826 ROBERTSON and 12 hands in a longboat took the English brig *Peruvian* with 2 million gold piastres aboard. He sailed the vessel to Marianas Island and buried the treasure. ROBERTSON then sailed for Hawaii and wrecked the vessel on the shore with all the hands except two men tied up below decks. He disposed of one of the crewmen, WILLIAMS, soon after. Nothing is known of the other man, GEORGE. ROBERTSON signed on as a crewman on a convict ship bound for Australia. There he met another Glasgowman who owned a yacht. ROBERTSON persuaded him and his crew to sail to Marianas, but on the way they had violent disagreements and ROBERTSON was thrown overboard. He was rescued from the sea by a Spanish vessel that just happened to be commanded by PACHECO, the officer that ROBERTSON had flogged many years previously. PACHECO, naturally enough, flogged ROBERTSON, who told him of the treasure during the flogging. They sailed for Marianas Island, but as they neared it, ROBERTSON, who was bound in heavy chains, threw himself overboard and drowned. PACHECO never found the treasure. Presumably it's still there.

ROBERTSON

? ROBERTSON. A crewman to Captain Thomas GREEN on the vessel *Worcester*. He was falsely arrested, tried, sentenced and hanged at Leith, Scotland in Apr 1705.

ROBINSON

Edward ROBINSON. b. Newcastle-upon-Tyne. A crewman to Major Stede BONNET. He was captured with BONNET on 27 Sep 1718 at Cape Fear River. ROBINSON was tried at Charleston and hanged on 8 Nov 1718 at White Point.

ROBINSON

Josiah ROBINSON. He was taken from the prize vessel *Tarlton* by Captain James SKYRM's ship

Ranger in Jan 1722. Captured by *HMS Swallow* on 1 Feb 1722 off the West African coast. ROBINSON was tried at Cape Corso Castle on 28 Mar 1722. He was found not guilty of piracy and acquitted.

ROBINSON

Captain Richard ROBINSON. An English pirate captain in the 1600s. His vessel *Bull, Bear and Horse* carried 4 brass cannon, 15 iron pieces and 4 or 5 'murderers'. ROBINSON sailed in company with Captain Peter EASTON until they quarrelled. In 1607 he was based in the Irish town of Baltimore, Bantry Bay. Almost everyone in the town was reputed to have engaged in trade with him. He gave £160 to his brother to invest for his two children, the interest to be paid to his wife in Plymouth.

ROCHE (or ROACH)

Philip ROCHE. b. Ireland. ROCHE took a French vessel in Cork Harbour with the CULLEN brothers. They changed the vessel's name and appearance at Dartmouth, Devon. They also sold some of the cargo, then sailed on to Rotterdam and sold the rest of the cargo. There they took a passenger aboard, but threw him overboard in the night. ROCHE left the CULLEN brothers with the vessel in France. He made his way to England and tried to claim insurance on the vessel in the name of John EUSTACE. He was arrested. ROCHE was held at the Marshalsea Gaol until his trial. He was found guilty and hanged at Execution Dock, Wapping.

RODERIGO

Captain Peter RODERIGO. A Flanderkin. He commanded the *Edward and Thomas*, a Dutch pirate vessel based in Boston. He took several English vessels along the coast of Maine. He was tried for piracy at Cambridge, Mass., and sentenced to death. He was later reprieved.

ROFFEY

Kerrill ROFFEY. A crewman to Captain Charles SWAN on *Cygnet*. After SWAN's crew split up at Mindanao, with much ill-feeling, ROFFEY remained there and was eventually picked up by a Dutch vessel. He worked for them, destroying spice trees in order to preserve the monopoly and maintain high prices. He later became a Captain in the Royal Navy.

ROGERS

Captain Thomas ROGERS. An English buccaneer. He commanded the buccaneer vessel *Forlorn*. In 1671 ROGERS routed the Spanish at Venta Cruz. He was one of Henry MORGAN's buccaneer captains at the sacking of Panama.

ROGERS

Captain Woodes ROGERS. Governor of the Bahamas. An important figure in the history of Caribbean piracy. ROGERS was a skilled navigator and a most competent sea captain. In 1708 he began a journey that was to take him around the world over a period of 3 years. The journey was a well-financed privateering expedition but was actually buccaneering in nature. William DAMPIER (in his old age) went along as the Navigator. ROGERS' most outstanding qualities were his great tact and humour, and a high diplomatic sensibility. In 1717 he was appointed Governor at Providence, Bahamas, with the specific task of stamping out piracy in the Caribbean. Armed with only one vessel and King George's offer of pardon, he succeeded beyond all hope. Pardoned pirates were given a small plot of land on Providence Island and timber to build a home. Many took his offer but reverted to piracy. ROGERS hunted them and hanged them as an example to their colleagues. ROGERS bankrupted himself in his efforts to improve the economy of the islands. The British Government would not bail him out and from 1721 for several years he was in a debtor's prison in England. He returned to the Bahamas and died on Providence (now Nassau) in 1729. His book 'A Cruising Voyage Round the World' is very readable. ROGERS life is fully treated in 'Dictionary of National Biography'.

ROLLSON

Peter ROLLSON. Captain John SMITH's gunner on *Revenge*. He was hanged at Execution Dock, Wapping, in Jan 1725.

ROOPE

Captain Gilbert ROOPE. He sailed in a squadron of Barbary corsairs under the patronage of the Dey of Tunis. This fleet included BISHOP and John JENNINGS. They took vessels off the Atlantic coast of France throughout 1610 and 1611. While cruising the Western Approaches his vessel sprang a leak and put into Baltimore, Ireland. JENNINGS' crew rebelled when he brought a woman aboard the ship. They said that the compass would not work in her presence. The crew voted ROOPE to take command but found him too severe and reinstated JENNINGS. Later a group of crewmen, including ROOPE, handed JENNINGS over to the Earl of THOMOND in exchange for a pardon.

ROSE

Captain Jean ROSE. A French filibuster. One of the captains in the huge fleet of pirates that plundered the Pacific coasts under DAVIS, TOWNLEY, SWAN and PICARD. ROSE was a leading captain in the French contingent.

ROSS

George ROSS. b. Glasgow. A crewman to Major Stede BONNET. He was captured with BONNET on 27 Sep 1718 at Cape Fear River. ROSS was tried at Charleston and hanged on 8 Nov 1718.

ROSSOE

Francis ROSSOE. He was tried in Jun 1717 with 4 other Carolina pirates for taking the *Virgin Queen*, *Turtle Dove* and *Penelope* in Jul 1716. They were all found guilty and promptly hanged.

ROUNSIVIL

George ROUNSIVIL. A crewman to Captain John AUGER. He had probably already taken a pardon from Woodes ROGERS at Providence in 1718. He was taken prisoner when AUGER's sloop ran aground on Long Island, W.I. He was tried and sentenced at Providence, but was eventually reprieved. Later he sailed with Captain Thomas BURGESS (another pardoned pirate) on a legitimate voyage for Woodes ROGERS. ROUNSIVIL died trying to save the life of BURGESS when their vessel was wrecked.

ROUSE

Walter ROUSE. A crewman to Captain Calico Jack RACKHAM. He joined the vessel at Negril Point on the day of its capture. Nevertheless, he was tried at St Jago de la Vega (Santiago) on 16 Nov 1720. The case against him was adjourned for want of evidence until Feb 1721. No further evidence was produced but ROUSE was still found guilty and sentenced to hang. He was probably hanged at Kingston or Port Royal, Jamaica.

ROW

Captain ? ROW. A Caribbean buccaneer captain. When Captain Bartholomew SHARPE and others assembled for their expedition to plunder the Pacific coasts of America in 1680, Captain ROW was there with his vessel of 20 tons and 25 men. In May 1685 ROW was with his ship at Panama as part of a huge Anglo/French buccaneer fleet which failed to take the town.

RUIZ

Fransisco RUIZ. One of Captain GILBERT's crew on the schooner *Panda* which took the Salem brig *Mexican* in 1834. RUIZ was tried in Boston, found guilty, but pleaded insanity. After a 60 day reprieve he was hanged on 12 Sep 1835.

RUPERT

Prince RUPERT of the Rhine, Duke of Bavaria, Duke of Cumberland and Duke of Holderness. 1618–1682. RUPERT was the son of the German Elector Palatine and Elizabeth, Queen of Bavaria, The Winter King and Queen, who lost their lands in the Thirty Years' War. The Elector, head of a large family, became a refugee in the Netherlands. Prince RUPERT was at the Siege of Rhynberg at the age of 14, but didn't start soldiering seriously until two years later, when he served in the Prince of Orange's Lifeguards. In 1636 he travelled to England, where King Charles I was his uncle. He gained a M.A. at Oxford and it was proposed that Madagascar be made a colony and he be made Governor.

RUPERT went back to soldiering on the continent and was at the siege of Breda, then invaded Westphalia. He was captured at Vlotho and it was reported to his mother that he was dead. She said, "Oh, I do hope so." fearing that he might have been converted to Catholicism. During his captivity he studied painting, played tennis, made love to the Governor's daughter and hunted. Being ransomed by Charles I must have seemed a disappointment.

At the outbreak of the English Civil war he joined Charles I at Nottingham in Jul 1642 and was made commander of the Royalist Cavalry. His adventures in that war justify a book to themselves. By the end of hostilities he was commander in chief of the

Royalist forces. General opinion seems to be that RUPERT's barbaric treatment of enemy prisoners (which he learned in his continental wars) did not suit the more gentlemanly behaviour of England's Civil War.

When King Charles surrendered to the Scots RUPERT and his brother Maurice went to France and took service with the Government there. RUPERT served at Landrecy in 1647. In Jun 1648 he sailed with Prince Charles (later Charles II) and the remains of the Royalist fleet against the Parliamentary navy, without success.

In Jan 1649 RUPERT arrived with his small fleet in the southwest of Ireland to support the local Royalists. BLAKE, the Parliamentary Admiral sailed after RUPERT. For the next two years BLAKE and RUPERT played 'Cat and Mouse' from Ireland to the Scillies, Spain, Portugal, Southern France and back to Portugal.

Eventually RUPERT sailed to Cape Verde, then the Azores and the West Indies. Throughout these travels he pirated any English shipping that he encountered, along with all Spanish ships.

During RUPERT's period of piracy he took many vessels and should have become very rich, his fortunes however, were very mixed. He lost ships as frequently as he captured them and returned to France in 1653 a skilled pirate but no millionaire.

In the winter of 1659 he returned to Germany and entered the Emperor's service in the army for the next few years. In 1660 he was back in England to celebrate the Restoration and be welcomed by Charles II.

Rupert's life from then onwards was still not boring. He commanded an English fleet against the Dutch, was appointed constable of Windsor Castle, was a founder member of the Hudson Bay Company, had an island named after him, became the Vice-Admiral of England and fought the Dutch at Texel, became First Lord of the Admiralty, was appointed a Governor of Tangier and a member of the new Council for Trade and Plantations.

RUPERT died in his bed, at home, on 29 Nov 1682 and was buried in Henry VII's chapel in Westminster Abbey. Oh, he was also tall and handsome and one of the best tennis players in England, wouldn't you know it?

Note: It's a safe bet the someone whose great-grandmother was Mary Queen of Scots, whose grandfather was King James I of England and whose father was the Elector Palatine, was not going to have an ordinary life. However, if you created a fictional character and attributed to them everything that Rupert actually did, then even the most adventurous of Hollywood directors would smile, hand the script back to you and suggest that you 'get real'.

RUSSEL

Isaac RUSSEL. He joined Captain Bartholomew ROBERTS' ship *Royal Fortune* from the prize galley *Lloyd*. Captured by *HMS Swallow* off the West African coast on 10 Feb 1722. He may have been a Royal Navy deserter because he was referred to the Marshalsea Gaol to await trial. The outcome of his trial is not known.

RUSSEL

John RUSSEL. Quartermaster to Captain Edward LOW. A brutal and intelligent man, RUSSEL later commanded his own pirate vessel.

RUSSEL

Robert RUSSEL. RUSSEL was carpenter to Captain Robert STEPHENSON, a pirate captain in the early 17th century. When STEPHENSON recruited RUSSEL he gave him the choice of being shot from a ship's gun, or becoming the ship's carpenter. The vessel was *Prong*, a 200 ton flyboat of 28 guns.

RUSSELL

Captain ? RUSSELL. A French-born Dorset pirate captain in the late 16th century. Russell commanded the *Daniel*, a smuggling and pirate vessel which was owned by Robert

GREGORY (Mayor and Member of Parliament for Southampton in the 1570s). I suspect that RUSSELL was more smuggler than pirate.

RYDER

RYDER the Pirate. In 1698 the merchant vessel *Beckford Galley* was taken by pirates off Madagascar. The pirate Captain was only known as RYDER the Pirate, and was described as 'a middle siz'd man of a swarthy complexion, inclinable by his aspect to be of churlish constitution, his own hair short and brown and apt when in drink to utter some Portugese or Moorish words'.

RYLEY

Bryant RYLEY. He joined the crew of Captain Walter KENNEDY from the captured slaver galley *Greyhound* of London on 16 Oct 1716.

SALTER

Edward SALTER. A crewman to the pirate BLACKBEARD. SALTER was wounded and captured on 1 Dec 1718 in the battle at Ocracoke Inlet, where BLACKBEARD was killed. He was tried and hanged.

SAMPLE

Captain Robert SAMPLE. A crewman to Captain ENGLAND on his ship *Royal James*. In 1720 they took the prize *Elizabeth and Katharine* off the West African coast. They fitted her out as a pirate ship and re-named her *Flying King*. SAMPLE was elected captain. In company with Captain Edward LOW, he sailed to Brazil and took Portugese shipping. They were sighted by a large Portugese man-of-war and LOW managed to sail clear. SAMPLE was forced to run his ship aground and 12 of his crew were killed. 38 of his crew were caught and executed. In 1717 SAMPLE was one of the pirates who surrendered to the Royal Pardon offered by Woodes ROGERS, Governor of the Bahamas.

SANDERS

Thomas SANDERS. An Elizabethan seaman who was captured by the Moors and used as a galley slave on a Barbary pirate ship.

SANTOS

Jose SANTOS. A Portugese pirate???

SAWKINS

Captain Richard SAWKINS. A Caribbean buccaneer captain. He took his ship of 16 tons, 1 gun and 35 men on Captain Bartholomew SHARPE's expedition to plunder the Pacific coasts of America. SAWKINS was killed leading the action at Puebla Nueva on 22 May 1680. Basil RINGROSE said, "a man who was as valliant and courageous as any could be, and likewise next to Captain Sharp, the best beloved of all our company". SAWKINS was known to throw dice overboard if he found them being played on a Sunday.

SAWNEY

Captain ? SAWNEY. An elderly pirate who lived on Providence Island. This was probably after he had taken Woodes ROGERS pardon in 1717. SAWNEY had the best hut on the settlement and was jokingly known as 'Governor' SAWNEY.

SAXBRIDGE

Captain Tibalt SAXBRIDGE. An English pirate captain in the early 17th century. His vessel

Phoenix was 35 tons deadweight. SAXBRIDGE was described as 'a little fellow' so he must have been very small in stature. In 1608, off Ushant, SAXBRIDGE was cruising with 2 vessels. When he called into Bantry Bay, Ireland, he had 300 men under his command. Later he was in Morocco, then the West Indies, where he lost 8 men ashore. SAXBRIDGE attempted to take a French ship off Newfoundland, but the Frenchman fought him and SAXBRIDGE was killed in the battle.

SAYER

Captain Ambrose SAYER. A Cornish pirate captain in the late 16th and early 17th centuries. SAYER was one of Queen Elizabeth I's privateers. He was captured by the Duke of Tuscany and imprisoned in Florence for 4 years. As a Protestant, he was handed to the Inquisition in Rome. After 3 years in their hands he was condemned to serve as a galley slave in the Spanish Sicilian fleet. In 1610, he and several other Protestants escaped from the galley and made their way to Algiers. For the next 3 years he took his revenge as the captain of a corsair ship. SAYER was captured at Sallee in 1613 and was shipped back to England. He was tried and convicted of piracy. It seems that he escaped again before his execution. Good for him.

SCOT

Captain Lewis SCOT. According to ESQUEMELING (an inveterate liar) SCOT was the first pirate to sack the Spanish city of Campeche.

SCOT

Richard SCOT. He was taken aboard Captain Bartholomew ROBERTS' ship *Royal Fortune* from a prize vessel in the Whydah Roads. Captured by *HMS Swallow* off the West African coast on 10 Feb 1722. SCOT was tried at Cape Corso Castle on 28 Mar 1722. He was found not guilty of piracy and acquitted.

SCOT

Roger SCOT. A crewman to Captain Bartholomew ROBERTS on *Royal Fortune*. Captured by *HMS Swallow* off the West African coast on 10 Feb 1722. He was tried at Cape Corso Castle on 28 Mar 1722. SCOT was found guilty of piracy and sentenced to death but no record was found of his hanging. He may have died of his wounds before the execution.

SCOT

William SCOT. b. Aberdeen, Scotland. A crewman to Major Stede BONNET. SCOT was captured with BONNET on 27 Sep 1718 at Cape Fear River. He was tried at Charleston and hanged at White

Point on 8 Nov 1718.

SCUDAMORE

Christopher SCUDAMORE. He was an apprenticed cooper in Bristol before he went to sea. Later he was a crewman to Captain John QUELCH on his pirate vessel *Charles*. SCUDAMORE was captured, sentenced and hanged with QUELCH at Boston in 1704.

SCUDAMORE

Peter SCUDAMORE. b. Wales. 1686/7. He joined Captain Bartholomew ROBERTS' vessel *Royal Fortune* from the prize galley *Mercy* at Calabar. Captured by *HMS Swallow* off the West African coast on 10 Feb 1722. He was tried at Cape Corso Castle on 28 Mar 1722. The evidence against him was that he wished to be the first surgeon to sign pirate 'articles' voluntarily. It was also stated that he tried to hatch a plot to take over HMS Swallow after the pirates were captured and before they arrived at Cape Corso. When a naval officer asked him what he was whispering about, he said, "horse racing". He was found guilty and hanged.

SEARLES

Captain Robert SEARLES. A captain on MYNG's expedition against the Spanish Main in May 1658. On their return to Jamaica, SEARLES bought one of the Spanish prizes, a vessel of 60 tons and 8 guns. He named her *Cagway*. In 1664 SEARLES brought 2 Spanish prize vessels into Port Royal, Jamaica. By coincidence, the Governor of Jamaica had just been ordered to encourage good relations with the Spanish. He returned SEARLES' prizes to their owners and removed his rudder and sails to stop his further plundering. It seems not to have worked for long, because in 1666 SEARLES and Captain STEDMAN, with only 80 men, captured the island of Tobago from the Dutch.

SEDGWICK

James SEDGWICK. A carpenter aboard the merchant ship *Prince's Galley*. On 15 Sep 1723 *Prince's Galley* was taken by Captain George LOWTHER. SEDGWICK was taken aboard the pirate vessel as a reluctant crewman, probably for his trade skills.

SEVER

Thomas SEVER. He was taken aboard Captain Bartholomew ROBERTS' vessel *Royal Fortune* from the prize galley *Cornwall* at Calabar in Oct 1721. Captured by *HMS Swallow* off the West African coast on 10 Feb 1722. SEVER was tried at Cape Corso Castle on 28 Mar 1722. He was found not guilty of piracy and acquitted.

SHARP

Rowland SHARP. b. Bath-Towne, N. Carolina. SHARP was a crewman to Major Stede BONNET. He was captured with BONNET on 27 Sep 1718 at Cape Fear River. He was tried at Charleston and found not guilty because he had received no share of the plunder.

SHAP-'NG-TSAI

SHAP-'NG-TSAI. The Admiral of a huge pirate fleet off Southwest China in the mid 19th century. The fleet was hunted by a Royal Navy squadron consisting of the steam sloops *HMS Fury* and *HMS Phlegethon* and the brig *HMS Columbine*. The pirates were cornered in the Tonkin River on 20 Oct 1848. A battle ensued and 1700 pirates were killed, 1000 escaped ashore. SHAP-'NG-TSAI appears to have escaped.

SHARP (or SHARPE)

Captain Bartholomew SHARP (or SHARPE). A Caribbean buccaneer captain. SHARP took his ship of 25 tons, 2 guns and 40 men on the great expedition to plunder the Pacific coasts of the Americas. Initially the expedition was under the command of Captain John COXON. COXON left the expedition, though he rejoined it later. SHARP took command after COXON left and retained it throughout. Two good accounts were written of the expedition, one by DAMPIER and the other by RINGROSE. The writers differ in their judgement of SHARP, but he succeeded in bringing his vessel back to the Caribbean around Cape Horn, with almost all of his crew. He returned to England after the adventure and was tried for piracy (He undoubtedly was a pirate at times). The fact that the Spanish fired at him first was enough to dismiss the charge, which had only been brought against him to appease the Spanish government.

SHASTER

Roger SHASTER. A crewman to Captain HEIDON on *John of Sandwich*. They were shipwrecked on Alderney in the Channel Islands. SHASTER was arrested and hanged at St Martin's Point, Guernsey, in 1564.

SHAW

John SHAW. A crewman to Captain George LOWTHER on *Ranger*. SHAW was captured with most of LOWTHER's crew on the island of Blanquilla in Oct 1723. He was tried at St Christopher (St Kitts) on 11 Mar 1724. SHAW was found guilty and hanged.

SHEEAN

John SHEEAN. Of Nantes. A

crewman to Captain Samuel BELLAMY on *Whydah*. SHEEAN was captured on Cape Cod the day after BELLAMY's ship was wrecked there. He was taken to Boston, tried and found guilty. SHEEAN was hanged on 15 Nov 1717.

SHERGALL

Henry SHERGALL. A buccaneer with Captain Bartholomew SHARP's expedition to plunder the Pacific coasts of the Americas in 1680/1. He fell from the spritsail-top on SHARP's ship on 12 Oct 1681 and drowned. It happened close to Cape Horn.

SHIPTON (or SKIPTON)

Captain ? SHIPTON. A crewman to Captain Francis SPRIGGS, who gave him command of a prize sloop. SHIPTON sailed in company with SPRIGGS and they took many vessels in the West Indies and Carolinas. SHIPTON was chased by a man-of-war off the Florida coast. One survivor told that 16 of the crew were captured and eaten by the natives ashore. SHIPTON escaped in a canoe with 12 of his men.

SHIRLEY

Sir Anthony SHIRLEY. In 1597 SHIRLEY landed an expedition on the then Spanish Island of Jamaica. They plundered the town of St Jago de la Vega (Santiago).

SHIVERS

Captain ? SHIVERS. He commanded the pirate vessel *Solidado* and sailed in company with Captain CULLIFORD on several Indian Ocean cruises. SHIVERS eventually accepted a Royal Pardon from Commodore LITTLETON at St Mary's Island, Madagascar.

SHUAN

Jean SHUAN. b. Nantes, France. A crewman to Captain Samuel BELLAMY on *Whydah*. SHUAN was captured on the night when *Whydah* was wrecked on Cape Cod. He was tried in Boston and hanged there on15 Nov 1717.

SHURIN (or SHUREN)

William SHURIN. b. Wapping, London. SHURIN joined Captain James SKYRM's vessel *Ranger* from the prize vessel *Jeremiah and Anne* in Apr 1720. Captured off the West African coast by *HMS Swallow* on 1 Feb 1722. SHURIN was tried at Cape Corso Castle on 28 Mar 1722. He was found guilty and sentenced to death but the sentence was commuted to 7 years transportation to the African colonies.

SHUTFIELD

William SHUTFIELD. b. Lancaster. 1682/3. A crewman on

Captain Charles HARRIS' vessel *Ranger*. Captured by *HMS Greyhound*. SHUTFIELD was tried at Newport R.I. He was found guilty and hanged on 19 Jul 1723.

SICCADEM

John SICCADEM. A native of Boston. SICCADEM was crewman to Captain Thomas POUND. He was found guilty of piracy at his trial, but was later pardoned.

SIMMONS

Nicholas SIMMONS. A reluctant crewman to Captain Francis SPRIGGS. SIMMONS was taken from the prize vessel 'Mary and John' but was left on that vessel under the command of 3 pirates. He was one of the captives who killed 2 of the pirates. The third pirate surrendered and the former captives sailed the ship back to Newport R.I.

SIMMS

Henry SIMMS. b. St Martins-in-the-Fields, London 1716. SIMMS was an old-Etonian, pickpocket, highwayman and pirate. A very colourful character. SIMMS was taken from school at the age of 14 and apprenticed to a breeches-maker, he ran away from his trade and became a pickpocket, later a highwayman. He was caught, imprisoned, escaped from gaol and impressed into the navy aboard *HMS Rye*. SIMMS deserted at Leith, Scotland and was arrested in Croydon, Surrey. He was sentenced to transportation to the colonies and shipped on the *Italian Merchant* to Maryland. He tried to raise a mutiny on the voyage. In America he was sold to the owners of *Two Sisters*, which was taken by pirates. Taken to Spain, he escaped at Oporto, was once more impressed into the Royal Navy and served aboard *HMS Kingfisher*. SIMMS was discharged at Bristol and his prize-money was enough to buy him a horse and a pair of pistols. He became a highwayman once again. SIMMS was caught and hanged on 17 Jul 1747, for stealing a silver watch and five shillings from Mr Francis SLEEP at Dunstable, Bedfordshire.

SKYRM

Captain James SKYRM (or SKYRME or SKRYM). b. Somerset. 1678. Nothing is known (by me) about SKYRM's early years but he joined Captain Bartholomew ROBERTS from the prize sloop *Greyhound* in Oct 1720. He was given command of the pirate ship *Ranger* and cruised in company with ROBERTS along the slaving routes off West Africa. *Ranger* was captured there by *HMS Swallow* off that coast on 1 Feb 1722. SKYRM lost a leg in the action but was taken prisoner with the rest of his crew. He was tried at Cape Corso Castle on 28 Mar 1722. SKYRM was found guilty and hanged.

SMALLBONE

An experienced seaman who sailed with Captain John COOK from Carolina in Aug 1683. SMALLBONE was responsible for saving their ship when, running under 'bare poles' in a storm, she broached and was in danger of being swamped by the great waves. SMALLBONE got the crew to mount the forward shrouds and spread their coats. This gave steerage enough to 'gain a point' and take the seas fore and aft. 20 years later, in 1703, SMALLBONE was suggested to DAMPIER as a Lieutenant for *Cinque Ports*. He sailed with DAMPIER, but not as an officer. In the Caribbean, a year later, SMALLBONE seems not to have been with DAMPIER, perhaps he died in the meantime.

SMITH

Aaron SMITH. A Caribbean pirate crewman who was tried at the Old Bailey in London in Dec 1822. SMITH was acquitted because he satisfied the court that he had been captured by pirates and forced to become one. After his release he wrote an account of his time with the pirates.

SMITH

George SMITH. He joined Captain Bartholomew ROBERTS' ship *Royal Fortune* from the prize vessel *Martha and Maria* in Jun 1720. *Royal Fortune* was captured by *HMS Swallow* off the West African coast on 10 Feb 1722. SMITH was tried at Cape Corso Castle on 28 Mar 1722. SMITH was proved to have been a leading member of the pirate crew. The records only say that he was sentenced to a lesser punishment than death. It was probably transportation for 7 years.

SMITH

Captain John SMITH (alias GOW). b. Cariston, Orkney Islands. 1690/91. SMITH was an experienced officer on both merchantmen and men-of-war. He shipped on the galley *George* carrying beeswax out of Rotterdam. SMITH and the crew took over the vessel between Santa Cruz and Marseilles. They killed the officers and re-named the vessel *Revenge*. They took ships off the Spanish coast, sailed for Madeira, then back to Spain and Portugal. They took many vessels and paid in beeswax for the goods they stole. SMITH wished to go back to the Orkneys, where he had a girlfriend. SMITH promised his crew that vessels of the Greenland fleet would be in the area. While SMITH was ashore in the Orkneys, courting his girlfriend, and his vessel was at anchor, some of the crew who were reluctant pirates got away in a boat and reached the Scottish mainland. These crewmen alerted the magistrates at Queensferry. SMITH had instructed the crew to clean the vessel's bottom while he was away, instead they went raiding ashore, even stealing a bagpiper. The vessel was blown onto Calf Rock and SMITH tried to bargain with the local landowner for a boat, but the landowner summoned the magistrates. SMITH and his crew were taken and shipped to London where they were held at the Marshalsea gaol. They were all tried and found guilty. SMITH was hanged at Execution Dock, Wapping on 11 Jun 1725. The order of the Admiralty Court was that SMITH and his lieutenant were to be hanged in chains as an example to other seamen. One of them was hanged at Greenwich, the other up the River Thames at Deptford.

SMITH

John SMITH. One of the mutinous crew of the *Antonio*. SMITH was hanged in Boston in 1672.

SMITH

John-William SMITH. b. Charleston, S. Carolina. A crewman to Major Stede BONNET. SMITH was captured with BONNET at Cape Fear River on 27 Sep 1718.

He was tried at Charleston and hanged on 8 Nov 1718.

SMITH

Phillip SMITH. A crewman to Captain John JOHNSON in the early 17th century. After JOHNSON's vessel took the prize *Black Buck*, SMITH won (at some gambling game) 680 of the 800 silver dollars found on the prize.

SMITH

William SMITH. He was taken from the prize vessel *Elizabeth* by Captain James SKYRM's ship *Ranger* in Jan 1722. *Ranger* was captured by *HMS Swallow* off the West African coast on 1 Feb 1722. SMITH was tried at Cape Corso Castle on 28 Mar 1722 and found not guilty of piracy. He was acquitted.

SMITH

Major Samuel SMITH. A Buccaneer. In 1641 SMITH was sent by the Governor of Jamaica to reinforce MANSFIELD's buccaneers, who had captured the Island of Old Providence from the Spanish. SMITH sailed later with MANSFIELD. In 1660 he was taken by the Spanish and held chained in a dungeon in Panama for 17 months.

SMITHSON

George SMITHSON. He was

taken from the prize galley *Sandwich* in Aug 1721 by Captain James SKYRM's ship *Ranger* which was in turn captured by *HMS Swallow* off the West African coast on 1 Feb 1722. SMITHSON was tried at Cape Corso Castle on 28 Mar 1722. He was found not guilty of piracy and acquitted.

SOCKWELL

Captain ? SOCKWELL. An English pirate captain in the early 17th century. His area of piracy must have been the Bristol Channel because SOCKWELL named himself the 'King of Lundy'.

SOUND

Joseph SOUND. b. Westminster, London. 1695/6. A crewman to Captain Charles HARRIS on his ship *Ranger*. SOUND was captured with the rest of *Ranger* crew by *HMS Greyhound*. He was tried at Newport R.I. SOUND was found guilty of piracy and hanged on 19 Jul 1723.

SOUTH

Thomas SOUTH. b. Boston, England. A crewman to Captain Samuel BELLAMY. SOUTH was captured on Cape Cod on the day after BELLAMY's ship was wrecked there. He was taken to Boston, tried and found guilty. SOUTH was sentenced to

death but for some reason was pardoned 13 days before the other crewmen were hanged.

SOWARD

David SOWARD. An elderly pirate when he took Woodes ROGERS' offer of pardon in the Bahamas in 1718. He was working on a turtling sloop when Captain Calico Jack RACKHAM enlisted his two crewmen as pirates. RACKHAM refused to take SOWARD because he was 'lame and disabled by a previous wound'. SOWARD must have spent his pirate plunder more wisely than most because, apart from his turtling sloop, he was also the owner of the sloop *Mary* that Captain John AUGER went pirating in.

SPARKS

James SPARKS. A crewman to Captain William PHILLIPS throughout PHILLIPS' cruise of the West Indies in 1723/4. On 14 Apr 1724 the captives on the ship overpowered the pirates and took over the vessel. SPARKS was thrown overboard in the action, whilst trying to defend PHILLIPS.

SPARKES

John SPARKES. A crewman to Captain Henry AVERY. SPARKES was known to have been a thief, even robbing his shipmates. From one fellowcrewmate, Phillip MIDDLE-TON, SPARKES stole 270 pieces of gold. He was hanged at Execution Dock, Wapping, in 1696.

SPRATLIN

Robert SPRATLIN. One of the men who crossed the Isthmus of Darien with Captain Bartholomew SHARP's expedition in 1681. On the return journey he became lost while the party were crossing the swollen Chagres River, but met up with Lionel WAFER's party later.

SPRIGGS

Captain Francis Farrington SPRIGGS. SPRIGGS sailed first with Captain George LOWTHER and later with Captain Edward LOW. In command of his own small vessel, probably a sloop because his crew were only 18 men, SPRIGGS parted company with LOW off the West African coast at Christmas 1723 and sailed for the Caribbean. He and his crew were considered particularly brutal and daring. He once sailed into Port Royal harbour, Jamaica, with the idea of sinking HMS Eagle, the ship that had taken LOWTHER's vessel. Two men-of-war were in harbour, but SPRIGGS escaped them. He cruised the West Indies and the Carolinas until 1725. His ship once captured a cargo of horses. The crew rode them around the deck

'like madmen at Newmarket'. SPRIGGS was eventually cornered by a man-of-war on the Florida coast, he and most of his crew got ashore and escaped into the woods.

SPRINGER

Captain ? SPRINGER. A buccaneer captain who fought bravely with SAWKINS and RINGROSE at the battle at Perico in 1680. He gave his name to Springer's cay, one of the Samballo Islands. This island was the rendezvous for the buccaneers who re-crossed the Isthmus of Darien on foot from SHARP's expedition.

STAKES

Henry STAKES. A River Thames pirate, not a deep-sea man. The gunner of a ship in the early 17th century. His ship took the *Cock of St Omer* at Ordfordness in 1613. STAKES terrified the captive crew by firing his guns point blank at them. Fortunately the guns were loaded with powder but no shot. He was brought to trial in London. Not a man to be compared with most of those here.

STANLEY

Captain ? STANLEY. A buccaneer Captain. With a few other buccaneers, STANLEY held the island of Old Providence against an attacking Spanish fleet for 5 days before being captured. With 2 other Captains, Sir Thomas WHETSTONE and Major SMITH, he was held in a dungeon in Panama for 17 months.

STEDMAN

Captain ? STEDMAN. A buccaneer Captain. In 1666, with Captain SEARLES and only 80 men, he captured the Dutch island of Tobago. Later, when England was at war with France, his small ship engaged a French frigate. With not enough wind to run away, his crew boarded the Frenchman and fought hand-to-hand for 2 hours before they were overwhelmed and captured.

STEPHENSON

John STEPHENSON. b. Orkneys. 1681/2. STEPHENSON joined Captain Bartholomew ROBERTS' vessel **Royal Fortune** from the prize vessel *Onslow* in May 1721. Captured by *HMS Swallow* off the West African coast on 10 Feb 1722. STEPHENSON was tried at Cape Corso Castle on 28 Mar 1722. He was found guilty and hanged.

STEPHENSON

Captain Robert STEPHENSON. An English pirate captain in the early 17th century. His vessel *Prong* was a flyboat of 200 tons

and 28 guns. STEPHENSON once offered a carpenter the choice of joining his crew, or being shot from one of the ship's guns.

STEVENS

William STEVENS. A buccaneer who joined Captain Bartholomew SHARP's expedition to plunder the Pacific coasts of the Americas in 1680/81. STEVENS died on 15 Jan 1682. SHARP's journal records that STEVENS "was observed, after his eating of three Manchaneel Apples, at King Charles' Harbour, to waste away strangely, till at length he was become a perfect skeleton."

STILES

Richard STILES. A crewman to the pirate BLACKBEARD. STILES was wounded and captured at the battle at Ocracoke Inlet on 1 Dec 1718, where BLACKBEARD was killed. He was tried and hanged.

STODGILL

John STODGILL. He was taken from the prize galley *King Solomon* off Cape Apollonia in Jan 1722 by Captain James SKYRM's vessel *Ranger*. Captured by *HMS Swallow* off the West African coast on 1 Feb 1722. STODGILL was tried at Cape Corso Castle on 28 Mar 1722. He was found not guilty of piracy and acquitted.

STOREY

Thomas STOREY. A crewman to Captain William COWARD. They took the ketch 'Elinor' in Boston Harbour. STOREY was tried on 27 Jan 1690 and sentenced to death. He was later reprieved.

ST QUENTIN

Richard St QUENTIN. A Yorkshireman. One of McKINLEY's crew who murdered Captain GLASS and his family on the *Earl of Sandwich*. He was arrested at Cork and hanged near Dublin on 19 Mar 1765. St QUENTIN's body, like the other pirates, was left to rot in chains as a warning to other seamen.

STRANGEWAYS

Melchior STRANGEWAYS. b. Gloucestershire. A late 16th century pirate who was based in Dorset in the 1570's.

STREATOR

Thomas STREATOR. A reluctant crewman to Captain William FLY. He was captured by FLY when the vessel *Elizabeth* was taken. FLY at first threatened to throw STREATOR overboard, but relented and kept him in chains. STREATOR was released when FLY's captives overthrew the pirates.

STRETTON

Thomas STRETTON. He was taken from the prize vessel 'Onslow' by Captain James SKYRM's ship 'Ranger' in Jan 1722. Captured by HMS Swallow off the West African coast on 1 Feb 1722. STRETTON was tried at Cape Corso Castle on 28 Mar 1722. He was found not guilty of piracy and acquitted.

STURGES

Captain ? STURGES. An Elizabethan pirate captain who based himself at La Rochelle. In company with the Portugese pirate CALLES, he took 2 Portugese ships, 1 French, 1 Spanish and 1 Scottish ship, all in the same year.

SUTTON

Thomas SUTTON. b. Berwick-upon-Tweed. 1698/9. A crewman to Captain Howard DAVIS, later a crewman to Captain Bartholomew ROBERTS on *Royal Fortune*. Captured off the West African coast by *HMS Swallow* on 10 Feb 1722. SUTTON was tried at Cape Corso Castle on 28 Mar 1722. He was found guilty of piracy and hanged.

SWAN

Captain Charles SWAN. A Buccaneer Captain who took his ship *Cygnet* around Cape Horn to join Captain Bartholomew SHARP's expedition to the

Pacific in 1680/81. William DAMPIER joined him as Pilot and Quartermaster, and Basil RINGROSE as Supercargo. SWAN did not sail back to the Caribbean, but onwards to the Philippines. There his crew mutinied and put him ashore with 35 crewmen. They sailed the *Cygnet* on, but only as far as Madagascar, where the worn-out ship sank at her moorings.

SWAN

On 9 Aug 1683 a group of 640 buccaneers, under Captains SWAN, TOWNLEY, DAVIS, and COOK, made a vain attempt against the town of Leon in Mexico. 540 men landed in 30 canoes and made a march of 20 miles across country. The Spanish were able to pick off some of the stragglers from the march. One of those killed was a seaman called John SWAN, who was 84 years old. I don't know which crew he belonged to, but given the hardship of the life, his longevity was amazing.

SWAN

? SWAN. He was Bosun of the merchant galley *George*, carrying beeswax out of Rotterdam. SWAN plotted with the pirate Captain John SMITH to take over the vessel. The plot was revealed to Captain FERNEAU, the ship's captain, who put SWAN ashore, not realising that SMITH, one of his officers, was the ringleader of the plot. SMITH later took over the vessel.

SWITZER

Joseph SWITZER. b. Boston. 1699/1700. A crewman on Captain Charles HARRIS' ship *Ranger*. Captured by *HMS Greyhound*. SWITZER was tried at Newport R.I. in Jul 1723. He was found not guilty of piracy and acquitted.

SYMPSON

David SYMPSON. b. North Berwick. 1685/6. SYMPSON was a crewman to Captain Howard DAVIS, and later to Captain Bartholomew ROBERTS on *Royal Fortune*. Captured off the West African coast on 10 Feb 1722 by *HMS Swallow*. He was tried at Cape Corso Castle on 28 Mar 1722 and found guilty. At his execution he saw a woman whom he recognised in the crowd of spectators. He commented that he had lain with her three times and now she was come to watch him hang.

SYMPSON

? SYMPSON. A crewman to Captain Thomas GREEN on *Worcester*. SYMPSON, along with GREEN and the rest of the crew, was falsely arrested, tried, sentenced and hanged at Leith, Scotland in 1705.

TAFFERY

Peter TAFFERY. b. France. One of the 3 Frenchmen who were reluctant crewmen to Captain William PHILLIPS. Eventually the captives overpowered the pirate crew and sailed the vessel to Boston. TAFFERY was tried at Boston on 12 Apr 1724. He was found not guilty of piracy and acquitted.

TAFFIER

? TAFFIER. A gunner to Captain ? KENNEDY in the West Indies in 1716. TAFFIER once knocked unconscious the captain of a captured vessel with the flat of his cutlass. KENNEDY, a pirate well-known for his dislike of violence, admonished TAFFIER for his brutality. There was a TAFFIER, who was also a gunner to Captain Samuel BELLAMY on *Whydah*. It's a reasonable assumption that they were the same man. TAFFIER is believed to have drowned on the night, in 1717, when *Whydah* was wrecked on Cape Cod.

TALBOT

James TALBOT. One of the mutineers on the *Vineyard* which was taken over by some of the crew en route from New Orleans on 23 Nov 1830. There is no mention of TALBOT after the mutiny, nor mention of him at their trial. Strange?

TARLTON

Edward TARLTON. Was taken aboard Captain Bartholomew ROBERTS' ship *Royal Fortune* from the prize vessel *Tarlton* of Liverpool. Edward TARLTON was the brother of Captain TARLTON, who was the Captain and probably the owner of the vessel. Captured by HMS Swallow off the West African coast on 10 Feb 1722. He was tried at Cape Corso Castle on 28 Mar 1722. TARLTON was found not guilty of piracy and acquitted.

Note: Edward's brother, Captain TARLTON was released with most of his crew and the vessel, though he would have been a better navigator or sailing-master than his brother Edward. The navy must have thought Edward was a volunteer pirate, or they would not have tried him. Perhaps he did volunteer to join them? I think an investigation into the TARLTONs would inspire a good historical novel.

TAYLOR

Captain John TAYLOR. Formerly a Lieutenant Royal Navy. TAYLOR sailed in the pirate fleet which included Captain Le VASSEUR and Captain Edward ENGLAND. They plundered East India Company and Compagnie Fransais vessels in the Indian Ocean, operating from the Seychelles, Reunion and Mauritius. TAYLOR captured the vessel ***Virgem de Cabo*** with treasure worth £100 million. He kept the vessel and re-named it ***Victory***. They overwhelmed the Dutch town of Fort Lagoa, in Lorenzo Marques Bay, in Apr 1722. TAYLOR then parted company with Le VASSEUR, sailed for the Spanish West Indies. TAYLOR's crew shared treasure of over £1 million plus 42 small diamonds per man when they dispersed. (One man was given a large diamond that weighed as much as 42 small ones, he felt he was being cheated and they smashed it into many pieces for him.) Each man's share was over £4000 in coin. Some of the crew left at Reunion or Madagascar, to stay in the Indian Ocean. Others travelled with TAYLOR to Portobello on the Spanish Main. TAYLOR took service with the Spanish Navy as a 'Guardacosta'. Legend says that he later traded in logwood at Honduras, and that he died in Cuba.

TAYLOR

William TAYLOR. A crewman to Captain William PHILLIPS throughout his cruise of the West Indies. TAYLOR was being shipped to Virginia 'to be sold' when his vessel was taken by PHILLIPS. He said that he 'was grateful to have been rescued by honest men' meaning the pirates. The pirates were overcome by captives and reluctant crewmen on 12 Apr 1724. The captives sailed the vessel to Boston. TAYLOR was tried in May 1724 and found guilty of piracy. He was sentenced to death, but the execution was stayed for one year pending a plea for the King's mercy. The outcome of the plea is not known.

TAYLOR

William TAYLOR. b. Bristol. He joined Captain Bartholomew ROBERTS' ship ***Royal Fortune*** from the prize vessel ***York*** of Bristol. Captured by ***HMS Swallow*** off the West African coast on 10 Feb 1722. TAYLOR was tried at Cape Corso Castle on 28 Mar 1722. He was found guilty and sentenced to hang, but the sentence was commuted to 7 years transportation to the African colonies.

TAYLOR

? TAYLOR. A crewman to Captain Thomas GREEN on the vessel ***Worcester***. He was falsely arrested, tried, sentenced and hanged at Leith, Scotland, in Apr 1705.

TEACH

Captain Edward (BLACK-BEARD) TEACH. b. Bristol. BLACKBEARD's original name may have been DRUMMOND. I know nothing (yet) of his youth, but BLACKBEARD joined the famous pirate Captain Benjamin HORNIGOLD in Jamaica in

1716 and quickly became his favourite. By 1717 BLACK-BEARD had his own ship and crew. He was a flamboyant dresser and favoured red velvet. From his shoulders hung coloured silk sashes, each holding a pistol. His beard grew almost to his eyes and was divided into narrow plaits, each with a ribbon. His wide hat-brim was festooned with cuttings of slow-match which he lit before facing his enemies, so that his huge bizarre figure was crowned with smoke and sparks. BLACKBEARD cruised off the Eastern Coast of North America, taking many vessels. In May 1716 he besieged Charles-Towne. A month later he surrendered to a pardon from the Governor of North Carolina and renounced piracy forever. He

married a 16 year old, his 14th bride, and settled down, but only for a few months. When he sailed again 2 naval sloops were sent to capture him. They cornered him at Ocracoke Inlet and a great battle ensued. Eventually BLACKBEARD was killed and his crew were taken. By the time he died he had 5 pistol balls in his body and 20 severe sword wounds. Lieutenant MAYNARD, commander of one of the sloops, had BLACK-BEARD's head struck from his body and the body thrown overboard. Legend says that BLACK-BEARD's headless body swam three times around the ship before it sank.

Note: A Highlander called Evander McIVOR was probably the person who actually struck BLACKBEARD down. McIVOR was a scarred celebrity when he sailed from The Downs aboard *Luxborough* in Oct 1726 on a slaving voyage. *Luxborough* caught fire on the homeward passage and 23 crew got away on the ship's yawl. Six survived, through cannibalism, to be picked up by a Newfoundland fishing boat. I don't think McIVOR was one of the six.

TEAGUE

Robert TEAGUE. A crewman to Captain John SMITH. TEAGUE was captured with SMITH's crew in the Orkneys. He was tried in London in May 1725 and was acquitted.

TEAT

Captain Josiah TEAT. An officer on Captain Charles SWAN's *Cygnet* which sailed from London in an attempt to trade legitimately with the Spanish in South America. Only when they were attacked at each Spanish port they reached did SWAN resort to piracy. In 1683 they met up with Captain John COOK's *Bachelor's Delight* in the Pacific and sailed together for some time. Later *Cygnet* sailed across the Pacific with TEAT in command of a small prize barque. By the time they reached Mindanao there was ill-feeling between SWAN and his crew. John READ took command of *Cygnet* with TEAT as Master. Eventually (maybe late 1688) *Cygnet* reached Madagascar and Captain READ sailed for New York. TEAT was at last Captain of the ship. TEAT and *Cygnet* joined the Madagascar pirates, but after all her travels, *Cygnet* was so rotten that she sank on her mooring at St Augustine Bay, Madagascar. TEAT's further adventures are not recorded.

TEMPLETON

John TEMPLETON. A crewman to Captain John QUELCH on his brig *Charles*. He was tried with the rest of QUELCH's crew at the Star Tavern in Boston in Jun 1704. When the court discovered that TEMPLETON was not yet 14 years old, he was acquitted.

le TESTU

Captain le TESTU. An early French privateer of Le Havre. Le TESTU led a crew of Huguenot privateers in the Caribbean and Central America. In Mar 1573 he and his men met Francis DRAKE near the Sacres River in Darien. Acting as a joint force they attacked a Spanish muletrain of 190 animals, each carrying 300 lbs of silver. After taking the treasure the parties split up.

TEW

Captain Thomas TEW. TEW's grandfather, Richard, emigrated from Northamptonshire to North America in 1640. In 1691 TEW arrived in Bermuda and raised money from important local investors to purchase and fit out the sloop *Amity*. He was given a commission to capture a French factory (a slaving station) on the Gambia River in West Africa. As soon as they sailed, TEW and his crew decided to turn pirate and sail for the Indian Ocean. There they took an Arabian vessel which gave prize money of £3000 per man. TEW's Quartermaster (whose name I don't know) and 23 of the crew decided to settle on the island of Madagascar. TEW and the remainder met up with the French pirate Captain MISSON, who invited TEW to come to Libertalia, the pirate Utopia that MISSON and CARRACIOLI had established in East Africa. TEW took part in the government of the town and sailed on missions to re-supply it with stores and manpower. He once took a slaver in the South Atlantic, sailed it to Libertalia and freed the slaves to swell the town's population. He later sailed back to Bermuda to pay off the investors in his original enterprise. Returning to Madagascar, TEW tried to get his old Quartermaster and crewmen to rejoin him, whilst ashore his vessel, Captain MISSON's *Victoire* was blown aground and wrecked. MISSON and CARRACIOLI later rescued him. Their infant democracy was eventually sacked by local natives and CARRACIOLI was killed. MISSON and TEW decided to give it all up and retire to live in North America. They loaded their huge wealth onto 2 sloops and set off. In high winds off the Southern African coast, MISSON's sloop overturned within sight of TEW and was lost with all hands. TEW continued to Rhode Island. From here on accounts differ. He either lived out his life on Rhode Island 'in great tranquillity', or he returned to piracy in the Red Sea, and while taking a Moorish ship which was putting up stiff resistance, his stomach was shot away and he died, still conducting the battle, with his hands full of his own intestines. You are the reader, you choose.

THOMAS

Captain THOMAS. An alias used by Major Stede BONNET,

when he sailed again after accepting a pardon from Governor EDEN of Bath Town.

THOMAS

John THOMAS. b. Jamaica. A crewman to Major Stede BONNET. THOMAS was captured with BONNET on 27 Sep 1718 at Cape Fear River. He was tried at Charleston and hanged on 8 Nov 1718.

THOMAS

Stephen THOMAS. He was taken from the prize ship *Dilligence* in Jan 1722 by Captain Bartholomew ROBERTS' ship *Royal Fortune*. Captured by *HMS Swallow* off the West African coast on 10 Sep 1722. THOMAS was tried at Cape Corso Castle on 28 Mar 1722. He was found not guilty of piracy and acquitted.

THOMPSON

Captain William THOMPSON. You can decide if THOMPSON was a pirate. He was Captain of the *Mary Dyer*, commissioned to take the treasure from the Cathedral at Lima to safety in a time of war, in 1821. Instead he took the treasure to the Cocos Islands and buried it there. The treasure, which included a six-foot high Madonna of solid gold, has never been recovered. THOMPSON died in Newfoundland in 1845.

THOMPSON

Captain ? THOMPSON. An English seaman who joined the Barbary corsairs, probably through capture, and turned Mohammedan. He commanded a corsair vessel and was captured off the coast of Ireland by a man-of-war in the reign of Queen Elizabeth I. He was hanged at Wapping, London.

THOMPSON

? THOMPSON. Was taken captive by Edward BENNETT on *Rampelagos*. He became a crewman to BENNETT and sailed with him until his capture by *Espiegle* (see CHAPPELLE and WALSH). After prison in Tasmania, THOMPSON settled in Samoa under the name of McCOMBER.

THORNDEN

Edward THORNDEN. He was taken from the prize vessel *Elizabeth* by Captain Bartholomew ROBERTS' ship *Royal Fortune* in Jan 1722. Captured by *HMS Swallow* off the West African coast on 10 Feb 1722. THORNDEN was tried at Cape Corso Castle on 28 Mar 1722. He was found not guilty of piracy and acquitted.

THURBAR

Richard THURBAR. Tried for piracy in Boston in 1704. (Was he one of QUELCH's crew, tried at the Star Tavern?)

THURSTON

Captain ? THURSTON. A buccaneer of Tortuga. He refused the offer of a Royal Pardon in 1670, when all privateer commissions were revoked. With a mulatto shipmate, DIEGO, using an obsolete commission from MODYFORD, the late Governor of Jamaica, he continued to take Spanish prizes and bring them to Tortuga.

THWAITES

Captain Joseph THWAITES. He was Cox'n to Captain HOOD, Royal Navy, and was promoted to Midshipman on *HMS Zealous* in 1763, in the Mediterranean. THWAITES was sent ashore in Algiers to buy sheep for the ship's rations, but never returned. HMS Zealous sailed without him, assuming that he had been murdered. In fact, THWAITES, who spoke Greek and Turkish, had entered the service of the Ottoman Empire. He turned Mohammedan and was given command of a 44 gun frigate. For several years he plundered shipping of all nations without mercy, killing the prisoners he took. From time to time he went ashore in Gibraltar and transmitted, through his agent, large sums of money to his wife and family in England. He also kept 3 young Armenian wives at his home in Algiers. International pressure was applied on the Dey of Algiers to quit piracy and THWAITEs realised that his time was running out. Taking all the treasure that he could carry, he boarded the American frigate *Constitution*, bound for New York. There he purchased land near New York City and had a handsome mansion built. A year later he was bitten by a rattlesnake and died in agony.

TOMKINS

John TOMKINS. b. Gloucestershire. 1700/01. A crewman on Captain Charles HARRIS' ship *Ranger*. Captured by *HMS Greyhound*. TOMKINS was tried at Newport R.I. and hanged on 19 Jul 1723.

TOMKINS

Captain Thomas TOMKINS. An English pirate Captain in the early 17th century. As a youth he served the Earl of Essex as a page at court. Later he fitted out a vessel *Margaret and John* to trade with the West Indies. Instead he sailed to the Mediterranean and turned pirate. In Mar 1605, he took the *Black Balbigna*, a Venetian argosy laden with cloth and gold coins. The prize was worth £75,000. TOMKINS landed his treasure at Lymington, Hampshire. 6 of his crew were caught and hanged at Southampton. Tomkins was captured in 1610, tried and sentenced to hang. He received a pardon, probably because of his family connections.

TOPPING

Dennis TOPPING. He shipped out of Providence in the sloop *Buck* with Captain Thomas ANSTIS, Walter KENNEDY and Howel DAVIS. TOPPING was killed as they fought to take a Portugese prize off the Brazilian coast. The rest of the crew, with gains and losses along the way, finished up as Captain Bartholomew ROBERTS' crew on *Royal Fortune*. Those that lived until 1722 were hanged at Cape Corso Castle.

TOWNLEY

Captain ? TOWNLEY. A buccaneer captain. TOWNLEY joined Captain John DAVIS voyage to the Pacific in 1684. He split with DAVIS and went off with the French party. He had disputes too with the French and split with them, only to meet them again when they were in battle with the Spanish 'plate' fleet. TOWNLEY managed to rescue the French from a defeat. He later took immense plunder at the town of Lavelia, near Lima, but was wounded conveying it back to his ship. He died of his wounds in Aug 1685.

TREVOR

Kidwell ap Cadwallader TREVOR. A Welsh pirate in the early 17th century. TREVOR was a crewman to Captain John JENNINGS. He was one of the party who handed JENNINGS over to the Earl of THOMOND in 1609.

TRISTRIAN or TRISTAN

Captain ? TRISTRIAN. A French filibuster. One of the French buccaneers who sailed on Captain Bartholomew SHARP's expedition to plunder the Pacific in 1680/81. TRIS-TRIAN obviously didn't cross the Isthmus of Darien with the main party, because when the group of malcontents under COOKE who left the expedition re-crossed the Isthmus on foot, they encountered TRISTRIAN's ship at Le Sound's Cay, on the Darien coast. COOKE and his men eventually took over TRISTRIAN's ship and put him ashore. TRISTRIAN and COOKE met again later, but seem to have forgotten their differences.

TRUMPET

John TRUMPET. He lived at Cochin, India. I think TRUM-PET was a retired pirate. He acted as an agent and a spy for the pirates of the Malabar Coast. He seems to have lived long and well on pirate plunder. He was the father of a large family and his daughters 'attended many pirate social functions'.

TRYER

Mather TRYER. A Carolina pirate. TRYER was tried for taking a sloop belonging to Samuel SALTERS of Bermuda, in 1699. He was found not guilty and acquitted.

TUCKER

Robert TUCKER. b. Jamaica. A crewman to Major Stede BONNET. TUCKET was captured with BONNET at Cape Fear River. He was tried at Charleston and hanged on 8 Nov 1718 at White Point.

TUCKER

Captain Thomas TUCKER. b. Newcastle-upon-Tyne. An English pirate captain in the early 17th century. TUCKER joined with Captain John WOODLAND in a venture to raid the 'Seven Islands' of Russia. They got as far as the Faroe Islands when TUCKER's vessel was wrecked in a storm. WOODLAND, instead of aiding TUCKER, robbed him and left him. TUCKER got a pardon in England in 1616, but had difficulty finding other employ. (I know the feeling).

TUCKERMAN

Captain TUCKERMAN. Sailed in company with Captain PORTER. These two novice pirates met with Captain Bartholomew ROBERTS and received from him lessons in piracy, good entertainment, and a pirate blessing. See PORTER.

TURNER

David TURNER. b. Britain. TURNER was a crewman to Captain Samuel BELLAMY on *Whydah*. TURNER is believed to have drowned on the night, in 1717, when *Whydah* was wrecked on Cape Cod.

TURNER

Lieutenant ? TURNER. One of BLACKBEARD's trusted officers. TURNER took command of Major Stede BONNET's *Revenge* when BLACKBEARD took the vessel from BONNET.

TURNLEY

Captain Richard TURNLEY. One of the pirates who took Woodes ROGERS' offer of pardon in Providence in 1718. It was TURNLEY who informed the Governor of Calico Jack RACKHAM's affair with Anne BONNEY. In revenge, RACKHAM and BONNET followed Turnley's sloop to a neighbouring island. TURNLEY was hunting ashore so the pair had to content themselves with sinking his sloop and capturing his crew.

TYLE

Captain Ort van TYLE. A Dutchman from New York. A most successful Madagascar pirate captain. He sailed in company with Captain James in the Indian Ocean. TYLE had a plantation on Madagascar and used his prisoners as slave labour there. One of his prisoners was the evil Welshman David Williams, who worked there for 6 months before escaping.

UPTON

John UPTON. b. Deptford, London. 1679. UPTON served in the Royal Navy as a petty officer until Jul 1723 when his wife died. UPTON discovered that she had several debts and that he was in danger of arrest by her creditors. Leaving his 4 orphaned children, he sailed from Poole, Dorset, as bosun on the galley *Perry*. It was captured on 14 Nov 1725 by the pirate Captain COOPER on *Night Rambler*. UPTON escaped from the pirates at the first opportunity, when the ship lay at the Mosquito Coast. He was captured by the Spanish but escaped from them too. A New York sloop picked him up and gave him passage to Jamaica. In Port Royal he was press-ganged into the Royal Navy aboard *HMS Nottingham*. He served as a Quartermaster for two years until someone said they recognised him as a pirate. UPTON was shipped to London, tried for piracy and hanged.

VALLANUEVA

Captain ? VALLANUEVA. A pirate captain from Dominica. In 1831 he commanded a small gaff-topsail-schooner named *General Marazon*, a vessel with one brass 8 pounder cannon and a crew of 44 men. His crew were a mixture of French, Italian, English and Creole.

VANCLEIN

Captain Moses VANCLEIN (or van KLIJN). A Dutch Frijbooter. VANCLEIN sailed in a mixed fleet under the command of L'OLLONAIS. Off the coast of Yucatan, VANCLEIN encouraged some of the vessels to leave L'OLLONAIS and sail with him to Costa Rica. There they sacked the town of Varaguas, but found only 8 pounds of gold to share between them all. Other buccaneer captains were less keen to follow him after that experience.

VANE

Captain Charles VANE. A pirate captain who cruised the Eastern coasts of North America, especially the Carolinas. He was exceptionally cruel and was known to have keel-hauled those who angered him. He was also the only pirate captain known to have cheated his crewmen in the share-out of plunder. He once tried, but failed, to take a vessel under the command of a Captain HOLFORD. VANE met with BLACKBEARD off the Carolinas, but they never sailed together. VANE's vessel was broken up in a storm on Baracho Island and he was washed up on the beach. As luck would have it, the first vessel that passed was commanded by Captain HOLFORD, who recognised him and left him there. The next vessel picked him up, but then met up with Captain HOLFORD, who took VANE to Jamaica in irons. He was tried there, found guilty and hanged on 29 Mar 1720.

VAN HOORN

Captain Jan Janszoon Van HOORN. A Dutch privateer. On 15 July 1633 Van HOORN landed at Trujillo on the Spanish Main with a fleet of freebooters and buccaneers. They held the town for 6 days while they plundered. They left discontented with their small rewards from the town. On 11 August 1633, along with the pirate Diego de los REYES and his crew, they attacked the town of Campeche. Eye-witnesses said they landed from 13 ships and were a mixed force of English, French and a few Portugese. The attack was led by Diego the Mulatto and Captain JOL. The invaders broke through the initial defences and engaged the local Spanish regiment in the main Town Square. More than 3 dozen Spanish were killed and the remainder fled. The pirates seized 22 vessels in the harbour. After this Van HOORN returned to Holland. JOL and de los REYES remained to plunder in the Caribbean. (see JOL and REYES.)

VANHORN

Captain Nicholas VANHORN. A Dutch Frijbooter of Hispaniola. In 1681 he sailed from England in command of the merchantman *Mary and Martha*. He put ashore the merchants in Cadiz, stole 4 Spanish guns, re-named the vessel *St Nicholas* and sailed off to plunder the Canaries and the Guinea Coast. VANHORN took ships and slaves then sailed to San Domingo. In Apr 1683 he took aboard 300 volunteers at Petit Goave and joined the buccaneer LAURENS fleet in the Gulf of Honduras. They learned that the city of Vera Cruz was expecting two ships from Caracas, so they crammed all of their men into two of their own ships and sailed into the harbour. The harbour-guards of the city lit fires to guide the ships into port. The buccaneers took the city easily and spent 4 profitable days plundering. A Spanish fleet of 14 vessels arrived off the harbour but dared not enter while the buccaneers were there. The buccaneers sailed away under the noses of the Spanish fleet. Not a shot was fired. In the share-out of the plunder, each man got 800 gold pieces-of-eight, VANHORN's share was 24,000. He and LAURENS came to blows about the share-out and

VANHORN was slightly injured on one wrist. He died two weeks later of gangrene poisoning.

VAN HORST

Simon Van HORST, of Amsterdam. A crewman to Captain Samuel BELLAMY. He was captured on Cape Cod the day after BELLAMY's ship *Whydah* was wrecked there. Van HORST was tried in Boston and hanged there on 15 Nov 1717.

VAN VIN

Moses VAN VIN. A Dutchman. Second-in-command to the buccaneer Captain NAU. He was with NAU when they were shipwrecked on the coast of Honduras and spent six months building a boat to get away. VAN VIN may have been left in command of the shore-party when half of the party could not get a place in the small boat. It is likely that they perished there.

VAUGHAN

Captain Alexander VAUGHAN. An English pirate captain in the early 17th century. "A greate and tall bigge thick man." I can find no more.

VAUGHN

A Dorset-based pirate in the late 16th century. I think it is possible that this man, the VAUGHAN above and William BAUGHE may be the same man, or two men, or three individual characters, or close kinsmen. You choose.

VEALE

Captain ? VEALE. VEALE arrived at New London on 1 Jul 1685. He was recognised as a pirate by the crewman of a ship he once robbed. VEALE made a hurried departure from the port.

VEALE

Thomas VEALE. One of 4 New England pirates, in the mid-17th century, who rowed up the River Saugus to Lynn Woods. They took with them their treasure and a beautiful young woman. At Dungeon Rock they built themselves a cabin and lived until the woman died, when they returned to the world. The other 3 pirates were caught and hanged in England. VEALE escaped and lived in a cave, where he is reported to have hidden his treasure. The cave-mouth was covered in the earthquake of 1658 and VEALE was never seen again.

VERNEY

Captain Sir Francis VERNEY. An English-born corsair captain in the early 17th century. He habitually dressed in a turban and curly-toed slippers. VERNEY grew tired of waiting

to obtain the family inheritance. He sold up and went to Algiers. There he 'turned Turk' and was given command in several forays at sea, taking English vessels amongst others. He disappears from history for a while and then re-appears in Italy in 1611. 4 years later he died in poverty (or at least reduced circumstances) at the Hospital of St Mary of Pity, at Messina.

VERNON

See William FERNON of Captain Bartholomew ROBERTS' *Royal Fortune*.

VERPRE

Captain ? VERPRE. A French Filibuster. He commanded *Le Postilion*, a ship of two guns and 22 men.

VIGERON

Captain ? VIGERON. A French Filibuster. He commanded *La Louse*, with 4 guns and 30 men.

VILLA RISE

? VILLA RISE. A Barbary Corsair. In 1621 he took the English ship *George Banaventure* in the Straits of Gibraltar. The captain of the English ship, RAWLINS, and some of the crew escaped from their captors in Alexandria. They got away in a stolen ship in a most daring manner.

VIRGIN

Henry VIRGIN. b. Bristol. A crewman to Major Stede BONNET. He was captured with BONNET at Cape Fear River. VIRGIN was tried at Charleston and hanged on 8 Nov 1718.

VIVIEN

Captain ? VIVIEN. A French pirate out of La Rochelle. VIVIEN joined Henry MORGAN at Isle La Vache, where the great buccaneer fleet was congregating for MORGAN's expedition against the Spanish Main. MORGAN was already under orders from Governor MODYFORD of Jamaica to detain VIVIEN for the piracy of a Virginia ship some time earlier. VIVIEN was arrested and sailed to Jamaica along with his ship. He was held there for trial but his ship returned to join MORGAN's fleet.

VIVON

Captain M. La VIVON. He commanded *Cour Vivant* of La Rochelle. In Dec 1668 his ship was seized by Captain COLLIER for having taken provisions from an English vessel. (Knowing the hatred between seafarers of both nations, I would not bet much money on VIVON's guilt).

WAFER

Lionel WAFER. 1660 to 1705. A Ship's Surgeon and Diarist on Captain Bartholomew SHARP's expedition to plunder the Pacific in 1680/81. WAFER was one of the disillusioned group which included DAMPIER and 42 others, who left the main party on the Pacific coast and re-crossed the Isthmus of Darien on foot to the Caribbean. WAFER was injured on that journey and spent some months with the local Indians of the Cuno nation recovering. He later joined DAVIS, COOK, DAMPIER and others on *Revenge*, then *Bachelors' Delight* for another expedition to the Pacific. WAFER seems to have been an active buccaneer until about 1688, serving two years in prison in Jamestown, Virginia, for piracy. WAFER published his diaries on his return to England.

WAKE

Captain Thomas WAKE. WAKE joined Captain Thomas TEW at Bermuda when TEW returned from the Indian Ocean to repay the investors in his initial voyage. WAKE sailed on TEW's second journey to the Indian Ocean. He had previously been pardoned for piracy by King James II.

WALDEN

John WALDEN. b. Whitby, Yorkshire. 1697/8. WALDEN joined Captain Bartholomew ROBERTS' ship *Royal Fortune* from the prize vessel *Blessing* of Lyminton. Because of his foul temper, WALDEN was known amongst the pirates as Miss Nanny. He lost a leg in the battle when *HMS Swallow* captured *Royal Fortune* off the West African coast on 10 Feb 1722. At his trial at Cape Corso Castle on 28 Mar 1722, John TRAHERNE, Captain of *King Solomon*, said that he had battered down their cabin doors with an axe, then cut their anchor cable, telling them "There are plenty more anchors in London, and who needs the strain of pulling it up in this hot climate". Not surprisingly, WALDEN was found guilty of piracy. He was hanged.

WALDEN

John WALDEN. He joined Captain James SKYRM's vessel *Ranger* from the prize *Mary and Martha* in Jul 1720. Captured off the West African coast by HMS Swallow on 1 Feb 1722. WALDEN must have been suspected of being a Royal Navy deserter because he was shipped to the Marshalsea Gaol in London for trial. The outcome of his trial is not known.

WALKER

Samuel WALKER. A reluctant crewman to Captain William FLY. WALKER was one of the captives who helped to overthrow the pirates and sail the ship to Boston. WALKER is not mentioned in the court proceedings.

WALKER

Captain ? WALKER. An English pirate captain in the early 17th century. WALKER seems to have had a working agreement with Captain William BAUGHE. In return for BOUGHE's assistance WALKER gave him a third of his plunder.

WALL

George WALL. A Boston fisherman, probably a retired pirate. He married 16 year old Rachel Smidt and sailed with her and one crewman. Their method of piracy was to shelter in the Isles of Shoals until a storm was almost blown out. They would then appear in the shipping lane with sails in tatters, the rigging tangled and only Rachel on deck as a maiden in distress. When a rescuing vessel came alongside, WALL and the crewman would board her and kill all the crew. This worked several times until WALL mistook a storm for a hurricane. He and the crewman were washed overboard and drowned, leaving Rachel as a genuine storm victim. She was rescued, to meet the hangman later.

WALL

Rachel WALL (nee SMIDT). b. Carlisle, Pennsylvania. Mar-

ried the George WALL above. After WALL's death, Rachel was picked up by a passing ship and brought into Boston. Nothing was known about her piracy because all of WALL's victims had been murdered. Rachel returned to her previous employment as a housemaid. Later she was caught stealing a bonnet. She was tried and sentenced to death. Rachel confessed to her piracy whilst in gaol awaiting hanging.

WALLIS

Daniel WALLIS. A crewman to Captain Charles SWAN on *Cygnet*. WALLIS left SWAN at Mindanao along with many of the crew, after much ill-feeling. This group, which included William DAMPIER was attacked by the crew of a Malay vessel, who stabbed five or six before they realised what was happening. DAMPIER said that WALLIS "leapt into the sea, who could never swim before nor since; yet now he swam well a good while before he was taken up." WALLIS met up with DAMPIER much later at Cape of Good Hope and they travelled home to England together. Several years after that DAMPIER refers to him as "a young man, now living at Weymouth."

WALSINGHAM

Captain Robert Walsingham. An English pirate captain in the

early 17th century. In Jun 1615 WALSINGHAM was one of 5 English pirate captains in an Algerian fleet of corsairs that attacked the vessel **Susan Constance** off Cadiz. WALSINGHAM was a leading figure amongst the Marmora pirates. He surrendered to the authorities in Bantry Bay, Ireland in 1618.

WANSLEY

? WANSLEY. A black crewman on the **Vineyard**, out of New Orleans. The vessel was taken over by Charles GIBBS, another member of the crew. The Master and Mate were both murdered by the mutineers during the taking of the vessel. WANSLEY was an active member of the mutiny and was tried for piracy and hanged at Rhode Island in Apr 1831.

WANT

Captain ? WANT. Mate to Captain Thomas TEW on his first trip to the Indian Ocean. On TEW's second journey to the Red Sea, in 1695, WANT commanded a brig and sailed in company with TEW's fleet.

WARD

Captain John WARD. b. Faversham, Kent. 1555. WARD was born into a poor fishing family but rose through the ranks in the navy fighting against Spain. In 1602 he left his wife and

family in Kent and went in search of adventure. He drank in Plymouth until his money was gone, then was arrested and gaoled. Ward was impressed into the Channel Squadron from gaol aboard **Lion's Whelp**, (under command of Captain SOCKWELL, who later became a pirate himself). Hearing the rumour that another ship in Plymouth carried gold aboard, WARD and some fellow crewmen took the vessel. It carried no gold, but there was no going back. They sailed and took some shipping off the coast of Spain. In Algiers they got a hostile reception from the pirates so they sailed on to Tunis. In 1603/4 WARD joined a fleet of corsairs under an arrangement whereby WARD used the harbour of Tunis under the protection of the Dey of Tunis and in exchange the Dey disposed of all WARD's plunder. No doubt it was advantageous to both. WARD asked King James I for a pardon in exchange for 40,000 crowns, but the Venetian Ambassador advised against it. Ward procured and fitted out a 60 gun vessel **Solderino** for himself. Unfortunately he was no shipwright and the extra gunports so weakened the vessel that in Feb 1608 she came apart and sank. WARD managed to escape to **Little John**, another of his vessels. He later cruised off Ireland with 700 men in several ships. WARD's end is uncertain. He may have drowned off Crete, or he may have been poisoned by the Turks. More probably he may have died of the plague in 1623. William LITHGOW (a traveller and diarist) had supper with WARD in WARD's Tunisian castle in 1615 and described the splendour in which he lived. WARD converted to Islam before his death and was known as YUSUFRAIS.

WARNER

Edward WARNER. A crewman to Captain Calico Jack RACKHAM. WARNER joined RACKHAM's vessel at Negril Point, Jamaica, on the day of its capture. Nevertheless, he was tried for piracy at St Jago de la Vega (Santiago) on 16 Nov 1720. The case was adjourned for want of evidence. No more evidence seems to have been produced but in Feb 1721 WARNER was found guilty and sentenced to hang. He was probably hanged at Port Royal, but I haven't found a record of it.

WARREN

William WARREN. A crewman to Captain Thomas POUND. WARREN joined POUND's ship at Lovell's Island. In the fight at Tarpaulin Cove, when POUND was captured, WARREN was seriously wounded in the head. WARREN was tried in Boston and found guilty, but later pardoned on payment of 13 pounds and 6 shillings.

WATERS

John WATERS. b. Devon. 1688/89. Waters was Quartermaster to Captain Charles HARRIS on his ship *Ranger*. Captured by *HMS Greyhound*. He was tried at Newport R.I. and found guilty. WATERS was hanged on 19 Jul 1723.

WATKINS

John WATKINS. He was one of the guard of English soldiers at Fort Loyal, Falmouth, Maine. Watkins became a crewman to Captain Thomas POUND. He was killed in the fight at Tarpaulin Cove in 1689 when POUND's vessel and crew were taken.

WATKINS

Thomas WATKINS. He was taken from the prize galley *Onslow* by Captain Bartholomew ROBERTS' ship *Royal Fortune*. Captured by *HMS Swallow* off the West African coast on 10 Feb 1722. WATKINS was tried at Cape Corso Castle on 28 Mar 1722. He was found not guilty of piracy and acquitted.

WATLING

John WATLING. A Caribbean buccaneer. WATLING went on Captain Bartholomew SHARP's expedition to plunder the Pacific in 1680/81. On 6 Jan 1681 WATLING was voted by

SHARP's crew to take over command from SHARP. He was killed on 30 Jan leading the second attack on the town of Arica. Before the attack on the town, WATLING had questioned two old residents about its defences. He shot dead one of them to encourage the other to be truthful. After WATLING's death, SHARP was begged to resume command of the crew. WATLING's head was paraded around the streets of Arica on top of a pole by the Spanish garrison.

WATLING

Captain George WATLING. The official guidebook to the Bahamas states that a British pirate Captain George WATLING took over the island of San Salvadore and named it after himself. The island was known as WATLING Island until well into the 20th century. It may be that the WATLING that the island was named after was John WATLING (above). As a buccaneer, he was likely to have done the island more good than harm, with the wealth that he would have brought there. Islands are more likely to retain the name of a benefactor than a tyrant.

WATS

William WATS. b. Ireland. 1699. WATS joined Captain James SKYRM's ship *Ranger* at Sierra

Leone in Jul 1721. Captured by *HMS Swallow* on 1 Feb 1722 off the West African coast. WATS was tried at Cape Corso Castle on 28 Mar 1722. He was found guilty and hanged.

WATSON

Henry WATSON. A crewman to Captain George LOWTHER on his ship *Ranger*. He was captured by the sloop *HMS Eagle* at Blanquilla in Oct 1723. WATSON was tried at St Christopher (St Kitts). He was found guilty and hanged.

WATSON

John WATSON. He was taken from the prize snow *Martha* by Captain Bartholomew ROBERTS' ship *Royal Fortune*. Captured by *HMS Swallow* on 10 Feb 1722 off the West African coast. WATSON was tried at Cape Corso Castle on 28 Mar 1722. He was found not guilty of piracy and acquitted.

WATTS

Edward WATTS. b. Dunmore. 1699/70. He joined Captain James SKYRM's vessel *Ranger* from the prize ship *Onslow* in Jan 1722. Captured by *HMS Swallow* on 1 Feb 1722 off the West African coast. WATTS was tried at Cape Corso Castle on 28 Mar 1722. He was found guilty of piracy and hanged.

WATTS

Samuel WATTS. A crewman to Captain Thomas POUND. WATTS joined POUND's ship at Lovell's Island.

WAY

John WAY. A crewman to Captain John QUELCH on his pirate brig *Charles*. WAY was tried at the Star Tavern in Boston in 1704.

WEAVER

Captain Brigstock WEAVER. Of Hereford, England. WEAVER was a crewman to Captain Thomas ANSTIS in the *Good Fortune*. When ANSTIS took *Morning Star*, WEAVER was given command. He proved to be a most able pirate and took over 50 vessels in the West Indies and on the Newfoundland banks, including *Don Carlos* and *England* in 1721 and a Dutch ship and *Dolphin* of London in 1722, all profitable prizes. By May 1723 WEAVER was a ragged beggar on the streets of Bristol. A Mr Thomas SMITH and a Captain EDWARDS gave him £10 to set himself up again. Dressed well, he met a Captain Joseph Smith, who appeared to know him and invited him to dinner. Over the meal, the man told WEAVER that he knew him to be a pirate, and unless he bought him 4 hogsheads of cider, he would inform on him. WEAVER had not the price of the cider, so he was arrested, tried and sentenced in London. He was hanged at Execution Dock. Hanged at the same time were Captain GOW and William INGRAM.

WEBB

Captain Christopher WEBB. An English pirate captain in the early 17th century. WEBB's vessel was the *Blue Man-of-War*. In 1610 he took two Spanish vessels homeward bound from Brazil.

WELLS

Lieutenant Joseph WELLS. An officer on Captain John QUELCH's pirate brig *Charles*. At Gloucester, Mass., WELLS attempted to escape captured on the vessel *Larimore*, but was caught and brought to Salem. He was tried at the Star Tavern in Boston in Jun 1704.

WELSH

Mary WELSH. The mistress of Captain Edward BENNETT (alias DON PEDRO, alias BENITO of the BLOODY SWORD). Mary WELSH was captured with BENNETT at Buena Ventura, Mexico. She was not hanged with him.

WEST

Richard WEST. A crewman to Captain George LOWTHER on

his ship *Ranger*. Captured by the sloop *HMS Eagle* at Blanquilla in Oct 1723. WEST was tried at St Christopher (St Kitts) on 11 Mar 1724. He was found guilty of piracy and hanged.

WETHERLEY

Tee WETHERLEY. A Massachusetts pirate who only had one eye (traditional, I thought). He was captured in 1699 with the pirate Joseph BRADISH, and they were put in prison. They escaped 2 months later and a reward of £200 was offered. The reward was claimed by a Kennekeck Indian called Essacambuit, who brought WETHERLEY back to prison. WETHERLEY was shipped to London in irons aboard *HMS Advice*. He was tried in London in 1700, found guilty and hanged.

WHETSTONE

Sir Thomas WHETSTONE. A nephew of Oliver CROMWELL. WHETSTONE was imprisoned in the Marshalsea for debt in the latter days of the Commonwealth. On the Restoration of the monarchy, he was given £100 by King Charles II (and, I suspect, told to push off). WHETSTONE sailed to the Caribbean and operated against the Spanish without a privateers commission. He joined MYNG's and MORGAN's fleet to take Santiago, Cuba and San Francisco de Campeche in 1663.

WHITE

James WHITE. A crewman to BLACKBEARD. WHITE was wounded and captured when BLACKBEARD was killed at the battle at Ocracoke Inlet on 1 Dec 1718. He was later tried and hanged.

WHITE

James WHITE. A Musician, probably a fiddler. He was taken from the prize galley *Cornwall* in Oct 1721 at Calabar by Captain Bartholomew ROBERTS' ship *Royal Fortune*. Captured off the West African coast by HMS Swallow on 10 Feb 1722. White was tried at Cape Corso Castle on 28 Mar 1722. He was found not guilty of piracy and acquitted.

WHITE

Captain Thomas WHITE. b. Plymouth, Devon. WHITE's mother kept a pub in Plymouth. He served at one time on a man-of-war. WHITE went to Barbados, married and joined a merchant ship. He made several voyages to West Africa on slaving trips. On one of them he was taken captive by French pirates, but was either put ashore or escaped on Madagascar. WHITE gathered together a crew and although he didn't really wish to become a pirate, he knew that the only way to leave the place was to take a vessel. They did so eventually, and knowing that they could not return to civilisation in a captured vessel, he and his crew cruised the coast of East Africa and the Red Sea. WHITE built himself a house and owned land and cattle on Madagascar. Later he joined Captain John HALSEY's crew as a seaman. He contracted a disease and died, but left money to a child he had in England. The money was safely carried to the child by the captain of the next passing ship.

WHITE

Robert WHITE. A crewman to Captain George LOWTHER on his ship *Ranger*. WHITE was captured by the sloop *HMS Eagle* at Blanquilla in Oct 1723. He was tried at St Christopher (St Kitts) on 11 Mar 1724. WHITE was found guilty of piracy and hanged.

WHITE

William WHITE. A crewman to Captain William PHILLIPS throughout PHILLIPS' cruise of the West Indies in 1723/4. The pirates were eventually overpowered by the captives and reluctant crewmen aboard on 14 Apr 1724. The ship was sailed to Boston and handed to the authorities. WHITE was tried and found guilty of piracy. He was hanged on 2 Jun 1724.

WHITTING

William WHITTING. A crewman to Captain John QUELCH.

At the time of his arrest WHITTING was "sick, like to die." I don't think he survived until the trial of QUELCH's crew in Jun 1704.

WIFE

Francis WIFE. A reluctant crewman to the mutineer Phillip ROCHE on a French vessel out of Cork in 1721.

WILCOCKS

? WILCOCKS. A crewman to Captain Thomas GREEN on *Worcester*. WILCOCKS was falsely arrested, tried, sentenced and hanged at Leith, Scotland, in 1705.

WILES

William WILES. A crewman to Captain John QUELCH on the pirate brig *Charles*. WILES was tried at the Star Tavern in Boston in 1704. He was found guilty, but later pardoned 'to join the Queen's service'.

WILGRESS

Captain ? WILGRESS. A buccaneer of Jamaica. WILGRESS was sent by the Governor of Jamaica to catch the Dutchman YALLERS. The Dutchman was working for the Spanish and was threatening the logwood cutters in their camps along the coasts of the Spanish Main. Instead of carrying out the Governor's wishes, WILGRESS went buccaneering on his own account.

WILLEMS

Captain Jan WILLEMS. A Dutch freebooter in the Caribbean. During 1681/82 WILLEMS sailed in a buccaneer fleet which included COXON, SHARP and Le SAGE, which took 12 Spanish merchant ships off Riohacha. In December 1683 he was with De GRAAF's large fleet which captured Spanish shipping in the harbour of Cartagena. WILLEMS gained a newer and larger vessel from that exploit.

WILLIAMS

Captain David WILLIAMS. Illiterate, ignorant, morose, easily affronted and a poor seaman. That's what his fellow pirates thought of WILLIAMS. He sailed first on a coaster from Chester to London, there he shipped on a vessel for the East Indies. As sometimes happens to unpleasant men, when he was ashore in Madagascar looking for water his ship was blown away from its anchorage. WILLIAMS was befriended by, and took service with, a local prince. Captured in a tribal battle by another prince, he was given to yet another prince. He eventually got away and joined Captain Achen JONES on *Bedford*. Later he sailed with Captain CULLIFORD and then Captain Thomas HOWARD. WILLIAMS was imprisoned on the Island of

Johanna for some time but escaped. He served Captain Thomas WHITE as Quartermaster, and later Captain John HALSEY. No captain kept WILLIAMS in their crew for very long. Eventually he got command of his own sloop. While ashore in Madagascar he was captured by Arabs who ruled locally. They tortured and killed him. None of those who had sailed with him mourned his death.

WILLIAMS

James WILLIAMS. b. Wales. A crewman to Captain John SMITH. When SMITH took over the galley *George*, on 3 Nov 1724, WILLIAMS killed those crewmembers who did not wish to turn pirate. He then had a dispute with SMITH and ran amok, threatening to fire his pistol into the powder magazine. The crew bound him in chains and handed him over to the next prize vessel that they took, with instructions to give him to the next man-of-war that they met. Thus WILLIAMS eventually got to the Marshalsea Gaol. He had only been there 2 days when SMITH and the rest of the pirate crew arrived there. WILLIAMS was tried and found guilty. He was hanged on 11 Jun 1725.

WILLIAMS

A Cornish pirate. WILLIAMS sailed from Jamaica with Captain

MORRICE and was eventually captured by the Dutch. He got to Boston, where in 1674 he joined Captain RODERIGO aboard *Edward and Thomas*, a Boston vessel. He was later tried for piracy but acquitted.

WILLIAMS

Captain John WILLIAMS (alias YANKEE). In 1683 Governor LYNCH of Jamaica offered WILLIAMS a free pardon and £200 if he would capture the French pirate Captain HAMLIN and *La Trompeuse*.

WILLIAMS

Joseph WILLIAMS. A crewman to Captain CORNELIUS aboard *Morning Star*. WILLIAMS was taken from a prize vessel by the pirate CORNELIUS and signed Pirate Articles so that he might challenge one of the pirate crew, Robert BLAND, to a fistfight. WILLIAMS lost the fight, but had to remain as a pirate. Some time later, at the Island of Johanna, WILLIAMS took command of the *Morning Star* from CORNELIUS, fearing, he said, that CORNELIUS would be overpowered by the slaves that they carried.

WILLIAMS

Captain Morris WILLIAMS. A Caribbean Buccaneer. In Nov 1664, WILLIAMS applied to Governor MODYFORD of Jamaica for permission to bring into Port Royal a Spanish prize, loaded with logwood, indigo and silver. The Governor refused him permission but WILLIAMS brought the prize in regardless. The vessel was seized and sold for the benefit of the Spanish owners. This was during one of the periods when England was trying to cultivate better relations with Spain.

WILLIAMS

Captain Paulsgrove WILLIAMS. b. Newport, R.I. A crewman to Captain Samuel BELLAMY on *Whydah*. He was given command of his own sloop, which sailed in company with BELLAMY. WILLIAMS seems to have remained subordinate to BELLAMY and to have been killed on the night, in 1717, that *Whydah* went aground at Eastham, on Cape Cod.

WILLIAMS

Paul WILLIAMS. An Irishman. WILLIAMS was said to have been a crewman to Captain ROBERTSON. He surrendered to the Governor of the Bahamas in 1717.

WILLIAMS

William WILLIAMS. b. Plymouth, Devon. 1681/2. WILLIAMS joined Captain Bartholomew ROBERTS's ship *Royal Fortune* from the prize vessel *Sudbury* in Jun 1720. Captured by *HMS Swallow* off the West African coast on 10 Feb 1722. He was tried at Cape Corso Castle on 28 Mar 1722. WILLIAMS was found guilty of piracy and hanged.

WILLIAMS

William WILLIAMS. b. Holland. 1691/2. All the detail I have on these two WILLIAMS, except the place and date of birth is the same. It may be that there were two William WILLIAMS taken from the same ship and hanged on the same day, but I suspect that between the date of the hanging and the publication of Daniel Defoe's 'General History of the Pyrates etc" a copy clerk made an error. You choose.

WILLIS

Robert WILLIS. A reluctant crewman aboard Captain George LOWTHER's ship *Ranger*. Captured by the sloop *HMS Eagle* at Blanquilla in Oct 1723. WILLIS was tried at St Christopher (St Kitts) and found not guilty of piracy. He was acquitted.

WILLIS

Thomas WILLIS. A crewman on Captain James SKYRM's ship *Ranger*. Captured off the West African coast on 1 Feb 1722. WILLIS was tried at Cape Corso Castle on 28 Mar 1722. He was found not guilty of piracy and acquitted.

WILLS

Captain Thomas WILLS. b. Devon. WILLS sailed from Topsham, Devon, in command of *Anna* of Topsham, loaded with cloth and barley for Portugal. In Oporto WILLS re-loaded for Brazil, but in Jan 1714 *Anna* was at Gambia trying to purchase slaves. They were denied the purchase of slaves and *Anna* sailed away and was not recorded again. Eight years later, when Captain Bartholomew ROBERTS' pirate ship *Royal Fortune* was captured off West Africa, Thomas WILLS was found aboard as a reluctant crewman. He claimed to have shipped out of Bideford as Bosun on *Richard*. WILLS was never accused of piracy, but his history from 1714 until 1722 might make interesting reading.

WILMERDING

Gustav Wilmerding. 1670–1726. A Danish pirate who sailed from home as a 12 year-old boy. On his first voyage the ship was taken by pirates and WILMERDING rose to command his own ship. He had no ambitions to return to Europe a wealthy man, as most pirates did. Instead WILDMERDING settled on the tiny island of Little Thatch in the Virgins and lived in great comfort and luxury. Local legend still claims that the sounds of his parties may be heard across the water on quiet nights. Decendents of Wilmerding are still to be found in the Virgin Islands. A most successful pirate. Like all sailing ships of that period, WILMER-DING's had musicians aboard, but he liked to engage ships to the accompaniment of drums and bugles. Because of this he was known as 'Ding-Dong WILMERDING'.

WILSON

Alexander WILSON. One of the mutineers on the vessel *Antonio*. WILSON was tried in Boston and hanged in 1672.

WILSON

George WILSON. b. Liverpool. WILSON joined Captain Bartholomew ROBERTS' ship *Royal Fortune* from the prize vessel *Tarlton* of Liverpool. Captured by *HMS Swallow* off the West African coast on 10 Feb 1722. He was tried at Cape Corso Castle on 28 Mar 1722. The charge against him was that when *Tarlton* was taken, he wanted to beat and then shoot the vessel's captain. Other crewmen from Liverpool felt the same. WILSON, a surgeon by trade, was found guilty and sentenced to hang, but obtain a stay of execution 'at His Majesty's pleasure'. He died before his return to England.

WILSON

James WILSON. b. Dublin. A crewman to Major Stede BONNET. WILSON was captured with BONNET at Cape Fear River on 27 Sep 1718. He was tried at Charleston and hanged on 8 Nov 1718.

WILSON

John WILSON. b. New London County. 1700/01. A crewman on Captain Charles HARRIS' ship *Ranger*. Captured by *HMS Greyhound*. WILSON was tried at Newport R.I. in Jul 1723. He was found not guilty of piracy and acquitted.

WINGFIELD

Captain ? WINGFIELD. He was hanged for piracy at Execution Dock, Wapping, on Wed 28 Mar 1759.

WINTER

Captain Christopher WINTER. A pirate captain based at Providence, Bahamas. WINTER took a sloop off Jamaica, the Mate of the sloop was Edward ENG-LAND, who later became a famous pirate captain himself. In 1718 WINTER accepted a pardon from Woodes ROGERS, but soon turned pirate again. Worse, WINTER accepted a Spanish commission from the Governor of Cuba and turned Catholic. He became a great hazard to shipping off the coasts of Jamaica. The Governor of Jamaica sent *HMS Happy* to Cuba to ask the Spanish to hand over WINTER to them. Needless to say, the mission was unsuccessful.

WINTER

James WINTER. A crewman to Captain John SMITH. When they took over the galley *George*, on 3 Nov 1724, WINTER cut the throat of the ship's surgeon. He was captured in the Orkneys with SMITH and taken to London for trial. WINTER was hanged at Execution Dock on 11 Jun 1725.

WINTER

William WINTER. See MUSTAPHA.

WINTHROP

Thomas WINTHROP. A crewman to Captain William FLY on *Elizabeth*. I can find no record of his having been tried with FLY at Boston in Jun 1726. He probably left FLY's ship with Mathew MITCHELL at Brown's Bank.

WISE

Francis WISE. b. Cork, Ireland. A crewman to Phillip ROCHE. There is no information about WISE after he left the vessel.

WISEMAN

Captain Geoffrey WISEMAN. An English pirate captain in the early 17th century. WISEMAN was one of the captains in Captain John WARD's fleet of corsairs.

WITHERBORN

Captain Francis WITHERBORN. A pirate captain who was captured by Major BEESTON and brought to Jamaica. Tried for piracy and sentenced to death, WITHERBORN was shipped to England for execution.

WITHSTANDENOT

T. WITHSTANDENOT. He was taken from the prize galley *Norman* by Captain James SKYRM's *Ranger*. Captured by *HMS Swallow* off the West African coast on 1 Feb 1722. WITHSTANDENOT was tried at Cape Corso Castle on 28 Mar 1722. He was found not guilty of piracy and acquitted.

WOLLERVY

Captain William WOLLERVY. A New England pirate captain who sailed in company with Captain Henley in 1683 off the Island of Eleuthera. On his retirement from piracy, WOLLERVY burned his vessel near Newport R.I.. He and his crew got ashore and dispersed with their treasure.

WOOD

James WOOD. A crewman to Captain John PHILLIPS. In Feb 1724 PHILLIPS took a prize snow bound for Barbados. He put 3 pirates aboard as a prize crew, WOOD was one of them. They attempted to desert from PHILLIPs but he gave chase and re-took the vessel. WOOD was killed in the fight.

WOOD

Richard WOOD. He was taken aboard Captain Bartholomew ROBERTS' ship *Royal Fortune* from the prize vessel *Porcupine* in Whydah Roads. Captured by *HMS Swallow* off the West African coast on 10 Feb 1722. WOOD was tried at Cape Corso Castle on 28 Mar 1722. He was found not guilty of piracy and acquitted.

WOOD

William WOOD. b. York. 1694/5. WOOD joined Captain James SKYRM's *Ranger* from the prize vessel *Onslow* in Jan 1722. Captured by *HMS Swallow* off the West African coast on 1 Feb 1722. WOOD was tried at Cape Corso Castle on 28 Mar 1722. He was found guilty of piracy and hanged.

WOODLAND

Captain John WOODLAND. An English pirate captain in the early 17th century. WOODLAND sailed in company with Captain Thomas TUCKER on a joint raid to the 'Seven Islands' of RUSSIA. TUCKER's ship was wrecked in the Faroes. Instead of going to his aid, WOODLAND robbed him and left him there.

WOOLMER

Captain ? WOOLMER. An English pirate captain in the early 1600s. WOOLMER was based in the southwest of Ireland, probably Bantry Bay.

WOOLWORTH

An English pirate captain in the early 17th century. "a tall man and well set, and hath a black head, and weareth a long locke on one side of his head."

WORLEY

Captain Richard WORLEY. He left New York in an open boat with eight others. They were provisioned with biscuit, tongue, water and small-arms. In Sep 1718 they robbed a shallop bound for Philadelphia and then two sloops. The Governor of New York raised a force against them. WORLEY found a sloop that he liked and left the area. After a spell in the Bahamas, WORLEY returned to the mainland and was met by two government sloops just off Jamestown. The Governor of Jamestown thought that all three vessels were pirates and panic ensued ashore. The men from the two government sloops boarded WORLEY's vessel and fought hand-to-hand until only WORLEY and one of his crew remained alive, but sorely injured. It was feared that

WORLEY and his crewman might die before they could be brought to trial, so they were brought ashore and hanged the next day, 17 Feb 1719. It was WORLEY who flew the 'scull and crossbones' as his personal standard. Other pirates added embellishments of their own but WORLEY flew the flag we all know as the pirate standard.

WORMALL

Daniel WORMALL. He was sailing master on Captain John QUELCH's brig *Charles*. He attempted to escape capture at Gloucester, Mass., by sailing off in *Larimore*. WORMALL was followed and caught by Maj SEWELL. He was tried at the Star Tavern in Boston in 1704.

WRIGHT

Captain George WRIGHT. A buccaneer captain in the Caribbean. In 1681/2 WRIGHT commanded a vessel in the large pirate fleet that included COXON, SHARP and Le SAGE. WRIGHT and Le SAGE left the fleet and took 12 Spanish merchantmen off Riohacha. They put the prisoners ashore then sold their plunder at Curacao. WRIGHT returned to Tortuga and Le SAGE to Saint Domingue.

WYNN

Henry WYNN. A seaman on the merchant vessel *Prince's Galley*. On 15 Sep 1723 *Prince's Galley* was captured by Captain George LOWTHER. WYNN was one of the crew who volunteered to join the pirates.

YALLERS

Captain ? YALLERS (YEL-LOWS?). A Dutch Buccaneer. YALLERS fled from Jamaica to Campeachy in 1671. There he sold his frigate to the Spanish Governor for 7,000 pieces-of-eight. He entered service with the Spanish and sailed against the English logwood cutters. He proved most successful at this and took more than a dozen of their vessels along the Mosquito Coast.

YEATES

Captain ? YEATES. From Carolina. YEATES was a crewman to Captain Charles VANE. VANE put him in command of a prize sloop and YEATES, resentful of VANE's treatment of him, his unequal sharing of plunder and his extreme cruelty, sailed away. With two sloops and a cargo of slaves, YEATES surrendered to the Governor of Charleston.

ZEKERMAN

Andrew ZEKERMAN. A Dutchman. One of McKINLEY's gang which murdered the crew and passengers of the 'Earl of Sandwich' bound from the Canaries to England. ZEKERMAN was said to have been the most brutal of this bunch of evil mutineers. ZEKERMAN was captured in Ireland with McKINLEY and three others. They were hanged in chains on the beach near Dublin on 19 Dec 1765.

ZUMIRO

Captain ? ZUMIRO. An English slaver who turned pirate.

Bibliography

J.M. von Archenholtz – The History of the Pirates, Freebooters and Buccaneers of America.

M. Ashley – England in the Seventeenth Century. 1952.

M. Azicri – Cuba. 1988.

Bahamas Ministry of Tourism – http://www.interknowledge.com

D. Botting – Pirates of the Spanish Main. 1973.

H.M. Chaplin – Privateer Ships and Sailors – The First Century of American Colonial Privateering, 1625–1725. 1926.

D. Cordingly – Life Among the Pirates. 1995.

D. Cordingly & J. Falconer – Pirates. 1992.

A. Cowley – Voyage Round the World.

E. Cree – The Cree Journals.

W. Dampier – Voyages and Discoveries. 1700.

T. Douglass – The Lives and Exploits of the Most Celebrated Pirates and Sea Robbers. 1845.

G.F. Dow – Pirates of the New England Coast, 1630–1730. 1923.

W. Effingham – A Narrative of the Attrocities Committed by the Crew of the Piratical Brig 'El Defencor le Pedro'. 1830.

J. Esquemelling – A History of the Buccaneers of America.

C. Ellms – The Pirates' Own Book. 1837.

B. Fuller & R. Leslie-Melville – Pirate Harbours and their Secrets.

A. Gill – The Devil's Mariner. 1997.

P. Gosse – The History and Lives of the Most Notorious Pirates. 1932.

P. Gosse – A Pirate Who's Who. 1924.

W. Hacke – Four Original Voyages. 1699.

J. Hepburn – The Black Flag. 1994.

A. Hyatt Verrill – Love Stories of Some Famous Pirates. 1924.

H.M. Government – Calendar of State Papers, Colonial Series, America and the West Indies.

Illustrated London News.

Charles Johnson (Daniel Defoe) – The Histories and Adventures And Dangerous Robberies

Committed on the High Seas by

Notorious Pirates. 1726.

King James II – A Royal Proclamation Against Piracy.

J. Keane – Tom Paine, A Political Life.

F.W. Knight – The Caribbean. 1990.

R. Lloyd – Dorset Elizabethans. 1967.

K.M. McCarthy – Twenty Florida Pirates. 1994.

D.F. Marley – Pirates, Adventurers of the High Seas.

J. Masefield – A Mainsail Haul. 1905.

R.D. Paine – The Book of Buried Treasure. 1922.

C. Platt & J. Wright – Treasure Islands.

S. Pepys – Diaries.

D. Pope – Harry Morgan's Way, The Biography of Sir Henry Morgan 1635–1684. 1977.

M. Rediker – Between the Devil and the Deep Blue Sea. 1987.

R.C. Ritchie – Captain Kidd and the War Against the Pirates. 1986.

N. Roberts – Blackbeard and Other Pirates of the Altantic Coast.

F. Sayfarth – Pirates of the Virgin Islands. 1996.

A.M. Smyth – The Book of Famous Pirates. 1940.

C.M. Senior – A Nation of Pirates. 1976.

E.R. Snow – True Tales of Pirates and their Gold. 1958.

E.R. Snow – Pirates and Buccaneers of the Atlantic Coasts. 1944.

N. Tattersfield – The Forgotten Trade. 1991.

G.M. Trevelyan – English Social History. 1944.

Dictionary of National Biography.

R. West – The Life and Strange Surprising Adventures of Daniel Defoe. 1997.

THE WAY OF ALEXANDER
by Charles Mercer
ISBN: 0-7434-9339-7

*A RIVETING ACCOUNT OF THE MOST FASCINATING
WORLD CONQUEROR IN HISTORY WRITTEN BY ON
THEPREEMINENT AUTHORITIES OF THE PERIOD*

Throughout the centuries, Alexander the Great has fascinated all manner of men all over the world. Handsome, youthful, he conquered the entire known world, then suddenly died at the age of thirty-two. The Way of Alexander the Great is an extraordinary book that in one volume pulls together the scattered images of Alexander and his life, and presents them with all the color and drama characteristic of his time. From Macedonia to Greece to modern Turkey, through Palestine and Egypt, all who stood in his way were conquered. Then, turning east he set his sights on defeating the greatest empire of the time: Persia. His success was breathtaking. How he managed it, how he conducted himself, and what it all led to are questions that challenge and worry men today as we view out own divided world.

THE WAY OF THE CRUSADES
by Jay Williams
ISBN: 0-7434-0485-0

A COMPREHENSIVE LOOK AT THE CRUSADES,
PORTRAYING BOTH ITS FAILURES AND ITS TRIUMPHS

Although the Crusades failed from a long-range military stand-point, these tragic Christian wars to recover the Holy Land from the infidel, left the world with memories of heroism and endurance, devotion and high adventure. The Way of the Crusades explores this remarkable period, shedding light on an era that was once portrayed as dark, recognizing the lasting achievements made in the field of the peaceful arts.

COMING AUGUST 2005

THE WAY OF CAESAR
by Irvin Isenberg
ISBN: 0-4165-0824-4

*AN ESSENTIAL VOLUME ON ONE OF HISTORY'S
MOST INTRIGUIN FIGURES FROM THE EDITORS
OF AMERICAN HERITAGE*

In larger quantities than most young men, Gaius Julius Caesar had brains and helpful family ties, but there were few signs that he would use them. Then suddenly, between the years 60 and 44 B.C., when he was in his forties and fifties, he began to excel in everything he attempted. As an orator, politician, military general, writer and statesman he stood above all men of his day. With an unerring sense of timing and tactics, he devoted himself to one supreme task: the transformation of Rome from a powerful but small republic into a world empires with himself at its head.